Global Economic Instituti

Globalization can have positive effects in many areas. This statement should not be as controversial as it often seems. In order for it to realize its potential, however, global institutions must be competent to deal with the problems caused by globalization.

This book examines global economic institutions critically. It presents an accessible, fluid history of globalization and explains how global public goods should be defined, how global economic institutions work, and it looks at the effect that major organizations such as the WTO, IMF, UNEP, etc., have on trade, finance, the environment, and so on.

The beauty of *Global Economic Institutions* lies in its unique approach and the author's ability to explain complicated economic and political systems and terms with commendable clarity and style. Students and academics interested in international business and economics will find this book a useful tool. Researchers, business consultants, policy-makers and so forth may yet come to see this volume as indispensable.

Willem Molle is Professor at Erasmus University, Rotterdam, and Director of ECORYS Research and Consulting, Rotterdam, the Netherlands.

Routledge Studies in the Modern World Economy

Global Economic
Institutions

Willem Molle

Routledge
Taylor & Francis Group

LONDON AND NEW YORK

First published 2003
by Routledge
11 New Fetter Lane, London EC4P 4EE

Simultaneously published in the USA and Canada
by Routledge
29 West 35th Street, New York, NY 10001

Routledge is an imprint of the Taylor & Francis Group

Typeset in Baskerville by Exe Valley Dataset Ltd, Exeter, Devon
Printed and bound in Great Britain by MPG Books Ltd, Bodmin

British Library Cataloguing in Publication Data
A catalogue record for this book is available from the British Library

Library of Congress Cataloging in Publication Data
Molle, Willem.
  Global economic institutions / Willem Molle.
    p. cm.–(Routledge studies in the modern world economy; 39)
  Includes bibliographical references and index.
    1. International trade agencies–Evaluation. 2. Financial institutions,
  International–Evaluation. 3. International agencies–Evaluation.
  4. International organization–Evaluation. 5. World Trade Organization.
  6. International Monetary Fund. 7. United Nations Environment
  Programme. 8. Globalization–Economic aspects. 9. Globalization–
  Environmental aspects. I. Title. II. Series.
HF1383.M65 2003
341.7´5´06–dc21   2003046541

ISBN 0–415–32349–5

Contents

PART IV
Evaluation 235

Figures

Tables

Boxes

Acknowledgements and invitation

In writing this book I have been supported by many, in particular students and colleagues.

My students at Erasmus University, Rotterdam have made many critical comments on earlier versions of the text and the present book owes much to them openly speaking their minds.

Many colleagues have helped me in making suggestions for conceiving or adapting (specific parts) of the book. I mention in particular Sebastiaan Princen (now with Utrecht University) and Max van der Sleen (of NEI/ECORYS) who have critically reviewed the whole draft text. Their suggestions helped to improve the internal consistency and to clarify the arguments.

Very valuable has been the secretarial support of Ineke van der Stap, who prepared the manuscript for publication.

I thank them all for their help. Of course, I am the sole to blame for any remaining errors and shortcomings.

I invite the reader to let me have the benefit of their criticisms. Please send me an email at the address indicated. I will be happy to discuss with you any proposals for improvement. Readers of a potential second edition would benefit from your help.

molle@few.eur.nl
willem.molle@ecorys.com

1 Introduction

1.1 Why this book?

The past decades have seen an upsurge of international transactions that have their origin and destination in very distant parts of the world. This phenomenon has become known as 'globalization'. It is a very pervasive tendency; people from all parts of the globe and all segments of society are confronted with it. International institutions supply the necessary framework for private, mainly business transactions. In other words, they set the rules by which the game is played. Business success depends therefore critically on the understanding of these rules. International institutions also supply a number of public goods. These are goods that will neither be produced by the private sector nor by national public institutions, because their use cannot be restricted to those who are prepared to pay for them.

So, for the setting of business strategies and of public policies it is essential to understand the why, what, when and how of the international institutions. Currently, the supply of textbooks and other literature is inadequate in providing this understanding. Many books either ignore institutions or take them for granted. Other books that address institutions tend to focus on a specific subdiscipline, such as monetary, trade, etc., thereby giving only a fragmented sight of reality. Yet other books deal specifically with the organizational characteristics of international institutions. So, most books leave in the dark their rationale, their dynamics and their impact on the economy in general and on firms and civil society in particular. To fill this gap the present book has been written.

Its objectives are to:

- present the essential features (driving forces and effects) of globalization which stimulate the emergence of new needs for public goods;
- develop the fundamental factors that shape institutions and the way they adapt to changes in their environment;
- describe the way in which the major global economic institutions have developed in the past and function at present;

- discuss proposals for changes in the system design so as to do away with present inadequacies and provide better solutions for present and future problems.[1]

In short, the objective of the book is to identify the need for and the prospects of achieving an improvement in global government.

1.2 What does it cover?

People tend to take for granted that private international economic transactions can be effectuated without problems and at low cost. However, this is far from self-evident. The possibility to enter into such types of transactions depends critically on the pre-existence of a number of international institutions; or at least of the effective coordination of relevant national institutions. So, an international sales agreement implies minimally common notions of property and contract, and an agreement on the national law that will be applied to adjudicate any differences between partners ensuing from the implementation of the contract. For a long time, simple institutions have sufficed to permit the international economy to function. However, with the increasing complexity of the economy, on the one hand, and the increase in the number of international transactions, on the other, the need for better and often more specialized international institutions has become apparent. To illustrate this we need but mention the rules that govern the electronic payments operations of the international banking system or those that govern transactions on the Internet.

Public goods can be provided at different levels. Traditionally, the national state has taken responsibility for the supply and sometimes also for the production of such goods. A good example is the reliability and stability of the financial system. The production of this good is realized on the national level by the public setting of standards for access to the trade and the public surveillance of the operations of financial institutions. However, with increasing internationalization the national dimension is no longer sufficient.

Increasingly, solutions have been found on the regional level, where neighbouring countries come together for coping with problems that transcend the national competencies. There are many books that deal already with this type of institutional solution. So, we will not deal with this aspect in detail.[2]

For coping effectively with the provision of international public goods (that means coping with some of the risks that globalization poses) truly global institutions are needed. An example is the reliability of the world financial system, which requires an international institution with a truly global dimension. Such global institutions are the subject of the present book.

Institutions are created by human action; they are designed and, if needed, adapted to serve better the needs of the global community; represented by many actors, such as firms, non-governmental organizations and national governments. Well-devised institutions are thus conducive to sustainable growth and are welfare enhancing.

1.3 What view does it take?

Globalization is a subject that arouses very heated debates. Some consider measures to facilitate the global organization of production as a conspiracy of big business against the citizen. They do not trust governments in their alleged action to safeguard values and public goods because they consider that governments have surrendered to the interest of big business (viz., silent take-over). Their conclusion, 'Better no order than one that is organized around particular interests'. Some of them take to the streets and turn the cities where heads of state meet to discuss global governance issues into besieged fortresses and battlefields. Their actions are relayed by international mass media. Their sweeping statements tend to carry the day. To those engaging in this turmoil, this book may seem of little avail.

The present book clarifies issues and presents solutions to problems on the basis of the results of theoretical and empirical analysis. It thereby acknowledges the views of different schools. It substantiates the positions presented by referring to authoritative studies made into the subject. Where relevant, it does not hide the uncertainties that persist in many fields. So, the book presents insights to a critical reader.

Establishing better government on the global level involves in the first place intergovernmental organizations (IOs). So IOs take a central position in this book. We are aware of the fact that many feel that IOs are part of the problem and not part of the solution. They consider that solutions need to be found not in the adaptation of existing or the creation of new global IOs, but in the empowerment of non-governmental organizations (NGOs). We agree that NGOs have a very important role to play. However, we think that in the end there is no way around the addressing the reshaping of IOs. And as institutions matter, such reshaping should lead to a reshaping of globalization in conformity with social preferences.

On the basis of the analysis presented and considering that globalization is a fact of life, I come to the following major conclusions and positions:[3]

- The present situation is not adequate.
- This is the case for organizations taken individually with respect to their specific field of competence. Each organization bears the marks of the historical conditions under which it evolved. On many points the governance does not respond to present needs.
- It is also the case for the organizations taken collectively as they do not provide consistent and comprehensive world government. They are a patchwork, not a system.

- Improvements will be very difficult. Theoretical arguments and historical examples show that change is inhibited by many factors. Yet on a number of points clear cases for change present themselves that are both economically desirable and politically feasible.

1.4 How to read it?

The structure of the book (see Box 1.1) follows closely the four objectives presented above.

We present in the first part the development of the global economy, the challenges it poses to governments and the evolution of institutions in a global context. This part starts with a chapter on the history (foundations and dynamics) of globalization and the gradual emergence of international institutions. This makes it easier to understand the present dynamics of the system. In the third chapter we describe the effects of globalization, focusing on the most pressing problems. We show here how globalization affects the ability of national states to influence policy and our conclusion is that there is a growing need for global institutions to recover collectively what has been lost individually.

In the second part, we turn our attention to the solutions that need to be found for such problems. To that end we have to analyse the foundations of global institutions. We devote a first chapter to the defining of the type of

---

Box 1.1 Road map of the content of the book

Part	Chapter	Subject
I		Defining the global problems
	2	The origin: trends in globalization
	3	Types of problems: the effects of globalization
II		Searching for solutions (theory)
	4	Collective action for public good provision
	5	Building adequate institutions (regimes) and governance structures
	6	Salient features of international organizations
III		Implementing the solutions (practice)
	7–10	Trade, finance, environment, transport
IV		Coping with insufficiencies
	11	Complementing the structure (filling in gaps)
	12	Redesigning the architecture

institutions that are needed for the provision of global public goods. Next, we deal with the economics of institutions in an international context. Based on several strands of theory we show that institutions are efficient solutions to a transaction cost and a coordination problem. We show how these factors point in the direction of the creation of a set of specialist agencies, each of them coping with global regimes. Finally, we present the architecture of the most important international organizations.

In the third part, we discuss the structure of the global 'system' of economic regimes. We thereby follow an approach that is problem oriented, not organization oriented. We devote a separate chapter to each of the most important economic problems the world system is confronted with. What we mean by this can be explained shortly by the international financial and monetary system. The main problem here is monetary instability leading to recurrent crises. The main organization that has to cope with this problem is the IMF. However, other organizations, such as the OECD and the G8, also assume responsibilities in this respect. Each chapter will present the main features of the development of an important regime; successively we deal with trade, finance, environment and transport, and telecommunications. Each chapter has a similar structure in four sections. The first is on the economic causes of the problem and its remedies. The next section covers such aspects as the sort of public good that need to be provided in order to cope with the problem. The third section is on the emergence of the organizations and regimes that have to make sure that this good is provided. The fourth section covers aspects of the tool kit (instruments) these organizations use to reach their aims. A final section gives an evaluation of the past (achievements), the inadequacies of the present and suggestions for the future adaptation of this specific regime.

The fourth part contains a general evaluation of the results of the analyses presented in the previous chapters. These chapters will make it abundantly clear that the 'system' is inadequate to deal with a number of problems. The first chapter of this last part deals with initiatives that have been taken to complement the existing set-up. The last chapter will be devoted to a broad ranging evaluation of the dynamics of the global institutional system and will discuss proposals for future change of the system as a whole, taking into account the discussions about individual regimes.

1.5 For whom is it written?

The book addresses mainly two categories of readers. The first category consists of the increasing number of students that follow courses in international economics and business. Both will find an essential complement to their core studies. Students of international economics will learn that the outcome of economic processes is dependent on the institutions that rule the transactions, such as trade and finance. Students of international business will find in the book the rules by which the competitive game is played;

their rationale, their effects and their adequacy. Students in disciplines like public administration, political economy, sociology and law will learn how institutions develop, and function against the background of economic problems and political processes. All categories of students will learn from the book to examine critically the strengths and weaknesses of the existing institutions and to evaluate the desirability and potential for improvement. All students will benefit from the experience the author has gained over several years when precursors of this book were used as teaching material in the course on International Economic Institutions at the faculties of Economics and Business at Erasmus University, Rotterdam.

Second, the book is written for all those professionally interested in the economic aspects of global integration in the widest sense. This includes such varied professionals such as staff members of international firms, national and international civil servants, researchers and consultants, journalists, and members of organizations that group business interests or the interests of civil society (NGOs). They will all be helped in preparing strategies, policies and actions by a broad view on and a critical assessment of the factors that shape the birth and subsequent development of global institutions.

Some general remarks concerning the set-up of the book are appropriate. They concern the way in which the material of the book has been organized and presented. The point of departure has been to facilitate fruitful and efficient study.

- Individual subjects can be studied without having to go through the preceding text. Before embarking on such a partial study the reader may find it useful to take notice of the key messages in the other chapters that are given in the summary at the end of each chapter.
- To facilitate access to the material and arguments presented, we have refrained from the use of mathematics and have written the text in such a way that that it can be studied with only a basic knowledge of economics.
- For a deeper and more complete study of specific subjects, ample references to more specific literature are given.
- The structure of the individual sections highlights the main features and arguments by presenting them as bullet points. We apply this method to present arguments *pro ad con*, to list relevant characteristics, etc.

Part I
The problem

Globalization and
its effects

2 The dynamics of globalization

2.1 Introduction

The objective of this book is to understand the way in which international institutions are created and developed. The present situation is the result of a long evolution. History has shaped this evolution under the influence of a set of long-term technological, political, economic and military factors. Understanding history helps to understand the present and hence to shape the future.

In the present chapter we will describe the historical development of globalization and of global regimes. Some fundamental factors drive globalization, such as corporate behaviour. Globalization of firms has been facilitated by two factors: decrease in distance cost and the liberalization of international transactions by new regimes. Before we embark on a description of the evolution of globalization over time we will briefly describe these fundamentals.

For the structure of the rest of this chapter, we follow the leading authors in this matter.[1] We distinguish between three periods: the nineteenth century, the period between the two world wars, and the post-Second World War period. For each of these periods we describe the evolution in a standard format:

- Issues of importance, major trends and ideas, driving factors;
- Indicators of globalization, notably trade, capital and labour movements;
- Institutions, regimes and organizations that emerged as a response to increasing needs.

We will conclude the chapter with a short section which summarizes the findings and evaluates the developments.

2.2 Fundamental forces

2.2.1 Definition

Globalization has many definitions. However, economic aspects dominate the definition we are going to use in this book. We define globalization as the gradual evolvement of the cross-border activities of economic actors that span the globe. These activities encompass mostly those of:

- *Firms.* Corporate involvement in globalization concerns mostly international trade in goods and services and investment in production in other countries. It also concerns international collaboration for the purpose of product development, production, sourcing, transporting, financing and marketing. We give two examples. The management of a Canadian shoe firm makes a direct investment by opening a production site in the Philippines. An international bank effectuates the payment by credit card by a Japanese salesman for a car rental in Argentina.
- *Individuals.* Persons migrate internationally for seeking better living conditions. They diversify their investments internationally in order to seek higher returns. They spread their consumption internationally, for instance by long-distance tourism to enhance satisfaction levels. For example, an Afghan intellectual migrates to the EU as a refugee, or a French student buys a specialist book he needs for his thesis in the US via the Internet.
- *Public authorities.* The (external) effects of global interaction tend to be increasingly international and even global. A case in point is global warming. National public bodies are less and less capable of coping with these problems, so there is an increasing need for regimes with a global dimension.
- *Non-governmental organizations.* The articulation of the needs of the civil society has traditionally be done on a national level. This is no longer adequate; problems in one country impact on the life of citizens in other countries. A case in point is shore pollution due to shipwrecking. Globalization has brought the need for worldwide action on such points.

2.2.2 *Technology: decrease in distance cost*

Major innovations in technology have lead to an explosion of productivity and to a considerable reduction in transport and communication costs. We will deal with them successively.

Productivity has been influenced by the main inventions that characterized the industrial revolution: the steam engine and mechanization of production. Later, this has been followed by the development of automation. Energy efficiency has played a major role here (compare the switch from coal to oil and electricity). The structure of production has also changed fundamentally from agriculture via manufacturing to information. In order to reap the ensuing economies of scale, production in large series became necessary. This required, in turn, large markets. Where national markets were too small the opening up of foreign markets became imperative.

The decrease in transport cost over time has been very significant. For the period between the two world wars a strong decrease in sea transport cost has been observed. For the period after the Second World War the decrease in the cost for all modes is given in Figure 2.1. The figure shows very clearly that present levels of the cost of transport are only a fraction now of what they used to be only a few decades ago. One should thereby take into account that the quality of the services that are delivered by both the transport sectors has considerably increased over time. For passenger transport one need but think of the increase in frequency of passenger flights and the comfort of the modern jet aircraft compared to the old propeller plane, the reliability and speed of modern container transport in specialist ships compared to traditional general cargo.

The cost of information and communication has also shown a decreasing long-term trend (see Figure 2.1). In recent years there has been a dramatic acceleration of this trend. The cost of a unit of computing power fell by 99 per cent between 1960 and 1990. Access to the Internet has reduced the cost of information dramatically. This has made it possible to offer a whole range of new services and to increase considerably the quality of the service (compare, for instance, the old-fashioned telegraph with the new broadband access to Internet).

2.2.3 Main facilitator: change in regimes[2]

The second factor inducing globalization concerns national and global regimes. This factor is the main subject of the present book.

International regimes have gone through fundamental changes. There has been a general trend towards more liberalization of trade, investment and capital movements. Evidence of this tendency is to be found first of all on the score of trade liberalization. The first method that was used to achieve this end involved colonialism. Next, the methods of regional integration and global multilateralism have been used. We give some examples of the latter. The post-Second World War agreements concluding in the

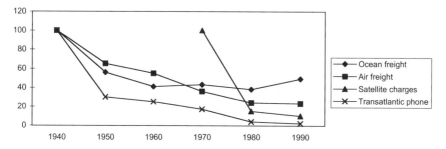

Figure 2.1 Decrease (index) in the cost of transport and communication by mode, 1940–1990.

Source: Adapted from Baldwin and Martin, 1999.

framework of GATT/WTO have resulted in a very considerable decrease of tariff protection (more than 40 per cent then, less than 4 per cent now). Moreover, many of the non-tariff barriers have been abolished. Second, evidence can be found on the score of liberalization of capital movements. Such liberalization has taken off only after 1970 and is, as yet, far from complete. However, the IMF has stimulated many countries to move further on this path. Capital and trade liberalization have reinforced each other. They have permitted the development of international (financial) markets that have, in turn, brought new services and lower transaction cost.

National regimes. The tendency of liberalization of international transactions has gone hand in hand with (and was reinforced by) a gradual liberalization of the internal markets of many countries, compelling business to improve competitiveness by doing away with rent seeking and with many types of (unneeded) transaction costs. This tendency has a different meaning in the various categories of countries. In developed countries the major example is the one of the EU 1992 programme for the completion of the internal market (Molle, 2001). Most of the centrally planned (and often largely closed) systems have recently collapsed and these countries are now completing their transition to open, market-oriented regimes. In many developing countries the experiments with different regimes (notably based on import substitution) have finally resulted in the recognition that an open system is most conducive to growth and development (see next chapter).

2.2.4 Firm behaviour

Increasing cost of research and development (R&D) and increasing economies of scale for production and marketing (brand names) push towards larger scale. Globalization permits firms to recover cost on volumes of sale extending far beyond the size of even large national markets. The decrease in the cost of transport and the liberalization of international transactions has permitted the spatial split of the stages in the production process and of production and consumption. The recent revolution in the information-processing and telecommunications sector has reinforced this tendency as it has made it possible to extend the capacities of management to coordinate complex international production and marketing systems.

Globalization is driven by firms pursuing strategies to exploit their competitive advantages outside their home country. They do so either to exploit the potential of the local market, or to use favourable local inputs, infrastructure and other conditions for efficient production. The explanation of this phenomenon can be illustrated with the help of the OLI paradigm (see Box 2.1).

2.2.5 Main indicators of global integration

The most important indicator of globalization is trade. Figure 2.2 shows clearly how over a very long period the growth of trade has always out-

---

Box 2.1 International production: the OLI paradigm[3]

The OLI paradigm addresses three questions related to foreign direct investment (FDI):

Which firms undertake FDI? Firms investing abroad must possess specific proprietary or ownership ('O') advantages to overcome the extra costs of operating in a different, less familiar environment. These advantages are generally costly to create, but can be transferred to new locations at relatively low cost. The analysis of 'O' advantages draws on industrial organization, resource-based, evolutionary and management theories. 'O' advantages reside mainly in firm-specific technology, in brand names, in privileged access to factor or product markets or in superior technological or management skills.

Where do firms choose to exploit their advantages, in the home country (by exports) or abroad? If they go abroad what sort of locations will they look for? They select sites with location ('L') advantages that best match the deployment of their 'O' assets. The analysis of 'L' advantages draws on trade and location theory. The main factors determining comparative costs are factor (for instance labour) and transport costs, markets (size and characteristics) and government policies (e.g. stability, predictability, tariffs, taxes and FDI regulations). Asset-seeking FDI is drawn to location with strong technological, educational or information creation activities.

Why do firms choose to internalize their advantages by direct investment in preference to selling them to other firms? The analysis of internalization ('I') draws on transaction–cost theories of the firm, and centres on the feasibility of contracting the sale of intangible advantages to other firms. The most valuable and new advantages tend to be internalized, since these are the most difficult to price and contract over time. The more mature ones are easier to price, less subject to uncertainty and less valuable to the owner: these are licensed more readily. Internalization can also explain vertical FDI, where a particular process or function is located abroad (rather than subcontracted to independent suppliers).

---

paced the growth of gross domestic product. There is only one exception to this trend, which is the period between the two world wars. This period was characterized by considerable impediments to trade following the economic crisis and the preparations for the Second World War. After the Second World War the growth figures increased considerably. In that period they were actually much higher than in the whole previous period. This

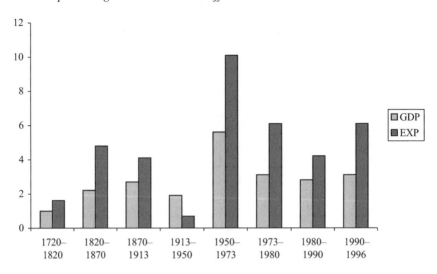

Figure 2.2 Growth of world production and trade (average % per year) 1720–1996.
Source: Adapted from WTO, 1998: 34.

reflects an acceleration in globalization that is due to both factors cited above: technology and regime change.

Other indicators are increasingly used as well. Some of them relate to the size of other flows such as capital. Others are related to the cross-border interconnection among firms such as assets, employees, subsidiaries. All these indicators convey the same message: a considerable increase of globalization over time with acceleration in recent years.[4]

2.3 A hesitant start

The globalization period starts effectively with the great discoveries by European explorers[5] (that is, from the end of the fifteenth century onwards). This is evident from the three basic indicators we use:

- *Trade* on the global level developed first in agricultural products for which the production depended on climatic conditions (spices, tea) and then in handicraft goods that were of low weight and high value (luxury goods, such as silk).
- *Migration* on a global scale started with the colonization of certain parts of the globe such as the northeast coast of North America and the plains of Latin America. Much of the migration has actually been forced migration in the form of the slave trade.
- *Capital* flows on a global scale developed from trade transactions. Capital transactions for investment purposes took off timidly with colonial activ-

ities (agriculture and mining). Of very great importance has been the transfer of gold and silver from the Spanish colonies to the motherland.

All this was achieved with only very embryonic institutions. In practice, these were limited to universal notions about property and transactions (exchange), on the one hand, and the acceptance of national government coercion powers, on the other. We will not go into further detail as to this period. Indeed, these global relations remained of limited quantitative importance given the technical limitations in production, transport and communication and the natural obstacles to international exchange.

2.4 The period 1820–1913

2.4.1 General[6]

The end of the War of Independence in America and the Napoleonic wars in Europe heralded a new era of relative stability. Notwithstanding the loss of its North American colonies Britain had emerged as the hegemonic power of the world. In this new era the industrial revolution (that had started in the previous century in Britain) spread over many countries. The profound changes in technology it brought with it affected almost all aspects of the economy and society. The breakthrough of steam power in domains such as manufacturing and sea and rail transport brought economies of scale in production and transport and led to a very significant decrease in the cost of production and distribution. Later in this century a further source of cost decrease was brought about by the generalized use of the telegraph.

Mass production demanded mass markets for raw materials (e.g. wool and cotton) and finished products (e.g. textiles). Transport capacity was there to accommodate these mass exchanges of goods (trains and steam ships). So, national boundaries were soon felt to be too constraining and a tendency towards the liberalization of international exchange became manifest. This political drive has been given its scientific foundation by some of the most reputed classical economists.

2.4.2 Trade

In the nineteenth century, the volume of world trade grew very fast. In terms of trade per head of world population the growth between 1820 and 1913 has been on average some 33 per cent every 10 years. Trade growth outpaced by far the growth of world output per capita, which can be estimated to average some 7 per cent per decade. This difference was greatest between 1820 and 1870. The main stimuli for this growth have been the entry of new countries into the international trading system and the increased international specialization of traditional trading nations.

The origin and destination of trade in the nineteenth century show very specific characteristics. Table 2.1 shows that during this period total trade

Table 2.1 Patterns of international trade, capital and labour movements (%)

	Trade[a]		*Capital*		*Migration*	
	I+E :2 *1876*	*I+E :2* *1913*	*Export* *1913*	*Import* *1913*	*Emigration* *1821–1913*	*Immigration* *1821–1913*
Europe	67	62	88	27	84	–
N. America	10	13	7	24	–	74
L. America	5	8	–	19	–	17
Asia	13	11	–	16	10	–
Africa	2	4	5	9	6	–
Oceania	3	2	–	5	–	9
Total	100	100	100	100	100	100

Source: Adapted from Kenwood and Lougheed, 1999 (various tables).
[a]Average of imports and exports.

was dominated by Western Europe. Countries specialized along the lines of comparative advantage. In a schematic way, one may say that manufactured goods (textiles, machinery, etc.) from mainly Western Europe were exchanged for mineral and agricultural primary products from other parts of the world. At the beginning of the century this trade in manufactured goods originated largely from the UK, later the rest of Western Europe and the USA took increasing shares in the total volume of exports. The exports of foodstuffs to Europe came from very different sources: some came from countries in the temperate climate zone, others came from tropical zones. Over time the share of foodstuffs declined relative to mineral products; this reflected the growing importance of metal and chemical products in the total activity of the developed countries.

With an increasing number of countries taking part in the industrialization process, trade in manufactures between European nations developed as well. The pattern of this trade was largely based on differences in stages of economic development. Some countries specialized in first-stage industrialization products, such as textiles. Other countries had already moved into higher-stage products, such as chemicals and machinery.

Trade openness resulted at the end of the period in a complex network of multilateral trade spanning the whole globe. This did not contribute much to the convergence of wealth levels. High value added production remained concentrated in the countries of the North Atlantic basin. The catching-up of the poorer countries has been inhibited by external shocks, most of which have originated in commodity markets, some in factor markets (Williamson, 1998).

2.4.3 Capital

At the beginning of the nineteenth century, foreign capital (both in terms of stock, the level of investment flows, and the yearly exchange of capital) was very limited. International exchanges developed gradually in the first and second quarter of the century, increased momentum in the third quarter and literally surged in the last quarter of the century.

Several mutually reinforcing causes for this complex phenomenon can be cited. We mention first the development of international trade and its accompanying financial flows (payments), which caused a basic infrastructure to be developed that could be used for financial deals of a different kind. Second, the international division of labour that resulted from the increased trade did give rise to an improved transparency about business opportunities and hence to a considerable growth in transcontinental direct investment. Third, the emergence and growth of specialized financial institutions in many countries caused the accumulation of savings to be operated more efficiently. The international linkages that these institutions developed made foreign investment more reliable and less risky. Fourth, the growth of operations of the financial institutions entailed a series of sophisticated specialized products that were better adapted to the needs of international borrowers and lenders. Fifth, the emergence of the City of London as the dominant financial centre where many operations were concentrated stimulated the development of a deep and diversified international market. Finally, the working of the gold standard as an effective international monetary regime (see Section 2.4.5) supported the development mentioned before.

The origin and destination of international capital flows showed a very distinct pattern. This can best be appreciated from the situation at the end of the period (see Table 2.1, middle column).

- *Supply*. The major lenders of capital were all in Western Europe. The United Kingdom accounted for about half of the total, and was followed at some distance by France and Germany. Other Western European countries were less important exporters of capital.
- *Demand*. The most important group of recipient countries were the Eastern European countries, such as Russia and the Balkans (including Turkey). This group was followed by North America and (at some distance) by Latin America and Asia. Other areas in the world captured only limited amounts of international capital.

During the nineteenth century the direction of some of the most important flows changed. Britain's exports shifted from Europe to the countries of the British empire and to Latin America. French investment shifted from Western European countries to Eastern European countries. The borrowing countries used the funds acquired on the international market mainly for three purposes:

- *Infrastructure*. Much of the investment in transport went into railway construction. Well known in this respect are the huge railway loans that

France gave to Russia. Even more sizeable was, however, the British investment in railways in the USA, the dominions and Latin America. The railways constructed with these loans helped the opening up to production and international trade of vast areas that until then had been excluded from the international division of labour. Other types of infrastructure also benefited from international loans, ranging from ports to telegraph and telephone.

- *Production.* Most of the investment in manufacturing and mining took the form of direct investment undertaken by companies eager to exploit certain local advantages. At first it concerned almost exclusively intra-European investment, later European (notably British) funds flowed into US companies as well. The financing of agriculture (sugar, rubber, coffee, tobacco) remained largely of the colonial type; funds of various activities in the colonies were accumulated and brought to London, where they merged with other funds to be invested in primary production in the colonies.
- *Administration.* Governments used the loans they obtained for a variety of purposes. Often they served to finance military and other, not directly productive, purposes.

The effects of these investments have been rather different according to the use to which the capital has been put:

- For the importing countries the effects of investment in productive capacity and in infrastructure was mainly positive, as it has permitted them to restructure their economies and to move into more productive activities. At the beginning of the century it permitted many countries that are now among the highest developed economies to industrialize (Belgium, Germany and others, such as Austria). Later these countries became themselves international capital exporters. However, the investments in primary production did little to improve local wealth levels, as most of the benefits accrued to the foreign investors. Finally, the effect of investment in government loans on the recipient country was often rather negative, as many of the funds were used for extravagancies and military operations.
- For the exporting countries the picture is not uniform either. Most of the investment helped the countries to develop a system that permitted them to acquire cheap foodstuffs and raw materials, which accelerated their industrialization and hence their movement to higher value added production. Moreover, lending abroad was only done where the loan provided a higher return than a domestic one. On the other side of the balance there are also costs; notably those of the defaults of important borrowers (examples are the Russian railways, but also many loans that had been used for military and related purposes). At this moment there is no conclusive evidence whether (and if by what size) the benefits have exceeded the cost for the lending countries.

2.4.4 Migration

The main feature of migration in this period is adjustment to the change in the production conditions in the home and destination countries. Migration accompanied the outflow of capital from Europe reported in the previous section. Thus the flow of workers and entrepreneurs was complementary to the capital that went from labour-abundant, land-scarce countries to resource-rich, but labour-scarce areas.

Migration in this period was considerable. Over the whole period the flows just described are estimated to amount to some 44 million persons. Most of the movement took place in the last decades of the nineteenth century and the first decade of the twentieth century.

The origin and destination of migration showed in essence a simple picture (see Table 2.1, last columns). Migrants originated for the largest part in Europe. First, they came mainly from the British Isles. Later, as conditions changed, most originated from other countries in Europe. At the end of the period they came predominantly from the poor countries of Central and Eastern Europe. The destination countries were notably in North America (primarily the US), but also in South America (Argentina and Brazil) and the Pacific (Australia and New Zealand).

The causes for this migration are to be found both in push, pull and friction factors.

- *Push factors.* In many countries the demand for labour fell short to the supply of labour. In some countries this took the form of a large agricultural labour surplus that could not be taken up in traditional and modern industry. The resulting overstretching of the possibilities of the land together with the import of cheap American grain led to an impoverishment of the rural population. In Ireland, a famine forced millions of people to leave the country.
- *Pull factors.* The immigration countries had large, untapped resources and the influx of labour permitted a labour shift to the most productive use.
- *Friction factors.* Barriers to migration decreased for several reasons. The steam ship lowered the cost of transport. However, to 'pauper' labour the cost of the voyage was nevertheless prohibitive. So, many private organizations came to help. Moreover, public support was given. In some emigration countries governments saw the emigration of poor people as a relief and gave subsidies to emigrants. In immigration countries, on the contrary, the influx was seen as an essential condition for further development and governments from countries, such as Australia and Brazil, gave incentives to attract immigrants.

Other intercontinental migration flows changed in size and character during the period. The slave trade from Africa to the Americas went on for the first half of the century, but under the pressure of the abolitionist it finally came to a halt. This caused, however, a big problem in a number of countries (e.g. in the West Indies and South Africa) that sought to attract Asian (often Indian) contract labourers. These numbers were, however, relatively limited (less than 1 million).

The economic effects of the mass migration just described are difficult to establish with some precision.

- For the recipient countries the effects are supposed to be positive; upsurges of immigration went hand in hand with a boost in investment and economic growth. Although there is no proof of a causal relation, there is much evidence of the capacity increases that were made poss- ible by immigrants, examples are the construction of railroads and the increase in agricultural production. On the other hand, the availability of abundant cheap labour has in some cases kept wages low and hence took away a stimulus for productivity increases.

- For the sending countries, the effects are also generally judged to be positive. On one hand, as most of the emigrants were desperately poor and had had little professional training or schooling, the loss of human capital was limited. On the other hand there were some positive effects in terms of incoming remittances. In a number of cases the emigration was used as a safety valve, which permitted the rest of the economy to change without having to cope with the social problem of mass poverty.

The mass migration flows did have a significant positive effect on the convergence of wealth (wage) levels between the countries that dominated the world economy (notably the Atlantic basin) (Williamson, 1998).

2.4.5 Institutions (regimes and organizations)

The increased interrelations between major economies required a number of rules. The most important were those that govern trade, payments and communications.

The trade regime evolved gradually under the influence of many contra- dictory pressures. It constituted in essence a patchwork of national policies, some of which converged to a multilateral understanding. The tensions were notably between:

- *Free trade.* Under the influence of the increased international depend- ency of its economy and supported by the theoretical writings of famous classical economists Britain adopted in the course of the century an increasingly clear-cut free trade policy. For a brief period after 1860 the example of Britain was followed by a large number of countries. The treaty between France and the UK of 1860 introduced the most favoured nation regime encouraging liberalization of trade on a multilateral basis. However, the world at large has never in this period seen a really free trade.

- *Protection.* Many countries decided to protect their economy from international competition. On one hand, agricultural interest demanded protection from cheap imports from the new economies, such as the USA. On the other hand, many countries that were building up their own industries used the infant industry argument to shelter them. These increasingly nationalistic tendencies were reinforced after 1870 by pressure groups asking for autarky in economic terms for military reasons.

The *financial regime* evolved gradually. A first essential feature to mention is that its proper functioning was based on the hegemonic situation of one country, not on formal international agreements. Indeed, the prominent position of the UK in international relations had made London the financial centre of the world. The city had developed new techniques and was able to handle efficiently a large diversity of international financial operations be they trade- or investment-related. The pound sterling was generally accepted throughout the international economy. A second feature concerns the international monetary standard. After some coexistence of gold and silver, the gold standard emerged as the (informal) regime for final settlement of balances between countries. As every national currency was defined in terms of its gold content, the exchange rate between any two currencies was defined as the relation between their gold parities (Bordo, 1999; Bordo *et al.*, 2001).

For *migration*, the patchwork of national rules can hardly be called a regime. Both recipient and sending countries set their rules in a unilateral way on the basis of national interest without much consideration of the wider issues involved.

However, not all aspects of international cooperation could be dealt with in such a loose manner. These concerned either aspects that were technically essential for facilitating relations or aspects that were considered from a moral point of view to be a global public good. For these aspects more binding international agreements had to be concluded and international organizations to be set up. We mention here:

- *Post and telecommunication.* Among the first international organizations were the International Telegraph (later Telecommunications) Union (1865) and the Universal Postal Union (1874). Both were established to harmonize the national regulations with respect to international traffic (rates, procedures, infrastructure, and so on). The harmonization has contributed to the high growth of PTT traffic at the end of the century.
- *Industrial property.* After the Paris Convention the International Union for the Protection of Industrial Property (Patent Union 1886) was ratified by most of the countries making up the then industrialized world. It established common principles with respect to the use of intellectual property. To prevent new inventions being used by countries

who do not share in recovering the cost, an international agreement
was needed that secured property rights to inventors.

- *Social policies.* The abolition of slavery was among the first steps towards
  the setting of worldwide labour standards. In 1890, a general act against
  slavery was signed.
- *Environment.* A special arbitral tribunal set up in 1883 to deal with the
  dispute between the US and the UK over fur seals in the Pacific heralded
  a new era in which international jurisprudence established principles
  for the common use and management of global natural resources. The
  efforts made were notably in the conservation of wildlife; examples are
  the multilateral conventions on African wildlife (1900) and on birds
  (1902).

2.5 The period 1913–1945

2.5.1 General

The first half of the past century is marked by political events. The period
of increasing global economic exchanges unexpectedly culminated in the
globalization of an internal conflict of a European multi-ethnic monarchy.
The conflict developed quickly into a war between European countries and
subsequently spread to involve countries from all over the world. From this
conflict the USA emerged as the major world power. However, its isolationist
tendencies meant that it did not assume the role of hegemonic power after
the First World War. So, many institutions based on the earlier hegemony of
Britain persisted.

The political changes have been paralleled by technological changes. In
this period the possibilities of production had been enhanced by improved
machinery, those of distribution by the emergence of motorised road traffic
and the airplane, and those of communication by the emergence of the
telephone. Although all these inventions were not yet producing according
to their potential they facilitated a further development of global exchanges.

In economic terms the most important event that has marked the period
is the great depression. Here, too, an event in a segment of a national
economy (the stock exchange in the US) sparked off a series of reactions
that threw the global economy into the deepest crisis in modern economic
history. The instability of the international economy coupled with unco-
ordinated and ill-devised national policies and inadequate international
regimes (gold standard) have aggravated the problems.

Out of the political and economic turmoil developed a whole series of
competing ideologies: communism in Eastern Europe, fascism in Central
Europe, corporatism in other Western European countries and liberal
capitalism in the US. Each of them had their economic doctrine as well,
they differentiated in the involvement of the state: from full control in the
communist system via strict planning and coordination in the fascist system

to strategic interventions in the liberal system. This produced an environment in which national protection took over from global freedom; as is witnessed by the increasing restrictions on finance and trade. This in turn had a severe negative impact on international relations and a divergent impact on the wealth levels of the most important economies of the time (Williamson, 1998; Wrigley, 2000).

2.5.2 Trade

The total volume of international trade continued to grow in the interwar years. This was notably due to a further specialization in the international economy and also to the entrance on the world stage of new trading nations. However, the pace of growth of international trade slowed down substantially; the average growth per decade declined to some 14 per cent for the period between 1913 and 1937. It thereby differed only marginally from the growth of output during that same period. So the major causes of this slow down must be sought elsewhere. One was the difficulty of re-establishing normal trading and payment conditions after the war. A second was the growing protectionism that occurred after the crisis of the 1930s.[7]

The *direction* of trade was profoundly changed as well. On the one hand, the dominance of Western Europe, which had a share of about two-thirds in 1913, declined to about half in 1937. On the other hand, the USA and the countries of the Asian, African and Oceania regions realized substantial increases in their shares of total world trade.

The pattern given above can be partly explained by the *composition* of world trade. By and large, the pattern of trade consisting of a primary product flow from developing countries to industrialized countries and a balancing flow of manufactured goods in the other direction was still dominant in this period. However, several elements of change indicate that this structure was increasingly under challenge. The share of developing countries in the world exports of primary products (covering a range of foodstuffs, metals and oil) increased significantly. However, due to the increasing attention on self-sufficiency, trade stagnated in non-tropical foodstuffs and in raw materials for which local substitutes (rubber, man-made fibres) were developed. In manufacturing products the share of Europe decreased very considerably. This was mostly due to the decrease in inter-European trade. Due to protectionism the possibilities of intra-industrial trade were largely foregone. A second reason was the emergence of new industrial countries. Paramount among these was, of course, the USA; but others to be mentioned include Japan and Canada.

The *commodity structure* of world trade in manufactures also changed rapidly in the period. The most important decrease in the share of total trade was recorded for textiles. The biggest increase was recorded for engineering products, including non-electrical, electrical goods and transport equipment. This shift was largely a reflection of the spread of industrialization. An increasing number of countries became capable of producing the goods that characterize the early forms of industrialization. However, for the more sophisticated modern products the world still had to rely on the most advanced countries.

2.5.3 Capital

The First World War changed the whole pattern of origin and destination of international capital movements. The European nations, including Britain, had all used much of their financial capacity for paying for their war efforts. For some (such as the UK), the position of creditors had weakened considerably. A particularly important feature in this respect is the Russian revolution, which forced countries, such as France and Germany, to write off the loans they had given to Russia in the pre-war period. Others, notably Germany, had become large debtors. The situation of the latter had been aggravated by its obligation to pay to the allied powers huge sums of reparations for war damages. The US emerged from the war as a major creditor, and after the war became the chief source of international loans. Much of the American capital was used in ventures in Latin America. In the 1920s and 1930s, the UK regained part of its role as a large investor in the countries of the British empire and France recovered as a source of loans for a variety of recipients.

The *composition* of capital movements changed. About one half of long-term investment was in the form of direct investment, oriented mainly to agriculture (rubber, coffee), mining (oil), and to manufacturing in emerging industrializing countries. Another feature to be mentioned is the emergence of heavy short-term capital movements. Much of this investment was in deposits or in securities traded on foreign stock exchanges.

The *pattern* of international investment just described brought with it increased risks of instability for three reasons:

- Investment no longer followed the trade pattern of the previous period, which had implied complementarity based on comparative advantage. American direct investments in Europe, for instance, were in activities that were in direct competition with American producers.
- Debtor countries that had invested in primary production became particularly vulnerable to an unfavourable movement in raw material prices.
- Recipient countries of short-term capital that had used this capital partly for long-term purposes became vulnerable to sudden withdrawals of this capital.

Given the interrelations that had grown and the severity of the crisis of the 1930s in the US, it is no surprise that the crisis quickly took a global character.

2.5.4 *Migration*

Migration *volumes* in the inter-war years were much lower than before. A first reason was the lower pressure from the emigration countries. Indeed, the First World War had led to an unprecedented loss of population in the belligerent countries. The second reason was the lowering of the demands of the immigration countries due to the great depression of the 1930s. In view of their heavy unemployment problems, the USA (which had tradition-ally absorbed the lion's share of migrants) restricted immigration by setting a yearly quota by country of origin. Figures of European emigration conse-quently fell from over a million a year before the war to some 130,000 in the 1930s.

The factors mentioned did have their influence on the *pattern* of migra-tion. Whereas the British Isles continued to send people to their traditional destinations, emigration from Germany and France decreased considerably. The population pressure on national resources remained, however, strong for countries such as Spain, Portugal and Poland. In the 1920s these countries continued to send relatively large numbers to the usual immi-gration countries in North and Latin America.

2.5.5 *Institutions (regimes and organizations)*

The international economy of the period between the two world wars showed increasing signs of weaknesses, as we have illustrated in the previous sec-tions. It would have been logical that some form of institutional response would be brought to these problems. However, the whole climate in this period was rather one of nationalism, and this was not very proficient for international institutional development. Moreover, as the international economy of the pre-war years had functioned effectively with a very light institutional superstructure, many thought that this would be feasible under the changed circumstances as well. Notwithstanding this general picture, some institution development occurred.

Trade relations were heavily distorted during most of the period as a consequence of the nationalistic reaction to economic problems. Multi-lateralism that had grown during the past period was the first to be sacrificed. A partial palliative to the problems that resulted was found in the conclusion of international commodity schemes by the exporters of primary products, such as metals (e.g. tin, copper), foodstuffs (e.g. sugar, wheat, coffee) or others (e.g. rubber), to control production and thereby sustain the prices. Another way to cope with problems was bilateralism, agreements between pairs of countries to try to balance their accounts.

International *financial relations* were governed by the gold standard until its collapse in the early 1930s. The workings of the gold standard in this period have been found to be particularly ill-adapted to the prevailing situation and caused very negative effects on growth and a historical high in unemployment (Bordo *et al.*, 2001; Eichengreen, 1995). The adaptation of a monetary arrangement to new needs is not easy; much depends on the scope for collective action of governments. This is in turn dependent on two factors (see Table 2.2). On the one hand (see columns), one distinguishes power relations or, in other words, the degree to which governments share responsibilities for the working of the system. On the other hand, one can distinguish the degree of coordination in day-to-day operations (see rows). A partial remedy to the ensuing international problems was the sterling area, initiated by the UK. It grouped not only Commonwealth countries but also a number of countries that had close economic ties with the UK (this corresponds to a shift from the left-hand upper part to upper and centre part of Table 2.2). To solve some of the problems of the global economy, international financial cooperation was pioneered. With the Tripartite Monetary Agreement (TMA) the USA, the UK and France (later joined by three other European countries) created a managed exchange rate system. In a sense the TMA heralded the advent of the International Monetary Fund after the Second World War (see Table 2.2; this represents a shift from the upper row to the middle row of the table).

In matters of *migration* no effort has been made to establish even the basics of an international regime. On the contrary, the nationalistic tendencies and militarist concerns in this period have strengthened the character of a patchwork of national rules.

The League of Nations, founded by the allies, came into operation shortly after the war. The scope of its activities and the effectiveness of its efforts have been very limited. The first reason was that the USA (which

Table 2.2 Comparison of international monetary arrangements according to the principles of collective action

Government conduct	Sharing obligations		
	Strong symmetry	*Intermediate asymmetry*	*Strong hierarchy*
Automatic mechanism	Ideal gold standard	Historical sterling gold standard	US $/Argentine peso 1990–2001
Intermediary co-responsibility	Flexible foreign exchange rates with target zones	Tripartite agreement (1936–45) Bretton Woods (1958–71) EMS (1983–89)	Bretton Woods (1947–58)
Discretion	Pure flexible foreign exchange rates	Floating foreign exchange rates with a predominant dollar (1973–85)	Floating of the Canadian/US dollar (1950–62)

Source: Adapted from Aglietta, 1995: 68.

emerged from the war as a leading power) refused to become a member. The league developed some activity in the negotiation of loans for countries that needed to stabilize the exchange rates of their currencies. It tried to promote the liberalization of world trade by calling a world economic conference, the effects of which, however, were limited and short-lived. Finally, the league entered into social affairs by creating the International Labour Organization (ILO). The ILO stated in the preamble of its constitution the principle of labour standards. It has not been able to put them into effect.

There is no progress to be mentioned in this period with respect to multilateral rules for the environment.

The turmoil of the 1930s created a tendency to integration areas, based on newly defined colonial ties. Dominant countries such as the UK and France (and even smaller ones such as the Netherlands) developed systems based on preferential trade and investment and some form of monetary cooperation (in some cases approaching monetary union). Integration on a regional basis, however, did not proceed in this period (Anderson and Norheim, 1993).

2.6 From 1945–present

2.6.1 General

During the second half of the twentieth century the trend towards globalization gained continuous momentum. The main causes for this phenomenon were the decreasing cost of communication and transport and a decrease in the level of protection.

The changes in the economic structure, largely determined by technological progress, have been very profound. In transport, road transport has gained a very strong place with the accompanying development of the car and truck manufacturing as major sectors of the economy. The picture of the change in transport is completed, on the one hand, with the growth of air transport and, on the other hand, with the development of the container, which has revolutionized combined transport of goods (land and sea). In the field of energy, the era has been dominated by oil (later also nuclear electricity). In manufacturing, the pre-war trend of mechanization had been supplemented by automation. Under the influence of the revolution of the information society, computers, media and telecom have stimulated the shift of the major economies from manufacturing to a very wide range of services.

This very rapid growth has produced new problems. Paramount among these is the occurrence of many global environmental problems such as depletion of natural resources and pollution of the soil and the air. New solutions have had to be found, resulting in new global regimes.

On the level of political developments we note that the political turbulence of the period 1913–40 ended in war between Germany and its neighbours. Given the international linkages of each of the belligerents, this war developed rapidly into the Second World War. The end of this war saw the confirmation of the US as the dominant world power. This time the US has accepted to play their role. As a consequence, a set of new institutions emerged. The other victor countries could not (USSR) or would not (UK) challenge this leadership. The USSR has created a zone of influence in which all countries adopted national and international regimes based on state production and central planning. These countries did participate in the new political (UN), but not in the new economic institutions (GATT).

In the course of the post-war period, we see a stepwise convergence of national regimes, facilitating international relations. The first such development was de-colonization. It created a large number of new independent states with considerable development problems. The second major event was the demise of the command economies. Most countries now have adopted some form of the liberal democratic system. A final important feature has been the demise of the import substitution policies of many developing countries, most of which have now opted for strategies based on world market access and global competitiveness.

In matters of the corporate structure the most important feature is the surge of multinational firms (MNF) during the period. MNFs are now responsible for a very significant part of total trade and investment. Their operations span the globe. However, the pattern of their operations has changed under the influence of a change of regime. As regards foreign trade and investment, a major shift has occurred from the 1970s onwards. Before that date most of the foreign direct investment was of the tariff (or rather obstacles) jumping type: multinational firms investing in a country to produce locally as an alternative to their exporting to that country. Since then, a much more intricate pattern has evolved whereby firms split parts of their production over different locations. The investment in production, distribution and other service facilities is of the optimal location type; whereby the best location in terms of cost and other important factors (access to finance to R&D) is chosen (see Box 2.1).

2.6.2 Trade

The total volume of world trade has increased very fast in the post-war period. Growth was not equal during the period (see Figure 2.2). Under the influence of the post-war reconstruction and the stabilization that the major international regimes such as the Bretton Woods institutions (see Section 2.6.5) provided, trade growth amounted to some 8 per cent per annum. Under the influence of the crisis of the 1970s and the collapse of the fixed exchange rate regime yearly trade growth slowed down to a low of some 1.5 per cent; in recent years it picked up speed again to some 4.5 per cent. Whatever the differences over time, the increase in trade has always far outstripped the increase in world output. Indeed, over an extended period the former has been almost double as high as the latter. In a sense the increase in the post-Second Word War period has compensated for the disintegration of the inter-war period. This becomes clear by comparing the figures for the end of the century with those for the beginning: the share of international trade in the GDP of some major trade partners has caught up only in 1990 with the 1913 figure (Table 2.3). However, it should be taken into consideration that the composition of the GDP has greatly changed. For the most developed countries a high percentage is now in services. If we correct for that we see for the largest of the most developed economies a dip in the interrelations due to the two world wars (1913–60) and a very clear rise in the degree of international interrelations since (1960–90).

The *patterns of origin and destination* of trade saw a fundamental change during the second half of the twentieth century and the beginning of the twenty-first. The dominant trade is no longer an exchange of manufactured goods against primary products. Most of the world trade is now intra-industrial trade between developed countries, which reflects the spatial division of tasks between the different affiliates of a multinational firm. Over the years the share of the newly industrializing countries has grown and an increasing number of countries have started to participate in this world system. It is particularly developed in the areas where economies of scale are present, both in production but also in marketing (international branding). Moreover, much of the trade is actually intra-regional (see Box 2.2).

The *composition* of trade reflects, on the one hand, the structural shifts in the global economy that have been recalled in the previous section. On the other hand, it is a continuation of the trends of the previous period. Growth is recorded for manufactured products in the field of metal engineering, transport equipment and electrical machinery such as computers (both consumer goods and investment goods). The increased share of services in the national economy has had its effects in trade; although the total trade in services is still low compared with manufacturing, some service sectors such as leisure (tourism), commercial (R&D, advertising, legal) and financial services (credit, derivatives) have rapidly grown in importance.

Table 2.3 Share (%) of trade in GDP and merchandise value added of selected countries 1913–90

	Trade to GDP				Trade to merchandise value added			
	1890	*1913*	*1960*	*1990*	*1890*	*1913*	*1960*	*1990*
UK	27	30	15	21	62	76	34	63
France	14	16	10	17	19	23	17	53
Germany	16	20	15	24	23	29	25	58
USA	6	6	3	8	14	13	10	36
Japan	5	13	9	8	10	24	15	19

Source: Adapted from Feenstra, 1998: 33–5.

Box 2.2 **Globalization or regionalization?**

Much of the increased trade is actually between countries in the same area. This leads some authors to refute the idea of globalization and to speak of *regionalization* of the world economy. This regional concentration is the effect of distance (transaction cost, see Chapter 4) and the creation of regional institutions (see Chapters 5 and 6). Areas that have embarked on successful regional integration schemes do indeed show both high shares of intra-regional trade and an increase over time in these shares (EU[8] and NAFTA). For schemes in other parts of the world the levels are relatively low and a trend towards an increase in the share of intra-trade in total either did not happen (ASEAN) or remained fairly timid (Africa). Mercosur (LA) takes a middle position. So, Table 2.4 confirms that there is indeed a trend towards regionalization in the world, but also shows that this trend is far from general.

Table 2.4 Share (%) of intra-regional trade in total trade of major regional groupings, 1970–2000

Area[9]	1970	1980	1990	2000
North America (NAFTA)	36	34	41	55
Europe (EU)	60	61	66	61
Asia (ASEAN)	23	17	19	23
Africa (SADC)	3	1	3	9
Africa (ECOWAS)	3	10	8	10
Latin America (Mercosur)	9	12	9	21

Sources: UNCTAD 1996/97, 2001.

Is this regionalization in conflict with globalization? The answer is: not necessarily. It depends on the external openness of regional blocs. We will illustrate this thesis with the example of the European Union. Over the period 1960 to 2000 the share of the external trade of the EU in its total GDP has oscillated around 10 per cent. Given the large increase of the GDP over that period and its reorientation to services, this figure means that the EU has very considerably increased its trade with other parts of the globe. The development pattern of this trade was, however, very different for different areas of the globe. The share of the OECD area in the total remained more or less stable; the share of Asia surged while the shares of Africa and Latin America actually declined (Molle, 2001; page 106–12).

2.6.3 *Capital*

The movement of capital has been gradually liberalized during the post-war period. This applies for all major types of capital flows.

Foreign direct investment has risen very considerably during this period. This is reflected in the doubling of the share of 'foreign' production in total world GDP from some 5 per cent in 1980 to some 10 per cent by the turn of the century. The most visible part of this FDI is mergers and acquisitions that have surged in the last decades as well (UNCTAD, 1993, 1999).[10] The first to develop FDI to a large extent were American companies that invested mostly in manufacturing in Europe and in primary production in developing countries. Two of the major determinants of FDI outflows are availability of capital and technological lead. After the war only the US fulfilled these criteria. However, after recovery other countries started to export capital as well. This was notably the case for EU firms which invested in the US for obtaining a presence in the most sophisticated market of the world. Other EU firms invested in emerging and developing economies mostly for cheap production of (parts of) manufactured goods that could no longer sustain the high cost levels in the EU. Japanese firms followed more or less the same model. Together, the countries cited dominated the pattern of FDI. Smaller players that have come to the stage recently are the Asian tigers such as Hong Kong, Singapore, Taiwan and South Korea. In recent decades the total flows of FDI have much increased under the influence of more and more markets opening up to foreign competition. This occurred first for developing countries abandoning the policy of import substitution and next for former communist countries giving up central planning. In the latter group the privatisation of state enterprises being taken over by Western companies contributed much to the growth of FDI.

Portfolio investments (consisting of investments by a private person or a company of one country in bonds or corporate equity in another country) have developed gradually over the decades. They have developed under the growing need for capital of both the private and the public sector in developing countries, notably emerging markets. They have even surged in recent years under the influence of a number of factors (Irwin and Vines, 2001):

- The liberalization of capital markets by the most important countries has permitted an increasing number of investors to diversify their portfolios internationally.
- The rapid growth of the capital markets in emerging economies, such as Hong Kong, Thailand and Malaysia in Asia and Mexico in the Americas has created new opportunities.
- The increase in the number of new products (such as derivatives) provided by international capital markets permitted intermediary services to adapt better to the specific needs of both suppliers and demanders of capital.

The present state of affairs, by which many intermediaries operate on the major stock markets of the world, does not provide a clear picture of the major countries which are net importers and those which are net exporters of capital. There is a very fine woven fabric of interrelations now spanning the globe.

Public capital flows cover grants and loans to governments of developing countries, mostly on soft terms, for development projects or for alleviating specific problems such as famine. Some of this flow has been in bilateral form, some of it in multilateral form.

- *Bilateral.* This aid is generally called official developed assistance (ODA). It has its origin with the governments of the developed countries. In the early post-war period the US was the biggest donor, in recent years the EU (both individual member countries and the EU as a whole) has become the main donor. In the 1970s, OPEC emerged as an important donor as well.
- *Multilateral.* This aid is given under the aegis of the World Bank (see Chapter 6) and its affiliate the International Development Association.

In recent years the level of official aid has tended to decrease as a consequence of a general disenchantment with its effectiveness, on the one hand, and the development of private sources of finance, on the other.

This freedom of capital movement has led to a larger vulnerability of the world financial system to crises, as is evidenced from historical data for a long period (Bordo *et al.*, 2001). During the post-war period of fixed exchange rates there were relatively few crises. After the collapse of this system in the mid-1970s the frequency of crises has increased and so has the severity. In recent years this tendency has become even more marked; it is related to a set of factors that we detail in Chapter 8 (Finance).

2.6.4 Migration

The total numbers of migrants remained relatively stable over the period up to 1990, with some increase afterwards. In relative terms labour mobility is of limited importance if compared with the flows of trade and capital; this is due to a considerable segmentation of labour market based on national restrictive immigration policies, on the one hand, and cultural factors that inhibit movement, on the other hand.

Intercontinental migration patterns have substantially changed during the post-war period. In the 1950s Europe was the main source of emigration. Some five million people felt that the resources of the war-ridden economies of Europe were insufficient to provide the standard of living that they could have in resource-rich countries that had not seen the devastation of the war. So the principal immigration countries were the US, Canada and Australia, but also Argentina and Brazil. Most of these migrants contributed directly to production in these countries as they had high skills both in agriculture and in various manufacturing industries. This European emigration dried up when Europe recovered from the devastation of the war. The subsequent rapid economic growth led to acute labour shortages and Europe became an immigration area.

In the 1960s many northwestern European countries developed links with countries of the southern and eastern facades of the Mediterranean basin to channel immigration. In this way millions of people entered Europe first as guest workers.

The economic crisis of the second half of the 1970s[11] put a stop to the need for foreign workers in Europe. However, little return migration occurred, and even after the stop on immigration many continued to come, either legally for family reasons or illegally. In this way the situation in Europe can be compared with that of the US where many Latin Americans cross the southern border without a permit.

In the 1980s and increasingly in the 1990s the picture of migration has become truly global. Indeed, large numbers of migrants fled from countries with poor living standards often coupled with security problems to the developed countries of the world. Some of this migration is organized, such as Asians working in the Middle East. However, much more migration is of an individual type. This new phenomenon has come about under the influence of a number of factors. First the push–pull factors: increased information (via satellite television) has meant that more people are informed about the wealth differences between their home countries and those of the developed world. Second, the friction factor has been diminished because of lower transport costs, more effective organizations (mobile phones) and more open borders (for Europe due to the fall of the Iron Curtain).

In the present century these latter trends are likely to become even more marked (Siddique, 2001).

2.6.5 Institutions (regimes and organizations)

Already during the Second World War a number of the foundations were laid to make sure that the international economy would not suffer from the problems of the inter-war period, and that it would be able to cope with the consequences of the war. The setting up of new international organizations was stimulated by two factors. First, there was no longer a hesitation as to leadership, the US had emerged from the war as the clear world leader and was prepared to assume that role. Next, the experiences of the inter-war and war periods had taken away the hesitation as to the basic conditions that needed to be fulfilled for governing international relations. These basically concerned the creation of regimes for trade and capital relations and a general forum for, among others, security matters. It was decided that specialist organizations would take care of different functions, thereby creating flexibility as to membership, rules, mode of operation and modalities of cooperation, etc.

The General Agreement on Tariffs and Trade (GATT), later recast as the World Trade Organization (WTO), had as its major task to promote the liberalization of international trade. To that end it started a number of rounds of tariff reductions. As a result, the tariffs on manufactured goods have been reduced to a very low level. The GATT/WTO had somewhat less success with non-tariff matters. It has even had less success in matters of trade in agriculture. Membership that initially was restricted to developed nations has increased over the years and encompasses now not only all the major economies of the globe, but also most less-developed countries (LDCs) and transition countries.

The International Monetary Fund (IMF) has been set up to pursue two main objectives. First, the creation of a multilateral payments system based on convertibility of the currencies of all trading nations. Second, the introduction of an international competence in orderly adaptation of exchange rates. The historical importance of this regime shift is illustrated by placing it in the systematic ordering of Table 2.2. The shift referred to here is from an automatic one (gold standard in top row) to a regime where there is coresponsibility of governments with the management of the exchange rate (middle row). The Fund was attributed the task to help member countries to restore balance of payments equilibrium and to realize exchange rate stability. The latter task implied the avoidance of competitive currency devaluations. The Fund had a limited role at the beginning of the third quarter of the century when exchange rates were fixed in terms of parities to the dollar and the most important source of a balance of payment disequilibrium were deficits on the trade balance. Its role changed gradually with the change in the hegemony of the US dollar (from last column in Table 2.2 to middle column). In the course of the last quarter of a century the task of the Fund has become more complex. It has to cope now with flexible exchange rates and with high capital mobility that can have a huge impact on the balance of payments with the risk of currency runs (shift from middle row of table to lowest row).[12] The Fund tries to realize its task by providing loans to member countries in difficulties and by regular surveillance of the situation on international financial markets.

The United Nations addresses a series of global concerns. The most important of them is security. As this book limits itself to economic issues, we will restrict ourselves here to the description of the most important competences of the UN in this field.

- *Trade and development.* In the 1960s the developing countries found that their interests were not taken sufficiently into account by GATT and they created, under the system of the UN, the United Nations Conference on Trade and Development (UNCTAD). UNCTAD has had some impact in terms of putting issues to the international agenda and in terms of stabilization of primary product prices. However, as an organization UNCTAD has faded to the benefit of the WTO.
- *Environment.* In 1949 the UN convened an international conference on the conservation and utilization of resources. It started an era in which

the United Nations took increasing responsibility for addressing world-wide environmental concerns. In the course of the 1950–2000 period a whole series of international conferences were held under the auspices of the UN (Rio de Janeiro, Johannesburg, Kyoto; see Chapter 9); some of which created organizations with competences in specific environmental matters. One of the more active among them has been the United Nations Environmental Programme (UNEP), launched in 1972. It coordinated the existing institutions, set a plan for action and adopted general principles to guide such action. Legal instruments were developed to enforce conservation of natural resources and environmental protection. In the last decade of the past century a new impetus was given by the United Nations Conference on Environment and Development (UNCED). It broadened the scope of the activities and developed methods for effective compliance.

- *High seas.* Here, several agreements about ocean transport have been made.

Together, the fortunate constellation of national regimes that were consistent with the international regimes has provided for a very high growth of the global economy in the 'golden' period of the third quarter of the twentieth century. Nationally, all countries followed economic policies that stimulated technology change and productivity increases coupled with active macro-economic stabilization. Internationally, there were stable exchange rates, increasing trade openness and monetary support for countries that needed the facility temporarily. Generally, this provided for full employment and growth in the advanced countries. The experience of the developing world is less unequivocal; in many countries problems tended to persist (see next chapter). The lessons of the crisis of the 1970s have brought an end to this constellation. A new paradigm emerged, putting the accent nationally on liberalization of markets and privatization of national industries and services and internationally on the liberalization of trade and capital flows. Whether the new paradigm will be more effective than the old is still a matter for debate.

Finally, regional organizations have been created during the period. Most of the early schemes were based on the idea that they would help industrialization through import substitution. They have, in general, been unsuccessful. Early starters (such as the EU) and more recent ventures in other continents (NAFTA in North America and Mercosur in South America) have been successful. They were based on the idea of open regionalism, that is that they were basically open to the world market.

2.7 Summary and conclusions

- The international economy has seen profound changes over the past centuries. These have been largely a response to fundamental changes that have occurred in matters of technology (notably transport and energy), in economic structure (from agriculture to information) and in politics (notably the demise of communism).

- Together these developments have produced a long-term increase in global interchange and integration. Over the last half century we see that global trade and capital movements have very quickly grown in size and complexity.
- Changes in the world economy have had important effects on the roles of the *major actors*, such as private firms, public authorities and representatives of civil society.
- The increase in international economic integration has been accompanied by the development of international economic institutions. The system of specialist international organizations created by a bold and imaginative initiative in the post-Second World War period has functioned reasonably well since then. Its scope has been gradually widened, while the structure of several regimes has also been strengthened.
- In subsequent parts of the book we will see that this fragmented, incomplete and inconsistent structure has not yet found answers to important new needs and is inadequate as a world system of government.

3 Coping with the effects of globalization

3.1 Introduction

Globalization is a very pervasive trend. We have seen in the previous chapter how it has developed over time. Proponents of globalization (among them very powerful ones) bring forward the benefits that it has brought. They point first towards the economic benefits, highlighting the growth of some countries that have opened their markets to international trade and investment. They point next towards the benefits in terms of peace and security, highlighting the low degree of armed conflicts between countries that have a strong economic interchange.[1]

Yet many others (among them very vociferous ones) are not happy with the effects of globalization. They actually blame globalization for many problems of the present-day situation. In this chapter we will go into some of their arguments. We will do that on the basis of a thorough analysis of the (mostly) empirical literature.

First, we will deal with the problem that globalization has left a number of developing countries (LDCs) out in the cold. Second, with the allegation that globalization has a series of negative influences on the labour market in both highly developed countries and LDCs. Third, with the argument that globalization erodes the possibility of welfare enhancing policies by national governments. Lastly, we will deal with the claim that globalization leaves capitalists free to act, which has negative consequences in terms of financial instability, pollution of the global environment, etc.

In the final section we will draw conclusions from our analysis and on that basis indicate the way forward for policy-makers. Our conclusion from the extensive review of the theoretical and empirical literature is that the positive effects of globalization are greater than the negative effects. So the logical way forward is to adapt national policies to further opening and to compensate for the resulting erosion of the capacity of national policy-making by strengthening the capacity of the multilateral institutions to cope with the major problems.

3.2 Unequal wealth distribution?

3.2.1 Does openness to trade stimulate development?

Economic theory states that international trade has a positive effect on the level of wealth. Such positive effects are enhanced in case there is freedom of capital movement in particular freedom of direct investment. Indeed, in this way capital can be used in the places where it has the best potential. The trend towards globalization has created new opportunities for trade and investment. However, much of the theory also says that these positive effects are conditional upon the absence of distortions (see for a review, for instance, Srinavasan and Bhagwati, 1999). The question about whether openness to trade does help growth is therefore largely an empirical matter. Here, much controversy has arisen between two views.

The proponents of openness claim that there is considerable empirical evidence that this enhanced openness to international trade and long-term capital flows has had positive implications for economic growth and living standards[2] (see, for instance, OECD, 1994; Frankel and Romer, 1999; Irwin and Tervio, 2002). Their views lead to a policy stand that favours export promotion and exposure to world markets. This has now become the dominant view, notwithstanding the fact that most of the remaining protection measures of the developed countries are in sectors that would be of most interest to the LDCs (mostly agriculture and textiles).

The opponents of openness claim that openness does not lead to more growth and is, moreover, responsible for some extra problems, such as widening income gaps within countries and increased vulnerability to external shocks (Rodriguez and Rodrik, 1999). Such shocks may have a lasting negative effect on growth rates. Openness also leads to a decrease in the capacity to cope with such shocks, because openness squeezes the size of government programmes (Rodrik, 1997). Their views lead to the policy stand that a protectionist policy coupled with an import substitution policy are quite valid instruments for enhancing growth in LDCs.

The search for the determinant factors of growth has received considerable attention both in theoretical and empirical studies. The results of a (selective) review showed that institutional factors are very important in this respect. . . . 'Monetary shocks, the variability of inflation, and the weight of public consumption in GDP have an adverse effect on income growth. Finally, political stability, openness to trade and various indicators of financial development seem to be associated with faster growth' (de la Fuente, 1997: 46). Other studies (WTO, 1998; IBRD, 1997, 2002) tend to confirm the positive role of openness and of institutional factors (see Box 3.1) and stress the role other (supply side) factors such as investment in human, physical and technological capital play in stimulating growth.

The present mainstream view (orthodoxy) is two-fold. First, the advantages of openness tend to be more important than the disadvantages. Second, adequate institutions (minimum government) and non-interventionist

Box 3.1 **Credibility, investment and growth**

For the World Development Report of 1997 a large private sector survey was held covering 3,600 firms, asking about the credibility of the state. This was measured on criteria such as predictability of rule-making, political stability, the fight against crime, liability of judicial system and freedom from corruption (IBRD, 1997). Countries were grouped in three classes of credibility. For each class the average rate of investment and the average rate of growth were calculated. The figures show very clearly that credible institutions have a very significant influence on both investment and growth.

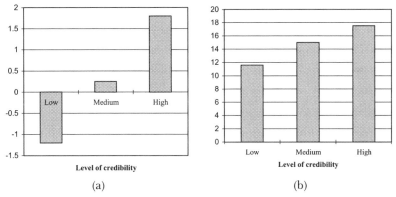

(a)   (b)

Figure 3.1 (a) Growth of GDP per capita (per year); (b) Growth of investment (percentage of GDP) by level of credibility.

policies are prerequisites for growth. There is much opposition against this view by countries that want to choose alternative ways to development. Their opposition is corroborated by the finding that none of the presently highly developed countries has actually followed these policy prescriptions in the past. So, it looks as if the rich countries have climbed in the past a ladder of protectionism and idiosyncratic institutions; a ladder that they kick away now that the poor countries want to climb it as well (Chang, 2002). Even now the highly developed countries do not follow an orthodox view in practice. They still apply protectionist policies in sensitive areas and use dense networks of institutions to foster the smooth functioning of their economies.

3.2.2 Does it lead to inequitable distribution and more poverty?

The question of the inequality has three aspects. The first one relates to the differences between countries and has to do with the claim that globalization leaves a number of countries out in the cold. We will show that this view is right. The second one is related to the difference between different groups within countries and has to do with the allegation that the populations of LDCs are poor and that openness actually increases the problems of the poor.[3] The third one combines elements of the previous two and deals with the general suggestion that globalization leads to a deterioration of the distribution of income in the world. We will show that the latter two allegations cannot be substantiated.

The first question, 'Has growth has been distributed in an equal manner over countries' is in general analysed with the help of indicators of convergence (less disparity over time) or divergence (more disparity over time). There is controversy here, both with respect to the conclusions and to the causal factors. Indeed, theoretical studies can lead to different outcomes, depending on the hypothesis made and the variables taken into account. So the question is how far empirical studies can enlighten us as to the validity of either thesis.

The problem is, however, that empirical studies also tend to come to different conclusions depending on the choices made as to the period, econometric specification, country sample, method and data used for the analysis. If we look at the very long term (1820–1990) we see divergence, stemming from the fact that the high-income countries of 1820 tended to grow faster than the low-income countries. The ratio between the rich countries and the poor countries rose from 2:1 in 1820 to 7:1 in 2000 (Maddison, 2001).[4] Diverging tendencies dominated the whole twentieth century (see IMF, 2000). Moreover, persistent problems seem to have been aggravated, as the composition of the lowest and the highest group had stayed remarkably stable over the whole century. For a more recent period, Park (2001) using data for the total set of countries in the world concludes that the global distribution of income has become more unequal from 1960 to 1976, but that since then the opposite tendency has set in. For the whole period 1960–90 his data show neither convergence nor divergence. Others (e.g. de la Fuente 1997, analysing notably the period 1960–85, or IBRD, 1992) find a general tendency towards more inequality, which is due to the growth rates of the high-income countries being significantly higher than those of the low-income countries (see also Table 3.1).[5] This trend seems to have been reversed in the last decade due a double effect: on the one hand, higher growth in Asia, and on the other, slackening growth in most of the highly developed countries.

As a consequence of this differential growth the disparities have increased. In 1960 the ratio of the share of world income to world population stood at 0.2 for the developing countries and at 2.7 for the developed countries. In 1990 the ratio for the former group had stayed the same while the latter had increased to 3.7 (Stewart, 1995). Calculating the disparity in another way leads to similar conclusions. Indeed, between 1960 and 1995 the ratio between the income of the 20 per cent of the world population living in the

Table 3.1 Growth of per real per capita income (average percentage annual change), 1960–2000

	1960–70	1970–80	1980–90	1990–2000
Developed countries	4.1	2.4	2.4	1.6
Developing countries:	3.3	3.0	1.2	3.0
Sub-Saharan Africa	0.6	0.9	−0.9	−0.2
East Asia	3.6	4.6	6.3	6.0
South Asia	1.4	1.1	3.1	4.6
Latin America	2.5	3.1	−0.5	1.9

Sources: 1960–90: IBRD (1992) *World Development Report*, p. 32; 1990–2000: estimates based on 1990/99 figures in UNCTAD (2001) *Handbook of Statistics*, pp. 290–99.

richest countries and the income of the 20 per cent living in the poorest countries has increased from 30 to 82 (UNDP, 1998). So, many LDCs have not been able to benefit from the opportunities that globalization has opened up. They have not been able to catch up with the most developed ones; on the contrary many of them have even lost ground. The most problematic aspect to this is that in the world a large number of people actually live on very low incomes. At the turn of the century it was estimated (IRBD, 2000) that about 40 per cent of the population of South Asia and Sub-Saharan Africa and some 25 per cent of East Asia and Latin America had to live on less than $1 a day. Together this afflicts more than 1.5 billion people.

Some authors have challenged the validity of the GDP/P figures for measuring convergence or divergence. They favour indices such as the quality of life index or the human development index. These also take such factors as health and literacy into account. Some of these indices (see IMF, 2000) actually show a general catching up of all poor countries with the rich ones. But even on these scores the differences between country groups are high: Africa and South Asia score on average only half of the figure of the group USA/Australasia/EU.

The second question, 'Is openness to trade detrimental to the equality of the income distribution in LDCs and does it worsen the poverty problem?', has no simple answer either. The theoretical work on the effects of trade liberalization on inequality in general (Fischer, 2001) and on poverty (see Winters, 2001) shows that there are many channels through which the independent variable can have an effect on the dependent variable. Much depends on the specific case whether the effect will be negative or not. The results of empirical case studies are very difficult to generalize. On aggregate level we find only a very general result, that poverty reduction owes much to growth in general, so that we actually can refer for the basics of a poverty reduction policy to the stimulation of the growth factors discussed in the previous sections.

The third question is: 'Has the era of globalization seen an aggravating poverty divide worldwide?' The answer to this question has been hampered for a long time by a lack of data. Recently, Bhalla (2002) has analysed a set of homogenized data for income categories, allowing a picture of the distribution of income over brackets for the world as a whole to be drawn up. These data show that the percentage of the world population living below the poverty line has decreased between 1980 and 2000 from 44 to 13. World income inequality has decreased in the same period at an unprecedented pace. The results are highly influenced by the good performance of the two most populous countries, China and India, both of which had a very good growth record. Their figures have dwarfed the bad results of the African countries. The conclusion of this study is thus that in an era of globalization large segments of the poorest people in the world have been able to improve their position significantly.

3.2.3 The effects of trade openness on LDC growth

Many LDCs that have failed to catch up with the richer countries blame globalization for this problem. They feel that globalization creates greater opportunities for the powerful, while limiting the leeway for LDCs to pursue policies that are geared to their specific needs and possibilities.

There is considerable evidence to the contrary as well, however. For many LDCs the access to the markets of the traditionally highly developed countries has opened up new job opportunities and has helped to restructure the economy towards higher value-added production sustaining higher salaries.

The trade policy of the LDCs is a major element to explain the success or the failure in this respect. We recall that openness to trade used to come up with a positive sign in the growth equations cited in the previous section. However, this may not apply to the subsample of LDCs, so a more detailed analysis of this group was in order. WTO (1998) have grouped 41 LDCs into four categories of openness to trade over three decades. They found that the average growth of GDP per head of each category was systematically higher the higher the degree of openness. The differences in growth between the categories, moreover, tended to increase over time. Authors associated with the World Bank (Dollar and Kraay, 2001) have grouped the data by three categories: rich countries, globalizers (increasing trade GDP ratio) and non-globalizers. The results are given in Figure 3.1, and show that:

- In the last two decades the globalizers outperform both rich countries and non-globalizer poor countries; the latter by a very large margin.
- Growth rates of globalizers show a positive trend over time, while growth rates of rich countries tend to decrease over time.

Simulation exercises also show that the LDCs as a group can gain considerably from further liberalization. A new round of multilateral broad-based tariff cuts is estimated to have considerable net benefits; the terms of trade losses and gains tend to cancel out, whereas the efficiency and pro-

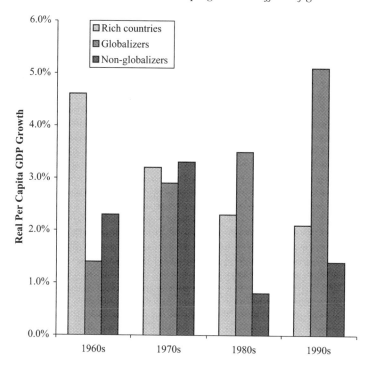

Figure 3.2 Real GDP per capita growth (percentage) per category of wealth and openness, 1960–2000.

Source: Dollar and Kraay, 2001.[6]

competitive effects can come fully into play (Brown *et al.*, 2001; Francois, 2001). 'To put the estimated net income effects into perspective; the projected annual income gains for developing countries would well out-weigh recent annual flows of official development aid to these countries. They would also be comparable to aggregate FDI flows' (Francois, 2001).

The positive effect of general trade liberalization measures on growth and hence on poverty reduction does not exclude that in individual cases the effect may be less positive. On the contrary, in some cases it may even be disastrous if countries are thrown into difficulties from which they cannot recover (misery trap). So the implementation of trade and development policies has to take account of such problems (see Box 3.2).

3.2.4 *The effects of openness to capital movements on LDC growth*

The issue of openness to capital movements is more controversial than that of openness to trade. This is related to the fact that capital is much more mobile than other production factors. The controversy comes about because of the difference between theory and practice:

Box 3.2 Trade and growth: a positive relation in general may imply a negative relation in particular cases

The relation of trade liberalization on growth and in particular on poverty alleviation is a complex one. In principle the further extension of the number of countries participating in trade liberalization and of the type of goods to which this applies should have positive macro effects. Yet it may be very problematic in individual cases. We will give here a few reasons why the putting into practice of liberalization measures may actually lead to problems instead of solutions.

Relative levels of protection may be poverty reducing
The entrance of China in the WTO and the elimination of the protection in textiles (see Chapter 7) may hit poorer-developed countries very hard, countries which have until now developed successfully as textiles and clothing (T&C) locations. Bangladesh, which is one of the poorest countries in the world, has profited from the existing quota system (and from the more lenient treatment of the EU of its exports) to build up a significant T&C industry. It now faces the possibility that a number of producers will relocate their production to China, as many consider that the conditions there in terms of stability of institutions, quality and price of labour force, and infrastructure are better.

Difficulties in restructuring
Trade liberalization strengthens the motivation for firms to modernize, but they may lack the means to do so successfully. Small countries, where growth has been restricted because of the small size of their domestic market, should be among the prime beneficiaries of the trade liberalization. However, due to constraints it may be difficult for these countries to fully realize the benefits. First, the potential for scale economies is normally associated with manufacturing. This may not be so important for poor, primary goods exporting countries with a small manufacturing industry. Second, the substitutability between import-competing goods and export goods can be low in poor countries. When the import-competing sector contracts as a result of trade liberalization this does not automatically release resources for the expansion of other sectors of the economy when the differences in product mix and skill requirements are wide. The building up of alternative competitive economic activities may be a very difficult exercise due to shortages in entrepreneurship, in capital, in infrastructure, in institutions, etc.

Source: Based on EU–LDC Network; Brief, November 2001 Issue on Trade and Poverty Reduction.

- *Theory* shows that the openness leads to a better allocation of resources and therefore to positive effects. It hints, moreover, at the dynamic effects of liberalization, creating new opportunities through innovative products and services.
- *Practice* shows that the movement of this production factor has in the past been related to considerable turbulence on financial markets and to crises. These, in turn, have had a very negative influence on the growth performance of the countries hit by them and on the countries to which the turbulence spread (see Chapter 8).

In the past these considerations have induced most countries to control capital movements. Recently, most developed countries and many LDCs have changed their policy towards openness. Most important factors creating this change were (Molle, 2001):

- Improvement in the balance of payments position;
- Poor efficiency of control instruments notably after information revolution;
- Deregulated domestic markets inconsistent with external controls.

The question now is whether openness to international capital movements is also beneficial to the growth of the LDCs. The effect of capital account liberalization on growth has been the object of a series of studies differing in methodology, time period, etc. A review of these studies (IMF, 2001a) finds a weak link between liberalization and growth. Positive effects may come about when capital openness is linked with higher domestic private investment, positive spill-overs of FDI and a boost to domestic financial depth (a measure for the quality of the domestic capital market). The positive effect is enhanced in case the country also pursues an openness policy with respect to trade. However, capital inflows can also lead to financial instability, which has a negative influence on growth. Indeed, when liberalization occurs in tranquil times, capital flows tend to increase and boost positive effects; the opposite is true in turbulent times. So, the net benefits depend very much on (1) the strength of the domestic macroeconomic policies; (2) the quality of the financial regime and structures; and (3) the good sequencing of liberalization.

So, this leads to the conclusion that the case for financial liberalization is at best a weak one, contrary to the case for trade liberalization (Bhagwati, 1998a).

3.2.5 The effect of openness to foreign direct investment (FDI)

The question, 'Which policy towards FDI?' has for a long time preoccupied governments of many developing countries. MNFs were supposed to exploit the resources of the host countries, both natural and human resources.

They were thought to manipulate the local institutions. The policy that many governments thought most apt to cope with these problems was to bind FDI in their country to a number of strict rules. These were often conceived as part of an import substitution strategy, implying that the investment had to target the local market and could benefit from trade protection.

In the course of the past decades the attitude of many governments towards FDI has changed considerably, mainly for the following four reasons (UNCTAD, 1999: 152):

- Increased awareness of the positive contribution that FDI can make to development and of the conditions under which such contribution can be made optimal;
- Increased capacity of governments to deal with MNFs; increased number of MNFs that follow codes of good corporate citizenship and hence increased mutual comfort in the relation between governments and MNFs.
- Shift from public to private sources of international finance and increased spread of the origin of FDI (an estimated 15–20 per cent of FDI now originates from developing countries.
- Conditionality of the financial support of international organizations (IMF and World Bank) and of the aid programmes of bilateral donors.

FDI has, in a number of cases, had very positive effects on the economy of the host country (see, for example, the case of China in Graham and Wada, 2001). In a number of other cases, however, it has had very negative effects. The positive impacts are basically due to increased competition, technology transfer and increased access to world markets. They are enhanced by spill-overs to local firms, worker training and management development (Lipsey and Muchielli, 2001).

The main difference between the occurrence of a positive and a negative effect seems to stem from policies of host governments. On the basis of the results of the analysis of a large set of cases, Moran (1998) concludes that FDI is likely to be:

- *Most successful* if the affiliate is wholly-owned and fully integrated in the global operations of the parent company. Export performance requirements have, in the past, encouraged this integration process. Joint ventures supposed to have helped the transfer of technology and the creation of a local supply and management capacity base have been less successful than fully foreign-owned firms.
- *Most harmful* when the investor is sheltered from competition in the domestic market and burdened with high domestic content, joint venture and technology-sharing requirements. There are political economy reasons why this negative effect risks to be perpetuated as this policy favours the creation of a constituency of rent seekers from protection.

The positive effect of FDI on development has induced many governments of both developed and developing countries to pursue policies to attract FDI. Much of this is necessary in the sense that FDI does not come about by itself. Other 'complementary' policies are needed in order to create a good environment for FDI (see Box 3.3). Yet other policies that entail subsidies are very difficult to pursue for LDCs, as their resources are limited, notably in comparison to those of the developed countries. In order to prevent an investment war replacing past trade wars, a regime for investment could be in the interest of all concerned. The architecture of such a regime will be elaborated in Chapters 11 and 12.

3.3 Negative effects on the labour market?[8]

3.3.1 Effects on (un)employment

Globalization is said to hurt workers. It is supposed to have a number of negative effects on the labour market. The more developed countries[9] are

---

Box 3.3 Success conditions for FDI

For FDI policies to be effective two types of actions need to be taken.

1. *Get the basics right by providing*
   - Sound macro and monetary policies;
   - Reliable and efficient institutions;
   - Strong commitment to openness.

2. *Link in FDI policies into other policies for development aimed at*[7]
   - Increasing domestic financial resources for development to supplement domestic savings and investment and, more basically, fostering enterprise development, as the creation of an efficient domestic supply capacity requires competitive economic agents;
   - Enhancing the technology, skill and knowledge base, given that these intangible resources are increasingly at the heart of the development effort;
   - Boosting trade competitiveness, as internationally competitive firms can contribute better to development by reaping the benefits of economies of specialization and scale, by broadening the demand base;
   - Maintaining competitive markets, to ensure that former statutory obstacles to investment and trade are not replaced by anticompetitive practices of firms; and
   - Protecting the natural environment, to maintain the basis for future growth and development.

:erned that globalization reduces their employment via increased petition of imports from low wage countries.[10] As local producers are n incapable of sustaining this competition, globalization is believed to lead to closures of firms and to delocation (transfer of activities from high-wage to low-wage countries). However, this will really 'hurt' only in so far as this labour is not redeployed in jobs that earn a higher income in the sector that can stand up to international competition or in one of the sheltered service sectors. The question is whether the fear of unemployment due to trade is confirmed by empirical data. To answer that question two types of study have been made.

The first type of studies started in the early 1970s. They were triggered by the steep increase in unemployment in all OECD countries that coincided with an increase in imports from developing countries. The implicit idea was that there was a causal relationship. However, the outcome of these studies (for a review, see OECD, 1979) did not support this view. Other factors, such as changes in demand and in technology, showed up as far more important. This need not be surprising in the light of the relatively small part that imports from LDCs actually have in total imports of large economic areas such as the EU or the US. Since then more theoretical and empirical work has been carried out. The available evidence suggests that globalization, in the form of increasing trade and investment with developing countries, is not the major determinant of unemployment.[11] Technology and openness do impose changes, but whether this leads to (un)employment depends on the (in)adequacy of national policies (Lee, 1996).

The second type of studies looks into *delocation*. The typical case of delocation concerns a firm that closes a plant, mostly a manufacturing plant in a traditional industry in a developed country and moves the production to a site in a low-wage LDC. The people made redundant blame their unemployment directly on globalization. Few large-scale studies into this phenomenon are known.[12] A study recently completed in Belgium concerned a survey of some 3,000 cases (see Sleuwaegen *et al.*, 2000; Pennings and Sleuwaegen, 2000) and produced several interesting results. For one, it showed the importance of the phenomenon; in the period 1990–5 almost 30 per cent of the total number of redundancies were related to relocations. These concerned mostly labour-intensive activities. Next it showed that only a limited number of these relocations were associated with the competition between the high-wage and the low-wage countries: most were actually due to restructuring within the EU. Finally, it showed that notably the more innovative, dynamic and profitable firms were involved in relocation. So, positive indirect effects tend to compensate for the negative direct effects. A similar study made for Italy (Schiattarella, 2001) did not find a negative correlation between Italian employment and relocalization either. However, there was an effect on skills in the sense that the particular industries studied shifted their labour demand to the higher-skill brackets. Whether this had a negative macro effect on the low-skilled could not be established by the study; to do so would imply a study of the demand for low-skilled labour by other sectors of the economy and of the dynamics of the relevant labour market. Other similar studies (see, for instance, those reported in Lipsey and Muchielli, 2001) show the complexity of the relations between mother companies and affiliates and tend to conclude also that FDI has for the most part a positive effect on both host and home countries.

3.3.2 Effects on (inequality of) wages

The second major labour market related concern of globalization is that it drives down wages.[13] The main interest has been with problems in the highly developed countries. The concern is with the following chain of events. Globalization enhances international competition from LDCs with developed countries. Some companies will not be able to resist so this will lead to a lower demand for labour in high-wage countries. This translates directly into lower average wages. However, this is not the whole story. Many think that globalization leads to higher inequality in the wage structure of the developed countries, which would be perceived as a negative effect given societal preferences. The simplified theoretical reasoning is as follows. Competition between developed countries with LDCs leads notably to a deterioration of the competitive position of the group of unskilled in the developed countries; the resulting decrease in demand leads to pressure on their wages (Wood, 1995; Walton and Balls, 1995).

However, the theoretical links are much more complicated. First, there is the relation between several types of institutions (policies), openness and inequality (Aghion, 1998). Next, there is the relation between trade and international production shifts (e.g. Feenstra, 1998). Under certain conditions the decrease in import prices in developed countries, due to a global increase in the openness to trade, can effectively lead to a local increase in the real wages of the unskilled workers there (Bhagwati, 1998b). Some have tried to do justice to this complexity by constructing general equilibrium models (e.g. Francois and Nelson, 1998). Thus, theory does have difficulty in clarifying the relations which explain this variety of effects (Wood, 2002).

We then have to turn to the results of empirical analyses. For the time being, the available evidence also permits a wide range of conclusions as to the effects on wages. For continental Europe we need to take into account that the labour market regulation (in particular with respect to minimum wages) has prevented a downward drift towards more divergence in wages between different skill groups. Here the effect may have been more on the score of unemployment; whereas in the Anglo Saxon world (UK and USA) the effects may have been more on inequality.[14]

Equally interesting, of course, would be to study the effects of globalization on average wage levels and wage inequality in developing countries.

The empirical data are much scarcer here, so that we cannot draw any firm conclusions on this subject.

3.3.3 Effects on migration

The third aspect we analyse is the effect of globalization on movement, in this case migration. In the post-Second World War period the increased openness of the various countries in the world on the scores of trade and capital relations has only partly found its counterpart in increased openness to the movement of labour (or people). This is neither the result of a lack of supply, nor a lack of demand. On the contrary, on the global level the pressures on both supply and demand sides have increased tremendously in the past decades (Ghosh, 2000). The push has increased as a consequence of improved information channels and decreased cost of transport. On the pull side we find both employers and those who consider that the present demography will not be sufficient to sustain the welfare state. In the end it is restrictive policies by host countries that determine the size of flows. These policies find their justification in the uncertain welfare effects of international migration.

In economic terms the migration of labour is seen as a mechanism for the improvement of the allocation of labour. It has positive effects as it increases the capacity of the economy to respond to new situations. However, this benefit is not obtained without cost. In labour-exporting countries the benefits are largely in the easing of the unemployment situation and the income from remittances; the costs are more long term and involve the loss of human resources and investment in education. For a labour-importing country, the main benefit is higher production. There are several cost factors. First, increases in public expenditure, as immigrants are thought to put higher demands on social services than indigenous persons; second, non-monetary costs in terms of social disruption and internal (in)security (e.g. for the EU, Huysmans, 2000); finally, slow-down of the adaptation of the sectoral structure of the economy to new technologies and world prices.

The quantification of these elements has proven to be a difficult exercise.[15] However, the available evidence suggests that the net benefits are at best fairly low. They are, moreover, dependent on the specific characteristics of the host country (labour market, social security benefit schemes, etc.) and of the length of stay of the migrant. These facts justify restrictive national policies and explain why there is not yet a worldwide regime for migration (contrary to trade and finance).[16]

Immigration also has a number of distributional effects. Some claim that it drives down domestic wages (and even capital income; Lundborg and Segerstrom, 2002) and that it increases unemployment. However, others (e.g. Agiomirgianakis and Zervoyianni, 2001) show that this need not be true and that labour can actually benefit. The available empirical evidence both from the EU (see, for instance, Tapinos and de Rugy, 1993; Zimmermann, 1995) and from the US (see, for a review, De Freitas, 1998) find that the negative effects on wages and unemployment are very small.

3.3.4 Effects on labour market institutions

Finally, we look into the effect of globalization on the way the labour market functions, that is into institutions. Labour market institutions differ considerably from one country to another. They have been developed over a long period in view of improving social standards and correcting outcomes of market processes in view of societal preferences (Teulings and Hartog, 1998). Many fear that openness is causing at best the erosion and at worst the total breakdown of these institutions. Some institutional arrangements are evidently more conducive to growth and employment than others. The main problems lie in the collective bargaining system and in labour market regulation.

As far as the bargaining system is concerned, the differences between countries (see OECD, 1997a) tend to be focussed on the level of concentration or centralization. In earlier studies a hump-shape relation has been found between unemployment and the level of concentration. On one side, we see that more concentration induces the taking into account of secondary effects. On the other side, we see that low concentration (bargaining at the firm level) induces taking the influence of competition into account. However, in the intermediate segment of concentration effects of wage setting can be shifted on others, leading to too high wage claims and hence to unemployment (Calmfors and Drifill, 1988). However, in more recent studies this hump shape no longer appears very clearly (OECD, 1997b).

Labour market regulation can have a significant influence on growth and thus on unemployment. It concerns employment protection, unemployment benefits (level and duration), payroll taxes and minimum wages. Strict regulation on these scores is mentioned as inhibiting employment (OECD, 1994). There is, however, some uncertainty as to the degree to which these factors (in combination with the bargaining system) influence employment (see, for instance, Fitoussi *et al.*, 2000).[17] Notwithstanding this, enhancing flexibility on many of the indicators mentioned and the lowering of labour related cost factors have a positive influence on competitiveness and hence on employment.[18]

Labour conditions. Many labour unions are against further globalization. Trade unions in high-wage countries fear that globalization enhances relocation, increases unemployment, lowers wages and has a negative impact on living and labour standards. Hence, they plead for both protection and for the introduction of labour standards in trade agreements (Cordella and Grilo, 2001).[19] LDCs are against such measures as they consider them as disguised trade protection. Non-governmental organizations

GOs) hold globalization responsible for the lowering of labour standards. Again a wide array of solutions is proposed in response. The argument is, further, that FDI in developing countries does often lead to exploitation of labour, including child labour.

Welfare state. Many fear that the pressure globalization puts on labour reduces the capacity of countries to sustain typical provisions of the welfare state such as insurance against illness, old age, unemployment, etc. Empirical investigations into this subject are scarce. Recent research (Rudra, 2002) on 53 LDCs shows that between 1972 and 1995 welfare spending did indeed respond negatively to greater openness to trade and capital. The reason is that the growing deterioration of the position of notably the lower skilled exacerbate the collective action problem, in other words their capacity to put pressure on government in their favour. This is different for developed countries, where the organizing capacity of the relevant groups is apparently stronger and institutions are more resilient.

3.4 Loss of sovereignty of national governments?

3.4.1 The fundamentals of the problem: system competition

National governments have to face an increasingly international business community that is less and less inclined to follow national rules. Multinational firms have the capacity to choose among several countries to locate their economic activity. They will choose their location on the basis of a set of criteria. Among them are cost considerations. Institutions concerning labour market regulation, taxes, environment, etc. influence these costs and hence location. International investors perceive some of these institutions as positive, others as negative.

Investors that do not like the regime they have to comply with can subtract from this regime by turning to some other location. So there will be competition between countries. With the need to create the conditions for growth based on FDI,[20] governments are induced to comply with investors' wishes by adapting national institutions and policies. The welfare effects of this can be of different nature. Some of it may be felt as neutral, for instance the switch to a new set of technical standards. Other aspects are felt as negative, for instance the lowering of labour or environmental (see Box 3.4) standards.[21] However, standards are only one aspect of the whole pattern. As a matter of fact, national systems that produce the environment in which MNFs work are a complex architecture in which elements of regulation of labour market, social security, innovation, dispute settlement, competition, taxes, infrastructure, etc., all have their place. The way each of these elements affects the choices of investors is very complex. So, there is room for countries to experiment in order to find a combination of positive factors for investment that come up as much as possible to societal preferences. On the other hand, there are also many inadequacies in system

Box 3.4 Does openness to global markets lead to a deterioration of the environment?

The relation trade environment is the subject of much controversy.

Many think that an open regime for trade leads to more pollution. The reasoning is simple; firms will move to counties with a weakly developed environmental policy. In this way they avoid abatement cost. Highly developed countries have, in general, a low tolerance level for pollution so firms will tend to relocate to the LDCs. These will become a sort of 'pollution haven'. The rich countries will then import the products of these firms from the LDCs. At the end of the day this leads to an increase in global pollution. The policy conclusion of this reasoning is clear: restrict free trade and apply checks on the way goods have been produced. If the goods have been produced under poor conditions import restrictions should be introduced.

Others think that trade helps improving the environment. The reasoning here is more complex. It starts with the consideration that trade increases wealth levels. It presumes next that wealth levels have a positive effect on the strictness of environmental policy. Abatement will be stepped up and pollution levels will thus decrease. This is reinforced by the fact that industries that are characterized by high pollution levels are usually very capital intensive. The conditions for such investments in LDCs are not always optimal. So we will see that firms will not move to LDC but prefer locations in capital-rich countries and accept the strictness of environmental policy. This reasoning leads to a quite different policy recommendation: stimulate open borders and transfer good practices in terms of environmental policy.

The two opposing views have up till now coexisted. Recently, some empirical work has been done (Antweiler *et al.*, 2001) that comes up with support for the second option. Their analysis of trade patterns, industrial structures and environmental policies of more than 40 countries (covering both developed and LDCs) for the period 1971–96 showed that the increase of national income with 1 per cent leads to a decrease in pollution of about 1 per cent. This relation holds only in democratic countries; so for many of the present transition countries pollution has increased in the past.

competition in matters of FDI. They call for an international regime. We will go in detail into this aspect in Chapter 11.

There is thus competition between national systems. To some, this competition is a healthy phenomenon. They (e.g. Ohmae, 1995) argue that the trend towards international openness is a fact of life and that both national governments and societal groups, such as labour unions, have to accommodate this, even when the effects are negative because there is no way to stop the trend. To others, such competition puts in jeopardy some essential public goods that only the government can provide. They argue that the trend has such negative effects that opposing forces should be mobilized. Among these authors are those who do not count on the national governments to reform international institutions because, in their view, the former have effectively been taken over by multinational industry (Hertz, 2001).

Good governance is not only needed to attract MNFs. The whole economic system works better under good governance. Econometric analyses show that GDP is higher the higher the scores of a country on aspects such as voice to interest groups and civil society, accountability, political stability, rule of law, absence of corruption, etc. (Kaufmann *et al.*, 1999a, 1999b, 2002).

3.4.2 *The aggravation of the problem: loss of instruments*

In modern societies governments have important roles to play. They have to make sure that a number of social objectives are attained. Such policy goals are based on democratic preferences and defined in terms of public goods (see next chapter). To give effect to their policies, governments use several instruments, including regulation and financial means.

In the past, governments tended to protect their economy from outside influences with instruments such as restrictions on the movement of goods and factors (labour and capital). For some time this has no longer been possible and an increasingly large segment of the national economy is subject to ever-stronger influences from abroad. In this way, globalization has indeed increased the vulnerability of national states (in particular small, open, developing economies) to external shocks (Kose, 2002). It has, moreover, made these states more receptive to influences from both policies and decisions of other governments and strategies and decisions of multinational corporations.

Globalization has, on the other hand, limited the capacity of governments to intervene. This applies to several segments of policy-making. The most obvious one is trade policy: to provide MNFs with an open regime, most trade instruments have been given up. Monetary policy is another case in point; under integrated financial markets an independent policy is only possible with flexible exchange rates. Now, many countries would like to stabilize the exchange rate and not be subject to speculations (see Chapter 8, for further discussion and proof).

This lack of intervention capacity due to internationalization is reinforced by a tendency towards denationalization and privatization. Examples of the first are monetary instruments that are now in the hands of independent national central banks. Fiscal policy is no longer used for immediate macro-economic effects, but is set in a long-term context of sound public finances that sustain a low inflation policy. Due to the trend towards privatization and more market liberalization, many possibilities of government leverage have now vanished as responsibilities have moved to the private sector.

Governments have thus lost a significant part of their regulatory capacity. The question is now to evaluate how far this is a problem in economic terms. To answer this question we have to check first how far the foregone national regulations were economically efficient. In case the result of that check is positive (which means that regulation reflected the basic preferences in society, for instance maintaining a balanced social security system), the loss of this regulation may imply a welfare loss. However, in case the regulation reflected only the preferences of the elite (income tax system), or the interests of special groups of rent seekers who wished to protect their privileged situations (for instance, trade unions having obtained high salaries for workers in sheltered industries), there may actually be a positive welfare result.[22]

3.4.3 The new role for national governments

In the light of the challenges of globalization governments need to find new ways to devise institutions. One strand of thought wants to solve this loss of national governance power by restoring the balance between the private and the public sector by curbing international activities of the private sector. However, all unilateral measures to cope with these problems tend to be of a protectionist nature, and the separating of the national economy from the world economy does imply foregoing certain benefits in terms of economic growth. Moreover, the effectiveness of this 'go-it-alone' approach is likely to be limited, as a single country will have to make bilateral deals with a variety of partners. Given the wide ramifications of modern business, the spill-over effects of decisions and the intricacies of the problems, it is very unlikely that the set of deals it is able to make will lead to an optimal solution. So this option is not a very attractive one.

Under these conditions the role of national governments is more streamlined and differently directed than in the past. They must orient their efforts towards the improvement of international competitiveness. This includes such factors as efficient product and service markets, sufficiently flexible labour markets, income redistribution (see, in this respect, also Lee, 1996; Memedovic *et al.*, 1998: 11), stable macro-economic and monetary conditions and finally adequate social standards.[23]

National governments have to play the game of competition of national systems. To that end they have to (Dunning 1997: 5, 13, 14) strike a balance between liberalization and regulation, in such a way that they:

• reduce cross-border non-tariff barriers, discriminating procurement policies, idiosyncratic technical standards and border controls;

- create new regimes for encouraging entrepreneurship and resolving conflict management, by selecting the best practices available;
- ensure that their institutional frameworks and governance systems do not disadvantage their own firms and citizens relative to those of other countries (for example, with respect to environmental regulations, competition policies, tax regimes, etc.);
- encourage and empower their constituents to upgrade and utilize the assets available to them to the fullest extent;
- ensure that the intranational distribution of economic activity is best suited to the needs of both the domestic and international market place;
- steer their economies through the waters of economic change with minimum social hardship and the maximum support for resource restructuring and manpower retraining.

3.5 Recovering collectively what is lost individually?

3.5.1 The need for global institutions

In the previous section we have seen that the national governments are no longer capable of coping individually with a number of effects of globalization. As a consequence, most national governments have cooperated internationally in order to recover collectively what is lost individually in matters of economic governance. Depending on the specific situation they have opted for one of the following two alternatives:

1   *Teaming up with others in the region.* Regional groups of countries tend to cover most of the international interwovenness and so the making of deals with a limited number of highly interrelated countries may solve a considerable part of the problems. Moreover, the coming to conclusions is in general easier the more the potential contracting partners are similar and the smaller their number. Finally, agreements on a regional basis can be based on similarity in cultures and governance structures, so there will be a higher level of trust among members of a limited group. However, they are only a second-best option in case of a truly global problem. Even so, they often serve as a pilot for global solutions.

2   *Making global arrangements.* Countries can make arrangements (rules and organizations) on a global scale (so universally accepted). In this way, countries are sure that they will contribute to and benefit from an efficient global system of governance. Moreover, the defecting of nations from such a system will be more costly than from more limited ones, as there are in principle no alternatives.

The previous chapter has shown that a whole series of global institutions ₁ve been created, each one of them dealing with a specific problem. But all ₁ been designed for either of the following two purposes:

- To improve the positive effects of global activity by setting the rules of the game. This takes away much uncertainty and conflict (for instance, regulating trade and trade disputes by the World Trade Organization).
- To reduce the negative effects. This can be done by preventing negative externalities (for instance, the setting of global labour standards by the International Labour Organization). It can also be done by curing possible negative effects (for instance, development aid by the World Bank to alleviate poverty).

However, there is no central authority on the global level. As countries are sovereign states, effective arrangements must make sure that countries also accept the rules for compliance or enforcement.

3.5.2 Inadequacies and challenges

Most observers would agree in general terms to the strategy that is described in the previous section. However, there are many critics as to the way this has to be put into practice. There are essentially three sorts of criticisms as to the present international organizations:

1   They do not address all the important problems. Indeed, as we have seen in the chapter on history, new problems come up in the course of time for which a solution has to be found. An important example in this respect is the global environmental degradation (e.g. climate change; see Chapter 9). Another problem is the increased vulnerability of the international financial system, which is due to increased mobility of capital, the sophistication of transactions and the increased inter-linkage between countries (Chapter 8). A sustainable environment and a stable financial system are examples of global public goods that need to be provided by adequate global institutions.
2   They do not do a good job. These criticisms lead to proposals for a change in governance and or instruments. An example here is the World Trade Organization, which enhances trade by taking away barriers. In case members do not come up to commitments the partner that sees its interests damaged may retaliate. This is not a very efficient instrument. It would be better economics if this instrument was replaced by fines (see Chapter 7).
3   They act mainly in the interest of specific groups. Such criticism has often been voiced with respect to the global financial system. If a developing country encounters financial problems the IMF comes to help but does so only by putting severe conditions on its internal policies. Now, these may be very harmful for the developing country while the international lenders to that country will not bear any risk. Coping with such problems leads to pleas for a change in the power structure and the rules of the decision-making bodies of these organizations (Chapter 8).

At this stage we will not take any stances in this debate. In the following chapters we will first provide the theoretical foundations, next analyse the situation for a number of specific global problems and only after that come up with our own conclusions.

3.6 Summary and conclusions

- Many are concerned about the possible negative effects of globalization on wealth (poverty) distribution and on labour conditions. They feel that they are threatened in their existence by international competition and that national governments are no longer able to protect them.
- However, sweeping statements such as: 'Globalization is grinding the poor'; or: 'Globalization hurts workers worldwide'; or 'Globalization destroys the capacity of governments to deal with human problems' are only partly and conditionally justified. The relations between variables reveal great complexity and the effects show great diversity.
- The answer to the challenges of globalization can best be based on the combination of the grasping of the beneficial effects, while avoiding (or compensating for) the negative effects. Such an answer should essentially be in two parts:[24]
   1   A recast of national institutions (and policies) aiming at the improvement of international competitiveness;
   2   A strengthening of the international (global) institutions[25] so as to improve their capacity to deal with a set of priority global problems.

Part II

The solution

International institutions

4 The provision of global public goods

4.1 Introduction

The good functioning of the economy is dependent on the quality of its institutions. The previous chapters have illustrated this with a number of examples. They have also made clear that the global institutional system has been able to find solutions to a number of problems, while leaving unsolved a number of others. It triggers the question why some things have worked out fine, while others have not. In other words: 'Which conditions need to be fulfilled to make institutional solutions effective?'

To answer these questions we need a clearer definition of the concepts (the tool kit) and the dynamics (the practices for using the tools). We deal with the tool kit first. The most basic tools (concepts) are property rights and transaction cost; their definition determines to a large extent the forms of production and allocation in the economy. Equally important is the concept of public good. We will present the specific characteristics of public goods in comparison with other types of goods. We will highlight in particular the international aspects of the various types, notably global public goods.

Next, we will deal with the dynamics of institution building. Questions such as: Who should take action? What would motivate actors? What forms of action are likely to be chosen? etc. Essential here is the collective character of the action. To get to a better understanding of this aspect we will describe the logic of group formation, the way groups tend to be formed and the likelihood of their being of limited size and of specialist nature.

Finally, we will describe the strategic games the major actors tend to play while seeing to the safeguarding of their interest. We will focus on the way in which they deal with transaction cost, both internal and external to the organization. Examples of such methods are commitment, delegation and incentive, and fine schemes.

We will round off the chapter with a short summary of the main findings.

4.2 Institutions are the answer to a transaction cost problem

4.2.1 From property to transaction[1]

Property rights are a basic notion in institutional economics. They define the way property is attributed and also the way it is enforced (Eggertson, 1996). The capitalist system is based on private property rights and their autonomous use.[2] In other words, the exclusive right of individuals, societies and groups (organizations) to own, control, benefit from (use) and dispose of (e.g. sell) their property as they think fit. The higher the confidence of people in the capacity to appropriate the benefits of the things they own, the higher the incentive for economic growth. Where protection of property rights is deficient people will be more hesitant to enter into various forms of production and exchange and economic growth will be hampered.

Property is not a static situation, however. Goods and services change owner as this creates wealth. It means that economic actors engage in contracts (Brousseau and Glachant, 2002). Property right systems structure economic transactions, including decisions concerning the exchange and accumulation of physical, human and intellectual capital (Weimer, 1997).

Institutions provide the structure for exchange that (together with the technology employed) determines the cost of transacting. These institutions vary according to the degree in complexity of economic exchange. The complexity in turn is a function of specialization of the economy. With the further development of the economy the number of transactions increases (see Box 4.1).

Box 4.1 Complexity and institutions

In primitive societies specialization is limited and institutions will thus be limited to essential conventions about (oral) contracting about immediate exchange, while group solidarity will take care of compliance problems. The pressure to lower transformation (production) cost leads to increase the degree of specialization. With increased specialization economic actors become more interdependent and the need grows for written contracts, for formal rules and for third party enforcement (state).

The greater the specialization of the economy and the larger the number and the variability of valuable attributes of goods and services to be exchanged, the higher the transaction cost. The higher also the need for reliable institutions that reduce transaction cost increases. Institutions need to be designed in such a way as to allow economic actors to engage in complex contracting with a minimum of uncertainty about the realization of the terms of the contract over the total duration of the contract. So the more specialized and complicated the organization of the economy, the more sophisticated the set of institutions and the more involved their interplay.

Transaction costs emerge because many factors impede the specification, planning, adapting, monitoring and enforcement of economic transactions. Essential in this definition of transaction cost are: 'the cost of measuring the valuable attributes of what is being exchanged and the cost of protecting rights and policing and enforcing agreements' (North, 1990a: 27).

Anything that adds to uncertainty and complexity of a transaction tends to increase transaction cost. Highly complicated transactions, such as a joint venture of an MNF with a local partner for which future revenues and products produced are all very uncertain, will bear high transaction cost. Small regularly made contracts, such as the buying of a good and its payment with a credit card, will have low transaction cost as the institutions exist to provide the service and the case is sufficiently frequent to make it possible to standardize the transaction.

With the increased sophistication of the economy one has to enter into contracts that deal with a very long term and with situations that cannot all be foreseen. Here, a reference to general institutions does not help out. Neither does an attempt to deal with such situations in a contract as it would become very detailed and so costly that economic actors would refrain from entering into negotiating. So the consequence is that complex contracts are always incomplete. In order to make transactions nevertheless possible, incomplete contracts set rules for the way in which one will complement the contract later. Such rules often concern stipulations about dispute settlement procedures.

4.2.2 Transaction cost considerations lead to the formation of organizations

Most transactions take place in a market. However, in a number of cases markets do not function well. Replacing markets by hierarchy is then the best way to decrease transaction cost. This leads to the formation and growth of organizations. The ones that will be most recurrent in the coming sections are:[3]

Firm. The rationale of the firm is that it reduces the high transaction cost of a market by replacing these transactions by a hierarchy. Ownership of assets to be used in all stages of production is unified. Hierarchy coordinates both decisions on daily production and on strategic investments. Disputes between parts of the organization are decided by fiat of the higher echelon.

Agency. Often economic actors cannot themselves see to all the decisions that have to be taken in their interest. They cannot cope with the transaction cost involved. So they have to resort to agents. Principal–agent relations change the nature of transaction cost. Complications arise because of information asymmetry (the agent has better information than his principal), about risk aversion (the agent being more risk averse) and the difficulty of monitoring output (the agent being out of sight). All these problems need specific solutions to which we will come back later.

Government bureau. The execution of certain tasks of modern government (for instance, the setting of rules, the provision of public goods, the redistribution of wealth, etc.) is usually entrusted to a public bureau. In this type of organization the aspects of hierarchy are most pronounced. This is because the authority of the state is to be used according to norms such as fairness, equal treatment, etc., that find their expression in rules and administrative controls more than in the type of incentives usual in private organizations.

4.2.3 Transaction costs govern relations between organizations

Internalizing transactions to limit cost will not be profitable for all transactions. Firms cannot expand without limits, as the negative aspects of hierarchy (e.g. low speed of reaction to new circumstances) will tend to exceed after a certain size the advantages of hierarchy. The same is true for other types of organizations, such as government bureaux. So there will remain a wide scope for the three types of actors just defined to enter into contracts with each other. As these transactions also bear cost, it is in the interest of the different participants to find ways and means to decrease these costs. This can be done in different ways. We illustrate the point with examples from employment contracts.

- *Private.* The private sector can deal with the problem of external transaction cost of organizations by providing services. Although the firm that provides a service causes cost to the organization that uses it, the service does produce value added as it takes away part of the transaction cost of the user. A case in point may be a lawyer who helps a firm to set up a complicated interim management contract.
- *Club.* Intermediary organizations provide another type of solution. They imply cost to members (contribution), but decrease their transaction cost as they defend the interest of members. Examples are trade unions that may help their members with legal disputes over their contract with their employer or branch organizations that help firms with specific information about relevant regulation in home and export markets.
- *Public.* The public sector can set specific and detailed regulation for different categories of transaction in order to bring down transaction cost and to safeguard a public good. A case in point is the legislation about the employment contracts and dispute settlement. These often involve both the judiciary or special (semi-public) agencies.[4]

The cases of employment contracts described are illustrations of a general phenomena. Other examples abound (see Box 4.2). Together they show that the three types of solutions are not mutually exclusive, but tend to complement each other. They show, moreover, that the borderline between the three can move over time; depending on specific configurations of problems, interests and institutions.

Modern societies have developed highly sophisticated sets of institutions to deal with external transaction costs. The more efficient they are, the better they will fulfil their role of lowering overall transaction cost and contribute to growth.

Box 4.2 Students abroad and transaction costs

Increasingly students complete part of the curriculum in a foreign university. This opens them to other views and improves their chances of getting a good job. However, there are considerable transaction costs involved that impede such transactions.

Student's perspective

He or she has to find out about a whole series of subjects, such as: (1) the type of studies one can do; (2) the quality and reputation of the university in general and of the professors in particular: (3) the recognition of these foreign studies by his home university; (4) the valuation of those studies by future employers; (5) the modalities and cost of inscription; (6) the connectivity of the course to the courses he has had previously, etc. Once this information leads to a positive decision to go, he has to find out about travel arrangements, and once in the new country, about mundane things such as lodgings, insurance coverage (health), etc.

University and professor's perspective

The university that receives an application from a foreign student to follow a course will have to check whether this student will qualify for it. It will have to judge the equivalencies of the exams he or she has already passed.[5] In cases where earlier contacts with another university have been established, such information may come at relatively low cost. In other cases it may lead to either extra cost to the university, which has to try to establish contacts or to risk accepting a student who brings down the reputation of the course. It may also lead to extra cost on the student who will be asked to pass additional exams in his new university before he is accepted on the course. Universities catering actively for foreign students will accept the occurrence of transaction cost, but will try to economize on them by setting up recruitment offices in selected countries.

Recent changes

Until recently, the cost of transaction on both the side of the student and of the university were such that only a very limited number of students actually followed courses abroad. However, two changes have brought transaction cost down considerably.

- Technological. Universities can now inform interested students around the world about their courses on offer and their conditions at very low cost via their websites. Students can retrieve and compare such information at very low cost as well.
- Institutions. In order to favour the exchange of students, the EU, for instance, has passed legislation on the equivalence of exams and has set up standard programmes such as ERASMUS in which universities can participate by bringing in their specific offers.[6]

The lowering of the transaction cost has made a large increase possible in the number of students who follow courses in another EU country. This increase in numbers has made it possible to lower other costs as the private sector has started to provide specific products such as short-term leases for housing, insurance, etc. Moreover, production costs have been reduced as a number of universities have started to set up specialized courses specifically geared to international programmes together with partner universities. In this way the present case can be seen as an example of the growth enhancing effect of good institutions.

4.3 Categories of property

4.3.1 A general scheme

Depending on the characteristics of a good, property rights have a different meaning and have different implications for transactions and institutions. These are given in a synoptic way in Table 4.1. In the top layer we distinguish two criteria for making categories of goods. In the second layer we specify the supply and provision conditions that go with these. In the third layer we specify the way the use is organized (allocation or rationing), while finally in the bottom layer we indicate the order by which the supply and demand decisions are taken.

We will go into the various aspects of this scheme in more detail in the coming sections.

4.3.2 The criteria for making a typology

The criteria that make the difference between the various categories of goods we distinguish are rivalry and excludability. We will define briefly the

Table 4.1 Types of property and conditions of provision and allocation

Name of good	Free	Private	Common	Club	Public
Excludable	no	yes	no	yes	no
Rivalrous	no	yes	yes	no	no
Provision (*supply*)	Nature, no problem	Private (autonomous)	Collective resources	Collective resources	Public funds
Allocation (*demand*)	Free, no limit to access	Private (autonomous)	Internal rules	Internal rules	Rules price subsidies
Order	Free	Markets	Group choice	Group choice	Public choice

Source: Adapted from Kasper and Streit, 1998: 180.

categories given in the columns of Table 4.1 and place them in an international context.

Free goods have been added to the categorization to facilitate comparison with the other types of good. By definition they have no element of scarcity so they are not the subject of economic analysis. They can thus be disregarded.

The *private good* is the most complete expression of property. The owner can sell it to somebody else; this transaction implies that the buyer becomes owner and that the seller receives money in return. Ownership implies that the use of the private good can be exclusively restricted to the owner. Another aspect is rivalry: if the owner uses the good (e.g. consumption of petrol in his car), somebody else cannot. With the growth of the global economy ever more goods are exchanged on the international scale.

The concept of *public good* is just the opposite. Here, we see that the consumption of the good is non-rivalrous, whereas consumers cannot be excluded from its use. There are a number of such public goods. Let us take the example of peace. Suppose the security of a country is protected externally by its army and internally by its police force. The state of security that results from it is a public good. It is non-excludable, as any citizen will enjoy the advantages of this. Moreover, it is non-rivalrous in the sense that the use of it by citizens, living in a border area does not impede at all on the benefits of the citizens living in a central area.

The increasing openness and complexity of international relations mean an increasing number of public goods have to be defined on the global level (see Kaul *et al.*, 1999). The definition of a global public good is fairly well circumscribed in economic terms as far as the element public is concerned.[7] However, the element global causes more problems (see also Box 4.5). For example, the international financial system is very vulnerable to crises, the effects of which may be felt in very different parts of the world (see Chapter 8). Indeed, there is a higher potential for contagion, as problems in one country may spread to other countries (think, for instance, about financial crises). The absence of solutions for the problems cited may produce a global *public 'bad'*. The opposite, a stable financial and monetary order on the global level, can then be considered as a public good, as any country or economic actor can benefit from it without it being depleted.

Common pool resources are property which is available to multiple users (a community) that may be composed of rivals, but who cannot be excluded from use. A case in point is the use of common grasslands where every member of a village community can herd his sheep. The problem is that they are subject to depletion (commons) or to congestion (urban roads) (see Box 4.3). On the international level[8] we can define the stock of natural resources as a global common. All nations can use this stock, for instance,

---

Box 4.3 The tragedy of the commons

The problem of the optimal use of the commons can be illustrated with the help of Figure 4.1. Let X be the quantity of fish caught in the oceans (horizontal axis). The cost and revenue of fishing are indicated on the vertical axis. The horizontal line MC represents the constant marginal cost of fishing boats per ton of fish caught. The downward sloping line MR represents the marginal revenue of fish brought to the market. The welfare created is represented as the difference between the cost and revenue, in other words by the size of the areas between the MR and MC lines.

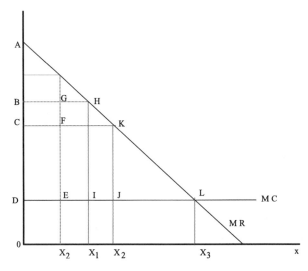

Figure 4.2 Tragedy of the commons.

We can now illustrate the welfare situation for the use of different quantities by different actors as follows:

1 A single fishing firm that would exploit the oceans as a private property would maximize welfare by catching X_1 fish. He would sell at price OB, have a cost of OD and hence his 'rent' would be the area DIHB.

2 If the oceans were exploited by two fishing firms that each have a significant capacity but have agreed on a certain distribution of the rents, then X_2 number of fish are caught and sold at a price OC. The rent of the two firms would be DEFC and EJKF, respectively. The sum of these two areas is about equal to the area DIHB.

3 If access is free, then the number of fishing boats rises until the sum of the producers' rents is completely dissipated, that is at the point L, where line MR cuts MC and where X_3 number of fish are brought to the market. Assume that this quantity of fish exceeds the quantity that is reproduced it becomes clear that the common resource is actually depleted.

Here we see the tragedy thesis; in comparison with a private property situation a common property produces an inefficient solution. The degree of overuse can be expected to grow due to technical progress; several inventions (such as radio location) have reduced the cost of fish caught (brought down line MC), which produces catches beyond X_3. As a consequence the deep seas have become increasingly overfished and a number of species are now on the verge of becoming extinct.

Source: Adapted from Tietzel, 2001.

the fish in the ocean. The problem with the use of the commons is that everyone has a private interest to maximize its use. Yet collectively this behaviour leads to a situation where the stocks are depleted. This may have a long-term effect in the sense that it can lead to the extinction of species (whales) and thereby to the loss of biodiversity of the natural system. In the same way individual countries may try to avoid paying the cost of air pollution abatement, as the beneficial effects are mostly spread inter-nationally instead of locally. This may lead to problems of global warming and the depletion of the ozone layer.

Club goods. These are excludable in the sense that non-members of the club have no access to them (for instance, the use of a tennis court). Assuming that sufficient facilities are available, the use of the court is largely non-rivalrous. If not, there will be a problem of congestion.

In case non-rivalry extends to the international level, and benefits remain excludable, we are in front of an international club good. This will occur notably where governments see the advantage in cooperating in order to get together a solution to a problem. A case in point here is the International Energy Agency (IEA) that was created in the mid-1970s by the major oil importing countries in order to safeguard the provision with oil in case of politically determined limitations in supply by the oil-producing countries.

Common pool, club and public goods together form a category which is often labelled *collective goods*. Their provision and allocation demands some sort of collective action, that is action by groups of individuals or organizations (see further Box 4.4).

4.3.3 The production/supply side

The organization of the production of the various types of good is quite different. We can illustrate this as follows:

- *Free.* Here, nature produces the good. This is the case for the light and the warmth of the sun, the air for breathing, etc.
- *Private.* Each private party decides autonomously how he will use resources to make sure the good is produced. If this is to be on a relatively large scale we see that firms are no longer owned by individuals, but become incorporated with more or less wide groups of shareholders.
- *Public good.* Supply of the good is done by the public sector. The mobilization of the funds needed is a problem in itself (taxation). The logical corollary of non-excludability is compulsory membership. Society at large will then decide on an equitable way of burden sharing. In some cases (see hereafter) the conditions are such that public goods are also produced by the public sector. In other cases the private sector may be asked to take part in the production under contract with the public sector.
- *Common.* Supply by nature (e.g. grass on common pastures). Often the maintenance of such commons is at a cost; here, we see that the limited group which is entitled to the use of the commons has to put up the necessary funds collectively.
- *Club.* Supply is made possible by the mobilization of group funds. The way in which these resources are mobilized will depend on the type of club. Some contribution system for members is elaborated, often in line with the objective of the club and the use members make of the club good.

The production of all types of good is the result of the cooperation of many actors, both private and public. On the one hand, private goods can only be efficiently produced in case public goods are provided. An example here is the orderly legal and adjudication system that is needed for arbitration and settlement in disputes of private parties. So, the provision of public goods is a prerequisite for efficient production of private goods. On the other hand, public (and club and common goods) can only be efficiently produced with the help of the private sector. Indeed, all three will use the possibilities of procurement with private suppliers to increase efficiency. That means that they buy private goods on markets (e.g. military equipment for defence, or laboratory equipment for scientific research).

However, this is not all. Some goods can actually be produced by the private sector (for instance, security). The public sector will then pay the private sector provider on a service contract. In other cases this is thought uneconomical. There are mainly three reasons for public production or, at least, public provision.

The market failure problem. Some factors inhibit markets to come to an efficient solution to transaction problems. These can be of different types. A good illustration is given in Box 4.4.

Box 4.4 **The dilemma of educational investment**

Suppose a person wants to enter into education to improve his job opportunities. Imagine that this person does not have the money to pay for tuition and subsistence cost. The likelihood of this person getting his training will depend very much on the way good education is classified. Let us consider here three cases:

Private. Considering his education as an investment, the person in question may consider borrowing the money he needs. He then makes a contract in which he obliges himself to amortise the loan on the basis of higher earnings in the future. However, who would be willing to provide the loan? As banks will have difficulty in assessing whether this person will be able to repay the cost later they will shy away from the cost of the transaction compared with potential earnings. So, there may be no possibility for bank financing. The potential employer who would be able to judge the capacities and would benefit from a better educated employee may not be willing to finance the investment either, because the person may leave before he or she has earned back the cost.

Club. If the training or education is very specific for an industry or even better for a type of job and is likely to be used only by a specific type of employers (e.g. textile weaving), employers' organizations may decide to solve the problem collectively. Only in cases where the cost of organization is low (number of employers limited) and benefits can be secured (few workers leaving the trade after education) is there a chance that a branch organization will be set up for the purpose.

However, in all cases where the benefits are very diversified and the cost of organization is high a club system will not come about.

Public. The development of a national economy depends on, among other factors, the quality of the workforce. So, it is in the public interest to improve the level of education. Where other actors fail to provide this good due to market failures and prohibitive transaction cost, the government will step in and assume the responsibility for making education available as a public good.

Intermediate cases may exist where a charity would organize scholarships. In some cases this becomes possible because uncertainty and transaction costs can be limited on the basis of the reputation of the school attended or the person making recommendations.

The free rider problem. Private actors will in general not be willing to produce a good that others may enjoy without the possibility of being charged for it. On the contrary, they are likely to wait for others to provide the good and then to enjoy its use, without having to pay for it (take a free ride). This can even lead to a behaviour that sends the wrong signals at a very early stage. For instance, people may not indicate their preferences in case they fear they have to be charged for use. As suppliers are in uncertainty about the real needs of people, we see that non-excludability leads to undersupply.

The collective action problem. For many public goods there is an imbalance between potential benefits and the cost of organization. Indeed, if the cost of collective action is high and the benefit small for each individual actor, then the organization for collective action for cost and profit sharing will not be easy. This problem will become bigger under a number of conditions. One is the case in which the positive effects are likely to take a long time to materialize. Another is the case where there is high uncertainty as to the rules of the game, so as to the likely distribution of the benefits or the capacity of an individual to privatize part of the gains (see Section 4.5).

4.3.4 The allocation/use side

The categorization of the various goods made in Table 4.1 also has a significant bearing on the way in which the use is organized. This has a particular importance on the global level.

- *Free.* There is, in principle, no economic problem as use is not rivalrous. So no action is needed. This may, however, change; for instance, the provision of clean air may become a problem if too many emissions are released into the atmosphere.

- *Private*. The private actor is completely free to decide on the use he thinks fit. He will use markets to come to transactions such as sales and hire. The same applies to the international level where firms enter contracts with each other and establish international firms to facilitate operations.
- *Public*. For a pure public good there is no rationing of demand. The defence system of a country provides security that can be used by everyone without problems to others. The global public good of climate stability will be available for everybody; irrespective of the use they make. In cases where government agencies provide the public good (e.g. fire brigades), access to use is regulated by collective choice and political processes. On the international level there is much uncertainty with respect to the rules that govern the use of public goods (see Box 4.5).
- *Common*. Use is regulated by internal procedures; these are often of a traditional type. The rules of the use of the global commons have to be determined by collective action of national governments. Many cases can be given of international organizations created for that purpose. One is the International Telecommunication Union (see Chapter 10) that has set rules for allocating the global capacity of radio and other communications over countries. Often the problem is attacked by partly transforming global common goods in 'private' or 'club' goods: a case in point is the allocation of sea resources to coastal states in a zone of 200 miles.
- *Club*. Here some sort of rule is set by internal institutions to avoid problems in use by members. To illustrate this one can cite the 'first come, first served' rule for the use of a court by members of a tennis club. To take an example on the international level: the International Energy Agency has worked out rules to distribute the available oil over each participating country in case of supply disruption.

Who would be the main beneficiary of improved public goods provision on the world level? Ideally, one would consider humanity as the recipient. However, this is very difficult to accept as humanity as a whole cannot easily articulate its needs and make a weighing between cost and benefits. So, intermediate organizations will act on behalf of the interests of humanity. Organizations in civil society (NGOs) have assumed this role. However, they tend to be dependent for their budgets on subsidies (from governments) and often lack a sufficient degree of democratic legitimacy. Business is interested in receiving certain rules of the game but that is restricted to certain issues. Governments will in most cases be the logical choice to act as the beneficiary. They have to deal with the problems back home, are aware of the limitations to take action and can provide the necessary legitimacy to act also on the international level. Consequently, the allocation of global goods has become mostly a matter of governments.

Box 4.5 The fight against HIV AIDS: a global public good?[9]

HIV (AIDS) is a highly contagious disease. Medical treatment is very costly and not fully adequate. In a number of countries the disease has infected so many persons that it seriously threatens the quality of the labour force and hence the possibilities of development. The fight against HIV has been declared a global public good (GPG). But there is considerable disagreement on this. One can distinguish three schools of reasoning:

Negative. However terrible and devastating the disease may be, this is simply not a global problem. The problem is a national one; it may actually even be a local one. Developing countries have more health problems than this one. The solution is with the treatment of individuals and in prevention.

Limited. The knowledge about how to produce treatment drugs or vaccines should be available to all. So the GPG challenge is to assure that such knowledge is made available at low or no cost, so that countries can produce drugs for local consumption.

Extended. The actual delivery of the drugs to infected persons should be seen as a GPG. This would not necessarily require the disclosure of the knowledge of the drug production, but would require the putting in place of all the arrangements required for purchasing, distributing and administering drugs to infected persons.

As can be seen, different views about the definition of GPG do have widely different implications in operational, financial and distributional terms.

4.4 Collective action

4.4.1 Best result with limited effort leads to GPG-specific solutions

The provision of global public goods will not come by itself. It will need in one way or another a collective action of the major actors. First in line, in this respect, are national governments. The decision to get together for a collective action follows very clear economic rules (Olson, 1965).[10] Each actor, while following a rational behaviour, will calculate whether for him the benefit/cost ratio of his efforts will be positive or not. These efforts are in defining the common interest and in convincing partners that they are to gain by cooperating to realize that common interest. Now, the chance that such a situation will occur is higher the clearer the benefit to the group, the smaller the cost of group formation and the more equitable the distribution of cost and benefits over partners.

One basic consequence of this rule is good specificity. The basic interests, the relevant cost benefit ratios and the distributional consequences are all likely to be very different from one global public good (GPG) to another. So institutional solutions will be sought for each GPG separately. This may lead to a wide diversity of coexisting specialist global institutions. We will come back to this issue in detail in the next chapter.

Once the need for a public good is established the question will be: how much of the public good should be provided? The economic answer to this question can be illustrated with the help of Figure 4.2. On the vertical axis we represent the total cost and benefits. On the horizontal axis we represent the output of the public good, for instance access to markets (trade) or lower pollution (environment). In this figure we give two curves. The upward sloping curve gives the marginal cost (MC) of joining; they rise as the activity expands due to the cost of negotiation, etc. The marginal benefit (MB) curve goes down; adding one more partner to a free trade agreement may not convey much benefit. The same can be true for an extra tariff reduction on a product that is not very important for the country. An

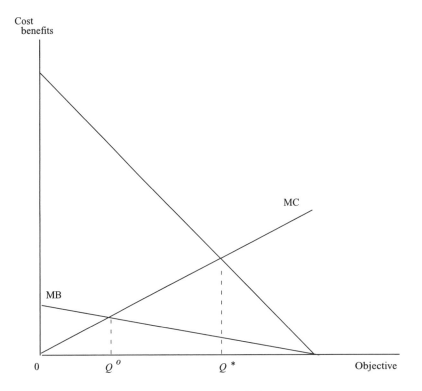

Figure 4.2 Cooperative versus non-cooperative solutions.

Source: Adapted from Barett, 1999: 199.

equilibrium at the world level would be at a point where the marginal cost (for instance, of abatement) equals the marginal benefit (for instance, of a better environment). However, with sovereign national states this point is unlikely to be very relevant. As a matter of fact, every country will make its own calculations. That calculation is different for two cases:

- *Non-cooperation.* Each country will provide an amount where their marginal costs are equal to their marginal benefits. The latter equilibrium is given in the lower intersection, providing Q^0 as provision level.
- *Cooperation.* Countries also take the efforts of other countries into account, so the curve of the marginal benefits moves upwards. This leads to a much higher provision level, Q^*.

So the conclusion is that countries have an interest in coming together and in making sure that the public good is provided.

4.4.2 Concluding international agreements

The production of a global public good calls for the conclusion of an international agreement. The first question is now: How likely is it that such an agreement will come about at all? The answer depends on the benefit–cost ratio of joining for each individual nation (Fratianni and Pattison, 1982). This can be represented graphically (see Figure 4.2). The equilibrium depends, of course, on the slope of the MC and MB curves. One can now identify the following cases (Barett, 1999):

- MC flat, MB steep. There is a great incentive for each country individually to start its part of the programme of collective good provision. The bonus for cooperation is small.
- MC steep, MB flat. Little action will be undertaken. The advantages of action are small and do not increase much by cooperation.
- MC flat, MB flat. Cooperation does create advantages over non-cooperation (large difference between Q^* and Q^0). However, the net benefits will still be limited.
- MC steep, MB steep. The difference in benefits between the two outcomes will be large. So it is really for this case that cooperation is most likely to occur.

However, even in the latter case there is no guarantee that the collective action will proceed. As a matter of fact, the problem with many collective goods is that once provided there is no possibility of excluding those who have not participated in its creation. So the free rider incentive may be very strong, leading many to adopt an attitude of wait and see whether others will take the burden of organization.

In order to create a regime (or an organization), actors have to agree on many issues, such as the way they are going to define the public good, the way they are handling the cost and benefits of the setting up of the regime, the issues of governance of the organization they may want to set up, etc. All this means negotiations. Negotiations on economic issues are no different from any others (Sjoestedt, 2000).

4.4.3 Action by how many? Clubs are trumps![11]

The next question that has to be seen is how many parties will be involved in the negotiations and are likely to become signatories of the agreement. Game theory has contributed much to answering this question.[12] There are very many cases that can be distinguished and the end result is dependent on many factors.

However, the limited number is likely to be the most common case. A small group can more easily define a common interest, while the cost of getting organized can be kept within limits. Moreover, a small group has greater possibility for coercion during the process of negotiation and of compliance once the agreement is concluded.

Notably, in case the cost and benefits are not identical for each potential signatory, it is not a good strategy to involve them all right from the start. In these cases a small (vanguard) group of influential countries, which have a very strong interest in results, will shape the agreement. They will not run the risk that the extension of the number will lead to a weaker and more ambiguous commitment. And they will accept that a number of countries will be free-riding on the benefits of their efforts. Moreover, the marginal cost and benefit of one more country joining the group may be small. Countries that see a benefit in joining will do so afterwards.

In some cases, where collective action proves difficult even for a small group, the stalemate can be broken by the determined action of a single major player, for whom the reward would be sufficient to pay the cost (an example is defence by a major player). Such actions then change the conditions for the other players, who may join at more advantageous conditions. Examples of this extreme case are rare, but intermediate cases where a hegemony weighs very heavily on the willingness of others to participate are very common (Eggertson, 1990: 312–14).

These dynamics may lead to outcomes that are at odds with fairness or with equity. Indeed, a small powerful action group that knows how to define and articulate its views may define the public good in terms of their own interest. Now, a larger group may very well have a more important interest, but as it cannot come to collective action it will see its wider interest being subordinated to the small group interest. Compare, for instance, a situation in the world where a small group has set the rules of a regime in its favour. As setting up an alternative organization is not feasible, others will tend to adhere to such a regime (notwithstanding the fact that to them it is only second-best), in order to grasp at least part of the benefits of the lower transaction cost that an international regime provides. A case in point is the membership of LDCs of WTO and the IMF. LDCs complain that the rules of the WTO and of the IMF (having been set by the most developed countries) are in the interest of firms in the developed countries and are not conducive to poverty reduction and balanced growth in the developing countries. The articulation and defence of such wider interest is often taken up by NGOs, which justify their funding from public sources and from charities and foundations.

The consequence of this preference for clubs is that, in many cases, regime formation follows rather the route of regionalism instead of globalism (examples are the EU, NAFTA, etc.). Although, according to some, regional regimes can only form a second-best option, they have the advantage of providing club goods to their members and serve as pilots for global solutions.

4.4.4 Large groups: difficult but feasible

Getting clubs organized can be difficult, notably in case there is no close relation between the users and the providers of the good. This will lead to a problem of undersupply of collective goods. The standard solution to this problem is production by the public sector and cost sharing by taxation. This can easily be done on the national level because over the centuries countries have developed elaborate institutions with strong coercive powers. The supply problem on the global level is different from the one at the national level. On the global level there is no structure like a sovereign state. So a new organization (or a set of new organizations) has to be created. Here, all the problems of collective action, in this case of many governments, arise.

As we have seen, the likelihood of collective action becomes lower the more diffuse the benefits, the lower the level of the benefits per individual participant in the action and the higher the cost of getting the different actors together. There are three reasons for this. Indeed, the larger the group:

- The smaller the part of the total group benefit any individual actor receives, and the less adequate reward for action in the interest of the group.
- The smaller the likeliness that a share of the good provided will fall on the small group that justifies the coming in an oligopolistic way together to form the nucleus for action.
- The greater the organization cost and thus the higher the hurdle that must be jumped.

These rules also apply to collective action of governments on the global level. Hence the prediction:

The larger the group, the farther it will fall short of providing an optimal supply of a collective good, and very large groups normally will not, in the absence of coercion of separate outside incentives, provide themselves with even minimal amounts of a collective good.[13]

The picture may be changed in case an organization does already exist. So the cost of organizing for a new subject are decreasing and the possibilities of coercion are increasing. An example in daily life is, for instance, that automobile associations now sell insurance and provide tourist bookings to their members. An example in terms of international institutions is, for instance, that the WTO has assumed new tasks in the course of its development.

4.5 Strategic games

4.5.1 Collective action games

Game theory[14] has been developed to support decision-making in situations where several actors (players) are involved. Each of the players has an objective function; in other words he has a set of preferences and strives for the outcome of the game (pay-offs) that suits this preference best. The outcome of the game will not only depend on the preferences of one player. As all players pursue their aims they interfere with each other. In such a situation of interdependence each player will choose a strategy that he expects will come to a result that comes as close to his preferred outcome as possible. Game theory analyses this interaction of players given certain assumptions as to rules of the game and information available. It tries to establish the dominant strategy (or best response) for each player. In other words it tries to determine the strategy that provides the highest pay-off given the strategies that the other players may choose.

In a sense, game theory is closely connected to institutional economics. It can take account of limited information, of transaction cost and of bounded rationality (see following sections). However, the more the game departs from the standard assumptions, the more difficult it is to generate meaningful solutions. Game theory analyses situations given certain institutions (rules of the game). By varying the assumptions on the rules, game theory can also help to devise better institutions. Games that states play in terms of negotiations on cooperation will take into account that there is no such thing as a global authority. In the following sections we will describe the complications of these games and the means that are used to come to practical solutions.

4.5.2 Individuals and organizations

The standard assumption about human behaviour in economics is that of the rational man. However, this is not the only relevant one. We see, for instance, in practice many cases in which man does not maximise his wealth, but shows altruism. Some have explained this by stating that some people do actually maximise utility, subject or some sort of moral code they apply. On the other hand, we see in many cases people that do not use high moral codes, but try to improve their position by opportunistic behaviour, by disguising specific features, by cheating and confusing the partner. Finally, we see that the human mind has a limited capacity to deal with complex information so that in many cases only reduced forms of the total information are actually taken into account.

The replacement of individuals by organizational actors does not need to alter much these behavioural assumptions. The decision-makers in these organizations, confronted with transactions between their own and other (types of) organization, are also subject to limited information and limited capacity to process that information. They will also be inclined to follow the types of behaviour (self-interest, opportunism, etc.), described hereafter.

In international institution formation the major actors are national governments or states. They interact with each other and with a number of other actors, such as MNFs and NGOs. The problem with games in international regimes is that national governments often have difficulty to specify their objectives (preferences). This is partly due to the time element (long horizon), partly to the uncertainty with respect to the power balance among the conflicting or rival interests groups within the state. Such a division of interests and standpoints leads to so-called two-level games (see Figure 4.3). On one level, governments (but also NGOs and MNFs) negotiate on the international level (represented on the three sides of the figure). On the other level, governments have a national negotiation interface for the acceptance of the international agreement (Putnam, 1988). This diversified 'rank and file' situation may induce governments (in practice, their representatives) to pursue aims that are perceived as irrational by other players.

The whole idea that international organizations are created for the provision of public goods and that they operate in the 'public interest' has been criticized by the Public Choice school as a normative theory (e.g. Vaubel, 1986). They view the actions of international institutions as collusions of national governments against majorities in their own countries made possible because the voters have much higher inform-ation cost. They suggest, moreover, that there is a big risk that the actions of international organizations will come under the influence of big international pressure groups (such as MNFs) because, to them, the lobby costs have decreased, while monitoring and compliance are much more difficult on the international level than on the national level. Finally, it has been suggested that the risk that bureaucrats pursue their own objectives of budget maximization and effort minimization applies a fortiori to international institutions (Fratianni and Pattison, 1982; Frey, 1984).

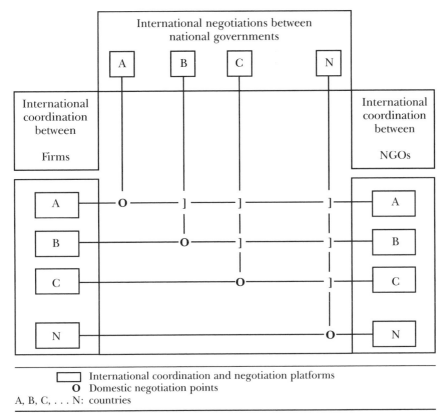

Figure 4.3 Two level games between major actors.

4.5.3 Bounded rationality

Playing strategic games is a very difficult exercise. We live in a world of great complexity and many times we have to take decisions without being able to judge either the conditions that will prevail in future or the real attributes of the goods or services we exchange. The problem (often termed information 'impactedness') can be split into three dimensions, each leading to a specific category of transaction cost:

- Pre-contract informational advantage for one of the parties. In terms of transaction cost this leads to signalling and screening cost.
- Non-observability of the agents' action, which may lead to moral hazard (one party will change its attitude once the agreement is concluded, leading to disadvantages to the other party). In terms of transaction cost this leads to the occurrence of monitoring cost.
- Non-verifiability of the output. This leads to auditing cost or to the increase of the risk premium, when auditing is not feasible.

So, in an imperfect world the cost of information, search and decision may be very high. They come from 'uncertainties that arise as a consequence of both the complexity of the problems to be solved and the limitations of the problem solving software (to use a computer analogy) possessed by the individual' (North, 1990a: 25). In such situations people will chose their optimal level of ignorance; they will be aware of the fact that they use subjective ways of making choices. It means that they operate with a bounded rationality.

4.5.4 Opportunism

Collective action is needed to come to some sort of contract about the way the major actors are going to deal with the provision of the GPG. Now, one of the problems with contracts is that they can rarely be fully specified. As a consequence there is always a risk that one of the parties to the contract tries to benefit from opportunistic behaviour. It means that the party will try to limit its contribution while assuming that the other party has no way of subtracting himself from his obligations.

A case in point occurs with asset specific investment. These involve contracts, where one party has to make an irreversible investment in assets that can only be used for the objective of the contract. For example, an MNF decides to invest in a country that promises a corporate tax waiver of 10 years and duty-free imports of intermediary goods. Once the investment is made the government may come back from its engagement knowing that the firm has already made sunk cost. It may even go further and actually proceed to nationalization (expropriation). Now, MNFs will want to avoid such risks, which will lead to underinvestment and thus to low growth in these countries.

Another case in point may be the mutual obligation of countries to invest in pollution abatement. Imagine one country has made an early start and fulfilled its part of the contract by adapting its power stations and by obliging its industry to limit emissions by investing in clean technology. The other country can choose to do nothing; it thereby limits its investment cost, increases its competitiveness because it has lower production cost and benefits from a cleaner environment. The risk of a partner adopting such an attitude may prevent the country willing to move to do so. Such distrust may prevent many such cooperative deals to materialize at all.

4.6 Mechanism to cope with transaction cost[15]

4.6.1 Commitment (locking-in)

A solution to the problem of opportunism is that all partners make a credible commitment that is observable ex ante and irreversible ex post.

One way of creating such international commitment is to establish national rules. Most credible are those that are enshrined into the constitution as these foresee, in general, increased majorities and other safeguards against sudden change. However, in international matters partners may feel that countries will still be tempted to defect and will consider a national barrier too weak to be credible.

The solution to this is to adhere to international regimes. Examples of such regimes are the commitment to trade liberalization (WTO, NAFTA) or to monetary stability (IMF, EMS). The degree to which international regimes are credible depends of course on the rules, the entry and exit conditions and the cost to countries that defect. Commitment does come at a cost, as it implies a loss of flexibility. Flexibility is important; what seems adequate now may prove very impractical under other circumstances. So, it is important to prevent long-term commitments that would become a nuisance to future generations. One needs to find a balance between the advantages of commitment and flexibility. This balance can be improved by making a commitment to an unconditional rule of a high order[16] and to a mechanism to deal with it and to provide flexibility in the framework of the system.[17]

4.6.2 Delegation

Credibility may also be acquired by handing over the decision to execute the contract to someone or some organization (agency) that has no possibility or incentive to deviate because it has different preferences to the principal. For example, a tenant may be obliged to give a bank deposit that he foregoes in case he moves and leaves without having repaired some damage he made to the property.

In politics such situations can often been found. The most obvious examples are:

- *Central banks*. The handing over of monetary policy matters to independent central banks has been shown to have a positive impact on the quality of the monetary policy. They are not subject to political influences and thereby can concentrate on the most important policy objectives, for instance the control of inflation (objective of the European Central Bank).
- *Competition agencies*. Political influences may distort the impartial execution of an antitrust policy. The quality of such a policy may be valued so high that the task is entrusted to a separate agency. A case in point is the Kartellamt of the Federal Republic of Germany.

The institutional solution of 'delegation has a number of problems' that may in practice take away some of its advantages. The problems are:

- Agency becomes a captive of the interests it has to check. Regulatory agencies of public monopolies, for instance, depend often on information held by the latter. After a while the regulatory organization tends to identify with the interests as presented by the management of the company it was supposed to control (see Box 12.5).

- Neglect of other interest. In order to be effective agencies often have one major objective. For instance, curbing inflation for a central bank. Other interests are then neglected (for instance, employment). Additional coordination mechanisms have then to be set up.

- Too detailed constraints on actions. In order to safeguard his interests, the principal may be inclined to specify very clearly the type of actions that are permitted under specific conditions. Although this may avoid mistakes and abuse, it may also lead to lack of dynamism and inadequate reactions to situations which have not been specified before.

- Alternative ways of control. Even if the agency that has been set up is independent in its day-to-day policy, it is often dependent on the polity for major decisions. Directors are often nominated by political bodies and their selection may be made partly on their being inclined to listen to political influences. In the same way the budget can be used: if the finance for a minimum operation is withheld the agency becomes ineffective.

These problems means that the 'delegation' solution has not been used very much in matters of international organizations. Exceptions are cases where the matter is highly technical (e.g. the Bank for International Settlements).

4.6.3 Repetition and reputation

In many situations where cooperation is beneficial, cheating is the temptation. Game theory has for a long time already identified that the likelihood to defect from one's obligations (or, in other words, the likelihood of deviating from cooperative solutions) is influenced by a number of conditions. The chances of defection decrease the more players are in repetitive games. The reason is that defection delivers short-term gains but they come at the cost of the loss of long-term cooperation, as partners will no longer trust the partner who has defected. A penalty on defection may be the exclusion from an organization, which means that the defecting member will forego the benefits of the club good. (For instance, consider a real estate surveyor who has fiddled the report on the quality of a house to obtain a deal, but may be expelled from membership of a professional organization of chartered surveyors.)

An important factor in transaction cost is reputation. A good reputation is built on past performance and takes years to establish. It may produce more rewarding contracts as partners will not feel the need to incur a series of transaction costs, such as elaborate verification before the contract or costly devices for ex post compliance. Defection on one contract means that this reputation will be foregone and with it the advantages it produced. Loss of reputation is therefore an important threat against defection. The effectiveness of the threat can be enhanced by making deviation public.

4.6.4 Incentive and fine schemes

The way to stimulate people in private sector organizations to comply with the objectives of the organization is to introduce an adequate incentive scheme. In the public sector, however, incentive schemes are very rare. Political processes and bureaucratic organizations (including international intergovernmental organizations) do rely more on monitoring, on commitments and constraints. This preference is due to the lack of competition and the problems involved in benchmarking.

There are situations where the incentives will not work. One may then try fines or penalties. Indeed, the risk of defection of a player will decrease the higher the cost of punishment. In the example of FDI, the home country of the firm that suffered expropriation may threaten to retaliate by doing the same with assets of the infringing country. In order to make this option feasible one must make sure that mutual hostages exist from the beginning. The penalty option is practised in the WTO where countries are allowed to retaliate in the event that their trade partner has violated the rules (see Chapter 7). A further option is to combine delegation with fines: lodge certain assets with an international organization. Examples in global institutions of such solutions are difficult to find as nations will shy away from it. However, in cases where integration is far advanced and solidarity between partners is large, they do exist. An example of such an obligation can be found in the growth and stability pact, where an EU member country may actually be paying a fine to the EU in case it does not fulfil its obligation to safeguard a balanced budget, thereby jeopardizing the macro economic stability of the union as a whole.

4.7 Summary and conclusions

- Economic problems on the global level can often be defined as the underprovision of global public goods.
- Public goods are goods that are both non-rivalrous and non-excludable. It means that the good is not depleted if someone uses it while nobody can be excluded from its use. Due to increased global interrelations the number of such public goods with a global dimension has increased.
- The provision of global public goods calls for collective action on the part of national governments. Such collective action is not simple. Therefore one often sees the emergence of separate collective action for specific global public goods (regime formation). Moreover, one sees the emergence of clubs; groups of countries for which the definition of

the benefits is easier and the cost of collective action lower (regional integration).

- Economic transactions lead to cost. Institutions are a solution to a transaction cost problem. The international institution that provides a particular global public good will have to deal with a series of transaction costs. The design of such global institutions can help to cope with such cost by using commitment, delegation and incentive and fine schemes.

5 Types of institutions and their dynamics

5.1 Introduction

The previous chapter has made plain that the provision of global public goods is dependent on the cooperation of governments leading to the setting up of global institutions. The objective of this chapter is to introduce the elements that determine the dynamics of institutions. The structure of the chapter is as follows.

We will start with a description of the role of institutions in the economy, highlighting the basic factors that lead to their creation and change. Many authors writing on institutions have struggled with the term. Few of the definitions used in the literature have received general acceptance. For obvious reasons we need a clear set of definitions. So, in the second section of this chapter, we will present the definitions that we have selected for use in the rest of this book.

For a proper understanding of the potential for and the barriers to cooperation one needs to distinguish several layers of institutions. So we will explain in the third section the essentials of this multilayered institutional configuration and show under what influences change occurs in each of them.

In the following two sections we will concentrate on the concepts that will have an important place in the analysis of the rest of this book. We devote a separate section to each of the concepts of regimes and organizations. We will describe for each in some detail the way they tend to be formed, function and develop.

We round off the chapter with a summary of the findings.

5.2 Some important definitions

5.2.1 Institutions

There is much confusion as to the definition of institution. Various authors use definitions and concepts that tend to use similar words for different meanings and different words for similar meanings. We have selected here the concept that is used by one of the most influential authors (North, 1990a) in this respect.[1]

Institutions are defined as the humanly devised constraints that structure political, economic and social interactions. They consist of both informal constraints (sanctions, taboos, customs, traditions, and codes of conduct), and formal rules (constitutions, laws, property rights). Important in this respect are not only the rules themselves but also the way in which they are applied or enforced; so aspects of implementation and compliance. The main rationale of institutions is that they reduce or remove uncertainty as to the behaviour of partners in the interaction.

5.2.2 Some more precise concepts

The problem with the term 'institution' as it is defined here is that it is too broad to be of use in concrete operational situations. Many attempts have been made to come to more precise concepts for specific institutions. Only one among them has become fairly generally accepted, that is the 'organization' (we will deal with this concept in Section 5.5). Less generally accepted is the term 'regime'. We have selected it nevertheless for use as there is considerable convergence in economics and in international relations on its meaning (we will give a more precise definition of this term in Section 5.4).

A third concept that has come to the fore is 'governance'. It is used in a considerable variety of meanings. In the more classical sense it means the way in which the regime or organization uses its instruments to realize its objectives. Recently it has increasingly been used in the sense of a network of interaction of regimes and organizations.[2] On the international level the network includes international organizations, national governments, firms and non-governmental organizations (NGOs). The whole system of interaction of these private and public bodies is then referred to as 'global governance'. We will not use the term here in this fashionable sense but stick to the more classical sense.

Note that the term 'governance' differs in all instances from the term 'government'. The latter refers to a hierarchical set of public administrations which pursue policies for the solving of societal problems. So government is about political leadership to reach societal goals, whereas governance is more about the deployment of instruments in implementing policies.

Many other concepts of institutions are used; most of them specific to one or other discipline. The term 'regulation',[3] for instance, is mostly used in a legal framework. Although the definition of the term regulation bears much resemblance to the terms we will use (see Box 5.1), we will avoid using it as we want to stress behavioural aspects, not formal aspects.

5.3 Factors of change for institutions at different layers[5]

5.3.1 Social embeddedness

At the highest or 'meta' level institutions indicate the norms, traditions and values of the society, often related to fundamental phenomena such as

---

Box 5.1 **Regulation**[4]

The term 'regulation' covers essentially the set of formal rules (legal and other). Formal rules comprise a whole hierarchy; they range from constitutions to by-laws and contracts. The constitutional order defines relations and ways of settling conflicts between actors with different rationales at different levels. These can be private–public relations, such as human rights, or public–public, for instance between federal, state and local. The higher their rank the more they have the character of principles; the lower their rank the more they specify allocation mechanisms (such as by-laws).

Rules bring predictability in behaviour, efficiency in contracting and conformity with social values. Political rules and economic rules influence each other. On the one hand, economic rules, such as property rights, are specified and enforced by political decision-making. On the other hand, economic interest groups will influence via the political structure the type of legal rules, such as taxation.

The international legal system differs from national legal systems in several respects. National systems have a central authority to establish the law and organizations to detect breaches, judge cases and punish violators. In international law neither of these exists; there is no central lawmaker, no central monitoring body, no courts with compulsory jurisdiction and no force to ensure compliance. Admittedly some embryonic elements do exist. Detecting breaches, for instance, is done by the trade policy review mechanism of the WTO. Judging cases is done by the dispute settlement procedure of the WTO. However, the possibility of punishing violators is almost completely absent. Thus most international law depends for compliance on the law enforcement mechanisms used within each national state.

---

religion and tradition (see Table 5.1). Meta institutions are taken as given by most economists; they tend to be the object of social theory. Meta institutions tend to give guidance to the actions of individuals and organizations. This may show up in differences in ideology, for instance, between liberalism and communism. Examples of differences between nations are the rather individualistic values that characterize the USA; the more social or equity-oriented EU values or the more collectivistic (group, organization) values that characterize the Japanese society. An example of a common (some say universal) value on the international level is the respect for deals (contracts). However, one has to be careful with the notion 'universal'. What may seem universal values to Western people, such as democracy, free markets, limited government, human rights, individualism and the rule of law, all meet with widespread scepticism even intense opposition in other cultures. 'What is universal to the West is imperialism to the rest' (Huntingdon, 1997: 184).

Table 5.1 Economics of institutions

Level	Type	Frequency (years)	Purpose
1	**Embeddedness:** values, customs, traditions, norms, religion ↓ ↑	10^2 to 10^3	Noncalculative; spontaneous
2	**Principles:** concepts (property, etc.) functions (polity, judiciary, bureaucracy) ↓ ↑	10 to 10^2	Get the basics right
3	**Governance:** play of the game (aligning governance structures with transactions) ↓ ↑	1 to 10	Get the implementation right
4	**Allocation:** prices and quantities; incentive alignment	Continuous	Get the marginal conditions right

Source: Adapted from Wiliamson, 1998: 26.

5.3.2 Principles

At the second level institutions provide the rules of the game that economic actors play. Meta institutions influence the elaboration of institutions on this layer. We give some examples. The consideration that humanity is the custodian of the global environmental patrimony (which has to be handed over intact to future generations) will lead to the adoption of the precautionary principle in environmental matters (see Chapter 9). The fundamental ideological values of liberalism will lead to the understanding that economic actors have to compete in a market, which leads to the adoption of the most favoured nation principle in trade relations (see Chapter 7).

Differences in the values and ideologies will make cooperation for regime development difficult. In the past this has been the case, for example, for trade; the differences between the ideologies of centrally planned and free enterprise countries precluded the realization of a global regime on trade based on the most favoured nation principle. Nowadays this distinction has lost most of its relevance, but on other scores such differences remain. For instance, the principles that guide competition are very different. The US and the EU are now rather strict against dominant positions; a country such as Korea has rules that are rather lenient. Such differences do influence greatly the possibilities to come to an international regime on competition (see Chapter 11). The Internet is another case of a 'culture clash', where strong differences in values do influence deeply the discussions about the creation of a regime (see Chapter 10). The US favours a 'light touch' approach, relying mainly on self-regulation. The EU favours an approach whereby the controlling function of government effectively safeguards minimum social values (for instance, a ban on paedophilia).

Principles have become increasingly the object of economic analysis (Rutherford, 1994). Important in this respect is transaction cost economics, dealing with subjects such as property rights and contracts (discussed in the previous chapter). Another branch of economics that deals more with the written rules is constitutional economics (Buchanan, 1991). This strand of thought developed from earlier work of the German 'Ordnung' school (Kasper and Streit, 1998).

5.3.3 Governance structures

At the third level, we find institutional arrangements that imply choices as to the way in which the cooperation to achieve the objectives is realized (Williamson, 1998: 37). In other words, how, by whom and to what end these forces should and can be controlled to achieve specific ends (Kirton and von Fuerstenberg, 2001: 3). In business terms one would find here different models of the organization of the firm (multidivisional and hierarchical or rather independent units in a network). Differences in governance structures would make a merger between the two firms difficult. The same exists in the public sector. The shift in ideology towards more liberalism has brought about a shift in the role of the state: from interventionist to regulatory (Majone, 1997). This in turn has had an influence on the choice of policy instruments. Where in the former situation a state might have opted for the use in environmental matters of the instrument of prohibition (e.g. prohibiting the use of certain fuels by public power stations) one may now prefer market-oriented instruments (such as the use of tradable permits). Differences in attitude between countries will inhibit the acceptance of an international regime on climate change (see Chapter 9). Another example of the influence of the higher layer on a lower layer is how the adoption of a principle determines the choice of the forms of governance. For instance, the polluter pays principle in environmental matters leads to the adoption of methods to charge the users of energy via carbon taxes rather than mobilize resources via the general tax system.

Discussions on governance often relate to the adoption of best practices: on the level of international organizations, for instance, the choice of ideology (liberal) and hence the principle (free capital flows) influence the ways the IMF tries to prevent and manage financial crises (see Chapter 8).

Economics has contributed much to the understanding of governance: first in the form of transaction cost analysis (see previous chapter), next by the theory of the firm (Coase, 1937: 52), where its rationale determines its governance structure, and finally also in the form of public choice (e.g. Vaubel, 1986). Important other contributions come from game theory.[6]

5.3.4 Allocation mechanisms

At the lowest (fourth) level we move from the discrete structural analysis to marginal analysis. At this level we find the way in which things are actually allocated, given the situations that prevail at the three higher levels. In matters of business we would find here, for example, the launching of a marketing campaign for a new car model in various countries, setting prices, dealers' margins, guarantee conditions, etc. In matters of public government we find here the adoption of best practices among the variety of measures that can lead to achieving a policy goal. At the level of international regimes one may cite here the allocation of pollution permits in one of the signatory states by a national system (see Chapter 9), or the allocation of special drawing rights by the IMF (see Chapter 8).

Economics has made many contributions to solving allocation issues. However, neoclassical economics has for a long time ignored the influence of higher level institutions, or at least assumed that allocation mechanisms function perfectly according some idea of individual behaviour in a largely capitalistic order. But more modern branches of economics, such as agency theory do take institutions into account by devising efficient incentives for agents that act on behalf of a principal. Evolutionary theories with a largely micro-economic orientation have directed most of their attention to specific organizational forms (Boyer and Saillard, 2002: 308).

5.3.5 Dynamics

Institutions are not universal and they are not created for eternity. They emerge at certain moments in time and under certain circumstances as a reaction to specific needs and they adapt as a consequence of changes in their environment. The frequency of change is dependent on the place in the four-layered structure (see middle column of Table 5.1).

The higher the level of the institution the lower the frequency in which they change. Values (social embeddedness) change only very slowly; this takes centuries or sometimes millennia. So, if on this level differences inhibit international collective action, progress will be almost nil. Principles (rules of the game) tend to be stable for at least decades, sometimes for centuries. So, if differences between countries exist at this level, one may at best hope for slow progress (compare, for instance, the issue of central planning and trade regime). Governance, on the contrary, is less stable; it tends to last only several years to a few decades. Differences on this level may be relatively easy to overcome, as opinions will change with the advent of evidence on best practices. Finally, on the level of allocation, decisions are part of an almost continuous process; so differences between countries are likely to be solved relatively easily.

International institutions that are successful in decreasing transaction cost will become valued. The opposite is also true; institutions that are no longer efficient will lose support. However, because the cost of collective action to change (and a fortiori to abolish) international institutions are high, they will (once created) tend to continue to operate even under conditions that would not be sufficiently benign to bring about their creation. We will go further into the factors of change in the subsequent sections of this chapter.

5.4 Regimes

5.4.1 Definitions[7]

The term 'regime' is widely accepted in the literature on international economic relations. It has acquired its titles of nobility in political science. We cite here the Krasner (1983) who defines regimes as, 'implicit or explicit principles, norms rules and decision-making procedures around which actors' expectations converge in a given area of international relations'. The term regime has also old roots in the work of eminent economists. We cite here in particular Nobel prize winner Tinbergen (1959), to whom regimes, 'on the one hand indicate certain procedures or a certain behaviour; on the other hand certain organizations'. Moreover, the term regime has acceptance in other disciplines, such as business and public administration, albeit with somewhat different definitions. The definition of regimes we will use is composed of the most salient elements from this literature that are common to several disciplines.

> Regimes are special sets of relational contracts. They govern relations between diverse entities such as governments (and assimilated public bodies), enterprises (MNFs) and other economic or societal interests (NGOs) in a given area of (international) relations.[8]

Their *form* is not fixed, they can be either:

- formal (e.g. the Bretton Woods exchange rate regime) or informal (such as the gold standard; see Chapter 2);
- explicit (for instance, written conventions) or implicit (that is, understandings about the way the convention is to be interpreted);
- well-structured organization (such as the WTO, see Chapter 7) or only an agreement (e.g the GATT) or a loose network or platform (the G8) (see Chapter 6);
- public (e.g. telecommunication) or private (e.g. Internet), see Chapter 11.

Their *purpose* is to:

- stabilize international relationships through mutually beneficial agreements, that

- reduce the uncertainty about the expected behaviour of interested parties, which contributes to
- solve problems of coordination about specific investments of participants and to
- lower transaction cost of obtaining specific goals.

They include:[9]

- norms (general injunctions or definitions of legitimacy);
- principles (stating purposes and basic rules of the game);
- rules (specific rights and obligations); and
- procedures and mechanisms (formal indications of instruments to meet objectives, for instance on decision-making, compliance and dispute settlement).

5.4.2 International aspects

Regimes cover a given area of international relations. Each of the two essential component terms can be defined in different ways.

Area. The fundamental aspect of issue specificity is a consequence of the logic of collective action (as we have seen in the previous chapter). Some regimes cover a fairly broad set of issues (such as trade), others are much more narrowly delimitated (for instance, air transport). There is no rigorous way to define functions; they relate to a series of policy areas such as trade (Chapter 7), finance (Chapter 8) or environment (Chapter 9).

International.[10] In the framework of this book we refer notably to regimes that have a global coverage. However, many international regimes have a more limited coverage, for instance a single continent. We will refer to such regional arrangements where useful.

Regimes at the international level are comparable to those at the national level, in the sense that they both specify norms, principles and rules. However, there is a big difference between international and national regimes with respect to the way compliance is realized. In the absence of a central authority at the world level, international regimes cannot be based on classical forms of coercion (such as police or military force). So compliance with most international regimes is based on aspects such as:

- benefits: for instance, the growth bonus due to specialization based on trade liberalization;
- reputation: living up to international agreements means that you are a reliable partner, which will be a basis for more mutually beneficial arrangements in future. NGOs play an important role in compliance for reputation reasons. They target both companies and countries that do not comply with a regime, for instance in matters of labour and environmental standards.

5.4.3 Private or public?

Private forms may be tried out before public (intergovernmental) cooperation is envisaged (Haufler, 1993). The motives of private actors to come to collective action are different for the two sides of the market.

- *Suppliers.* A field in which private regime setting is quite common is the setting of technical standards. Sometimes this is left to competition in the market (for instance, with video tapes) sometimes a small number of major firms come together (for instance, with compact disks), sometimes there are industry-wide organizations that set standards (for instance, in electricity generation and distribution). However, where safety aspects for a wider public are present, standard-setting organizations tend to become public (for instance, in matters of the safety of electric appliances).
- *Users* (consumers). In some cases the regime comes about because of strong needs of a particular set of users. A very good example on the international level is the Internet (see Chapter 10 for more details).

A third category of (semi) private actors pressing for regime setting consists of those who feel the negative (external) effects of the activities of suppliers and/or users. They are often represented by NGOs. NGOs rarely direct their actions towards the development of private regimes; they tend to claim a strong say in public regimes.

There are considerable problems involved in the setting up of private sector regimes. These are in the fields of:

- *Creation.* The negotiating cost of many participants become quickly prohibitive, so it is unlikely that regimes of this type will be created where needed.
- *Development.* There is a risk that the regime will be 'hijacked' by a small interest group that will not take into account the interests of a wider number of stakeholders. Private sector regimes may quickly develop into cartels that restrict competition, which damages the interests of consumers. Such situations will trigger action by the public authorities. In order to avoid antitrust charges, private actors will be reluctant to take initiatives.
- *Operation.* Self-organization leads to a lack of consistency between the various segments that cater for themselves. The partial solutions to sectoral problems may not be adequate in an international, and even less in an intersectoral situation.
- *Legitimacy and compliance.* The effectiveness of a regime depends on the quality of its compliance mechanisms. Compliance issues can often not be solved without the involvement of the public sector. As the public sector is likely to have its own views on the way a regime should best be set-up, it is likely that it will take the leading role itself.

So, we come to the conclusion that private actions for international regime formation are not common and that in most cases national governments are the key actors. They will take into account the economic and societal interests as voiced by business and civil society.

5.4.4 How are regimes created and once created, how are they changed?

Regimes come about in many different ways.[11] We give here a general view of the factors that have proven to carry most weight in empirical studies.[12] We will do so with the help of steps in the total sequence of events that tend to determine the articulation of the demand for a regime:

- *Awareness*. The awareness that there is a real problem comes often only after major disasters, that have a high bearing on the mass public. Examples are maritime safety (the Titanic), the environment (the Amoco Cadiz) or a financial crisis (e.g. Asia, Tequila, etc.; see Chapter 8).
- *Knowledge*. The changes in values and positions that lead to regime formation and regime change are often based on scientific evidence. The clearer and more unequivocal the problem can be defined, the easier it will be to find a cooperative solution. If on the contrary countries have a different understanding of the problem and of the best way to solve it (or have different sets of values), regime formation will be very difficult.
- *Attitudes*. Change in ideas about major issues (such as care for the environment due to increase in wealth levels), change in political trends (such as the end of the Cold War) lead to changes in positions in internal political structures that change the attitude of governments.
- *Rising levels of interdependence*. Interdependence decreases the ability of states to realize their goals autonomously. So they will be inclined to cooperate. They realize that the cost of non-coordinated policies can be very high. Interdependence changes the power of internal coalitions, giving more weight to those interested in cooperation.
- *Interest*. Regime formation is more likely the higher the interest of the parties involved. Interest increases with benefits and benefits increase with the intensity of transactions between participants (benefits are the mirror image of the transaction cost a regime takes away). It increases also with the importance of the market failures an international regime can take away. The factor interest is generally confirmed by empirical studies as the most important.

5.4.5 Conditions for success and further development

Collective actions for the set up of regimes are more likely to succeed when certain conditions are fulfilled. As such we mention:

- *Effectiveness and efficiency.* The regime has to show that it actually can deliver the public good ('common interest') in a way that is cost-effective. In other words, it has to show that it lowers the transaction cost to participants or that it reduces risks. If the benefit/cost ratio is low then, at best, a simple regime will result. However, if this regime is successful it will provide experience that lowers the barriers (transaction cost) to a stronger regime in the same area or to a new regime in another area. As the number and importance of interdependent policy areas increase, the cost of extending existing regimes will tend to be lower than those of the setting up of new regimes. Once established, regimes may lack the degree of efficiency that was planned for. Such a situation may persist for quite some time; actually as long as the nuisance it creates is less than the cost of collective action to change it.

- *Power.* Cooperation (or the organization of international negotiations to come to a regime) is costly and different participants will make personal cost/benefit calculations in order to decide whether they will move or not. The cost of collective action can be much reduced when there is a dominant power that has an important interest in common action and that is prepared to take the leadership. However, empirical studies do not provide support for the proposition that success in regime formation depends on a single dominant party. On the contrary, a rather symmetrical power distribution seems to be more conducive to regime growth.

- *Equity or fairness.* Cooperation will not achieve results when participants do not feel that they can reach a fair deal (see Box 5.2). In general, this means that the benefits and cost have to be distributed among participants according to some criterion of fairness (equal access to resources, to pollution rights, etc.).

- *Repeated cooperative games.*[13] The abilities of states to make agreements are thwarted by externalities, uncertainties, informational asymmetries and opportunistic behaviour (see previous chapter). When cooperative games are played, regimes can develop; when dilemma-type games or antagonist games are played, regime formation is unlikely. Integrative bargaining permits parties to come to package deals, which are often easier to conclude than more focused ones. Of course, the negotiation and reaching of an agreement will be easier the more there is experience with the process, so the existence of previous agreements is a facilitator to new agreements.

- *Effective compliance mechanisms.* The risk of opportunism and cheating of subscribers to a regime makes negotiators hesitant to conclude deals, unless compliance can be guaranteed. So cooperation is more likely the better the chances of compliance. These, in turn, depend on several factors. First, the higher the advantages countries draw from the regime, the more the regime will be self-policing. Second, the longer the transition time accorded, the more room countries will have to adapt their internal structures. Third, the speedier the detection of and the higher the penalty on infringement, the lower will be the inclination not to comply. Finally, the higher the flexibility with respect to ways and means, the higher the compliance.

• *Possibility of de-seating free riders.* Even in the clear case that it is in the interest of everybody to cooperate, a country may prefer to stay out. It will postpone the taking of action (in environmental regime building, for instance by subsidizing the change of technical installations in order to reduce emissions). It will let others bear the cost of actions, while sharing in the benefits (for instance, of clean air, a global public good because non-excludability and non-rivalry prevail).

Particularly important with respect to the factors 'effectiveness, power, and equity' is the distribution of cost and benefits over incumbents and newcomers. The group of countries that has created a regime to suit their interests will after some time become incumbents. Those who stayed out because the set up did not suit their needs may end up with a difficult

---

Box 5.2 The distributional issue in international regime formation

The provision of global public goods is very much dependent on the cooperation of a large number of countries (see Chapter 4). The degree to which such cooperation will come about is, in turn, very dependent on the distribution over countries of cost and benefits of such goods. Many distributional conflicts occur between countries of different levels of development.

Developed countries have a low tolerance level for the non-provision of certain public goods. Indeed, as welfare levels increase, one attributes a higher value to immaterial things. These may apply to fairly concrete notions such as clean air, but also to more abstract notions such as long-term sustainability (e.g. biodiversity).

Developing countries consider their contribution to the provision of a global public good often as an unfair constraint on their growth potential. They see the developed countries as the cause of the public bad and think that these countries should bear the burden of coping with it while also providing room for the LDCs to use a fair share of the worlds' resources. A case in point is pollution; the most important polluters are the developed countries. They should not try to limit the expansion of pollution by newcomers, but restrict their own emission. A similar situation prevails for the depletion of the tropical forests.

choice. They have either to set up an alternative regime or accommodate the existing one. The first alternative is very difficult given the cost of collective action (see previous chapter). If realized it may prove ineffective (compare for instance GATT and UNCTAD in Chapters 6 and 7). So, if a particular group of countries feel they do not get a positive reward for their participation in a regime and are unable to change it, they will try to obtain wavers of certain rules, long transition periods or compensation (for instance, financial help).

5.4.6 *Do international regimes matter?*[14]

International regimes govern relations between diverse actors, such as national governments, multinational firms, etc. In so doing they stimulate the decrease of transaction cost and the provision of certain public goods. These aspects of regimes do influence national governments in mainly three ways.

Enhancing capabilities. Regimes are a source of influence of states whose policies are consistent with that regime (in particular its rules and decision-making procedures). We give an example of a strong state and one for a weak state. A strong rich state that has been able to shape a regime to its ideas will see these ideas about policies put into effect by the other countries that have adhered to the regime (compare Chapter 8 IMF). A weak state may use a regime as a device for the reduction of its vulnerability to outside influences. A good illustration of this case is the country that has adhered to an exchange rate stabilization regime and experiences that the regime wards off most attempts at speculation against its currency, which enhances its capacity to pursue its domestic policies.

Shifting interests. Regimes may alter calculations of interest by assigning property rights and altering patterns of transaction cost. A good illustration of this case is the introduction of tradable emission permits by the climate protection regime (see Chapter 9). Regimes also alter conceptions of self-interest by the exchange of information, by mutual persuasion and by the accumulation of scientific knowledge. Evidence of this happening is available for the trade rules of the WTO (Chapter 7), and the measures to avoid global warming (Chapter 9).

Altering governance. Regimes may alter the balance and workings of domestic policies and can have effects on states' action by:

- Altering bureaucratic practices and rules (or habits)
- Promoting learning about cause–effect relationships
- Altering ideas about legitimacy and values of practices
- Becoming embedded in higher level normative frameworks
- Enhancing the political or administrative capacity of governmental or nongovernmental organizations within countries.

5.5 Organizations

5.5.1 Definitions

The term organization is used in a whole series of disciplines. We will not expose all the various definitions that are available, but just present the following somewhat mainstream definition: 'Organizations are more or less durable, planned arrangements to pool productive resources in order to pursue one or several shared purposes'. These resources are coordinated within some kind of hierarchical order (structure of power). They involve a set of routines to overcome coordination failures among agents by a mix of incentives and commands. In other words, the action of the partners involved is coordinated according to specific rules about decision-making and control.

Organizations are based on a set of rules, a constitution. In private organizations these have the character of voluntary contractual commitments. In public organizations they often are compulsory and are based on political authority. Such rules cannot cope with all the complex interactions that characterize the modern international organization. It is indeed impossible to spell out and negotiate completely the large variety of relational contracts that occur. So international organizations rely very much on procedural rules (Kasper and Streit, 1998: 258).

Organizations are the players in the game. Examples of organizational players are firms and government departments. They play by the rules set by the regimes discussed in the previous section. They themselves set internal rules for optimizing the effect of their agents. These rules often become part of the total governance structure of a regime.

Organizations are commonly defined by two elements. First, by the purpose they pursue, implying a search for efficiency through routines. Second, by the type of order they establish that is by the carrots and sticks they use to make actual behaviour comply with expected behaviour.

There is a relation between regimes and organizations. The notion 'difference in purpose' of the definition of organizations matches often the notion 'specific area of international relations' from the definition of regime. Second, the compliance of regimes is often given substance in organizations. However, as we will see in the upcoming chapters, there is no one-to-one relation between regimes and organizations.

5.5.2 The rationale of organizations

Organizations are formed for good economic reasons. Economic interaction would be problematic without them. This may be illustrated with an example from the private sector and one of the public sector.

The private firm is formed because it is an efficient way of producing goods. Imagine a person wanting to engage in the production of a good. He may want to limit risk and bring together the various production factors on a daily basis. He would than have to decide every day which amount of capital he needs and would have to discuss with his banker the arrangement on a short-term basis. He will also need to negotiate with people whose labour he wants to hire. He will have to acquire information about their professional qualities and their personal integrity. Because he is not sure about their qualities he will have to monitor production closely. It is clear that this involves extremely high information, transaction and monitoring costs. Making a permanent organizational arrangement in the form of a firm can do away with most of these costs (Coase, 1937 [1988]). Durable relational contracts within such organizations enhance the value of property rights for the various partners: labour can show what its productivity is and get remunerated in function of that. Capital prices can be set on the basis of the trust that a firm has built up with the banker by paying back its loans in time. Inventors will see their rewards improved, as sales of the product are developed on the basis of their ideas by a well-established firm will be much higher than those sold by a one day offshoot.

In the public field we also find the need for organizations. The provision of a public good (for instance, the set up of an efficient financial system) is needed to avoid a situation whereby economic agents have to decide every day again about the way in which they are going to settle their contracts (barter). So, a country will establish a national currency. In order to facilitate exchange it will issue bank notes and will set up a good system for electronic financial transactions. A central bank will then be created as an organizational form to cope efficiently with problems such as trust in paper money and in the quality of the prudential control of the financial institutions.

5.5.3 *International organizations*

The modern economy has become increasingly global in character (see Chapter 2). It is no surprise that organizations also take an international dimension. For the provision of private goods by private firms this means the formation of multinational firms (see Box 2.1 for a description of the rationale of the MNF). For public good provision, it implies the setting up of international organizations (IO). In line with the general definition of organization we define international organizations as purposive entities, with bureaucratic structures and leadership permitting them to employ their resources to deliver a public good and to respond to events. IOs are mostly cooperation forms of national governments. Much in the same way as the public organizations described in the previous section are efficient solutions to a national coordination problem, international organizations are an efficient institutional solution to an international coordination or cooperation problem.

International organizations provide the following functions to the participants:

- information on developments relevant for the attainment of the objectives

- platforms for consultation and negotiation
- rules for coming to decisions (voting procedures)
- fixing of contributions and access to resources
- legal forms of agreements
- monitoring of compliance of members
- rules for dispute settlement
- minimal mechanisms for enforcement
- some provision for accountability and liability for actions
- operational activities.

International organizations tend to differ as to the way each of these elements is specified. Important elements that are common to all international organizations are:

- *Lack of coercion.* All international organizations rely on national governments to comply (see Chapter 6 for the details). This difference in institutional strength influences strongly the capacity of IOs to provide effectively a public good.
- *Indirect accountability.* Within a democratic state the government is responsible vis-à-vis the parliament for its actions. On an international scale this cannot be done, and the actions of the international organization have to be made accountable via the national governments and their elected body.

5.5.4 Membership

International organizations can be divided into three categories according to the degree to which they are restrictive in their membership:[15]

- *Restricted.* Most organizations tend to deliver advantages to members only and thereby discriminate outsiders. Some do this for reasons of effectiveness. A case in point is OPEC, which only covers the largest oil-producing countries with a view to maintaining high prices for oil. Other organizations restrict membership because they want to create a strong sense of community in order to improve the internal cohesion and thereby create efficient institutions.
- *Conditionally open.* These organizations have a predefined set of conditions for membership but are in principle open for all those who accept to commit themselves to observe these rules. They are designed to foster collaboration of like-minded countries and to cope with the problem of free riders by exclusion. They can be compared with clubs: a price must be paid to get access to the organization (in other words, access to the advantages of an excludable club good). States that do not want to pay this price (in other words, that do not follow the rules) are excluded from these advantages. A clear illustration of this case can be

found with a regional organization, like the EU. The adherence to the European Monetary Union (that means the adoption of the common currency, the euro) is only open to members who accept the monetary rules of the European Central Bank and the macro-economic rules of the stability and growth pact.

- *Open*. These organizations are mainly for information exchange and consultation. They are not good at actions. They have often a limited resource base. They arise where the options of 'restricted' and 'conditionally open' are not feasible. Here, any autonomous state can apply. A case in point is the UN, which has fairly minimal conditions and excludes only pariah states.

5.5.5 Factors of change

Organizations change under the influence of external and internal factors. Change depends very much on the type of organization.

Private organizations such as firms, including MNFs, operate in a competitive environment. So they will be constantly looking for the best way to provide the needs of the consumers of their products and services. Moreover, they will be constantly searching for ways to improve the efficiency of their production and marketing and will adapt their governance structures accordingly. They will also increasingly take into account the views of civil society as consumers and investors check critically on the values that the company applies. Illustrative in this respect is that many firms have started to report on their contribution to sustainable production and consumption. As the economy is always in flux, firms will have to adapt constantly to the changes in their environment.

Public sector organizations are in a different rationale. They respond to political criteria. When a majority find it necessary to create certain agencies or departments or to change their governance, the state power will be used to do so. Lack of efficiency is less of a drive for change here than in the private sector, notably because efficiency is difficult to measure. On the other hand, lack of effectiveness will quickly lead to complaints and political action to force government to make the necessary organizational changes.

International organizations are in general created for the provision of a public good. Given the cost of collective action only one organization will be created. IOs are thus not subject to competitive forces as they are the sole provider of that good. So the factors that trigger change in the private sector are absent here. The factors that bring change in the public sector on the national level do not operate very well on the international level either. The political and bureaucratic processes in IOs have to operate in the absence of a clear political authority that can show leadership and force change. Change is thus dependent on major changes in the environment of IOs. On the one hand, the change in values and or principles can cause redesign of governance structures of international organizations (see, for instance, the

IMF, Chapter 8). On the other hand, the emergence of new public goods can lead to such change (see, for example, the UNEP, Chapter 9).

5.5.6 *Coordination*

Coordination can best take place in the framework of an existing organization with known and stable governance practices.[16] Coordinated policies tend to be more effective than independent ones. There are mainly three ways in which coordination can take place:

- *Inform.* A rather passive way, in which one hopes that other members of the organization will change their behaviour on the basis of better knowledge of our position (in plain language: talk).
- *Convince.* Active consultation is sought and arguments are exchanged between members so as to bring partners to the conclusion that coordinated action is in their common interest. 'Convince' involves elements of monitoring of developments, the exchange of best practices and the deliberate willingness to be open to new ways of doing things (in simple terms: argue).
- *Exchange.* Although partners' preferences may be different for a specific project, they may be ready to change their preference in exchange for something they value more. A variant to this is compensation; cooperation can be achieved in case a partner is compensated for the (perceived) loss, foregone benefit or lack of opportunities (in somewhat negative words, 'bribing' into agreement).

In most of the international organizations such forms of coordination are at work. Most of this concerns monitoring; that is, the degree to which the behaviour of the members of an organization corresponds to the rules and objectives set. In some cases this leads to regular consultations (for instance, the IMF); in practice the consultation process tends to boil down to exchanges between the country involved and officials of the international organization.

5.5.7 *Compliance*

Organizations use also different means for stimulating compliance. We may list them as follows:

- *Coercion.* This is mostly done in a hierarchical situation, where orders are given, or in a situation of dependency, where the power of the hegemony is used to force compliance (in colloquial terms: arm twisting). A case in point is the IMF that lends money to countries in difficulty. If that country does not agree to the conditions the IMF can withdraw support. As alternative financial help will be hard to find, a country will in general comply.

• *Sanctions.* This instrument is not used very much in international organizations. The WTO admits retaliation in case a country does not live up to the result of a dispute settlement procedure. Most organizations have as their ultimate sanction only the expulsion of the violating member from the club. This withdraws the benefits of the club good. A variant of this instrument are fines, but these are practically nonexistent in matters of IOs.

• *Incentives.* This instrument is the opposite of sanctions or fines. It is used in various forms, notably in the pecuniary form: the World Bank can give debt relief to countries complying with environmental programmes.

• *Indirect rewards.* Compliance to standards, for instance, signals to the international community that you are part of a respectable set, which leads to lower cost of capital or higher inward investment. This element is akin to reputation (see Section 5.4.2).

5.6 Summary and conclusions

• Institutions condition actions for the provision of public goods.

• Institutions exist at different levels of specificity. At the top level we find values and ideology, next we find basic principles followed at the third level by aspects of governance and on the fourth level by aspects of allocation. High-level institutions determine to a large extent the character of the institutions at a lower level.

• As the general definition of institution lacks operationality we use two more specific definitions:

  – *Regimes* are defined as special sets of contracts that govern the relations in a given area of international relations. They are important as they set the rules of the game.

  – *Organizations* are more or less durable, planned arrangements to pool productive resources in order to pursue one or several shared purposes. Organizations are actors in the game.

• International economic institutions will evolve only gradually under external influences and will tend to:

  – give answers only to the most pressing needs; the factor interest is the most important motive for action;

  – be organized on a functional basis as an answer to a sectoral problem;

  – become facilitated by unity of values, by the effectiveness of pre-existent structures, by the equity of outcomes and finally by the

strength of the mechanisms that are put in place to enhance compliance with objectives.
- be positioned at some distance of optimality, given the diversity of the interested parties; risks of cheating and opportunism, etc.

Once created, regimes matter. They create conditions and set the rules and thereby influence the behaviour of actors in such a way that they become conducive to the reaching of objectives.

6   Main organizations

6.1 Introduction

International organizations have developed in the past as a response to specific needs. So there is a range of organizations, each of which assumes responsibility for a certain economic policy field. They do not coincide with a specific global problem. In each of the coming chapters we will discuss in detail one such problem and the organizations dealing with it. To facilitate the placing of these discussions in a wider framework we give in this chapter an overview of the total global organization structure on the basis of the legal building blocks.

To that end we describe first the general architecture of the system. We will see that the various organizations fall into different categories. We will deal with each category in a separate section. First, we will describe the roles of the major specialist independent organizations that deal with the trade system. Second, we describe the organizations that deal with the capital/finance issue. Third, we deal with the organizations that care for the other global public goods (environment, transport and communications, and labour). Last, we describe a group of intergovernmental organizations which have a less than world coverage, but who are nevertheless influent in global matters, such as the OECD and the G8. For each of these organizations we will briefly describe in a standard format its essential characteristics, subsequently its origins, its objectives and tasks, its membership and power structure, its internal structure and its instruments to enhance compliance with its objectives.

The chapter will be complemented with a picture of the representation of private interest; that is of business and NGOs (non-governmental organizations). In that section we will see how these 'private' organizations influence the activities of international 'public' organizations.

Finally, we will give a short summary of the basic findings.

6.2 The general architecture

6.2.1 The structure of the UN system

6.2.1.1 Emergence

The ravages of the Second World War had made clear that an international body should be established that could deal with security issues. Moreover, many countries wanted this organization to take over the responsibility of many multilateral agreements that were not part of a coherent institutional set-up. It should be more effective than its unfortunate predecessor the League of Nations. In 1945 the United Nations Charter was signed.

6.2.1.2 Objectives and tasks

The UN is, in principle, comprehensive in the sense that it can cover all functional areas that come into the realm of an international organization. In principle, it can be compared to a national government that is also comprehensive in its functional coverage. However, in practice the UN does not cover all areas. The major aims of the organization are:

* Maintenance of peace and security
* Promotion of better standards of living
* Encouragement of economic and social progress.

6.2.1.3 Membership and power structure

Membership has been expanding from an initial fifty-one to a quasi-complete coverage of the globe now. The UN system attributes one vote to each member, irrespective of the size of the country. For economic matters this is considered to lead to unbalanced results, which is the reason why the strong economic powers tend to avoid using the UN platform.

6.2.1.4 Internal structure

The United Nations is a complicated organization (see Table 6.1). Its essential constituent elements are of the following types:

* *Central organs.* The General Assembly makes recommendations on all UN matters. A limited number of members sit on the Security Council. Next we mention the Economic and Social Council and the International Court of Justice. The daily work is done by a secretariat headed by the Secretary General. The Economic and Social Council forms the coordinating machinery for the specialized agencies and the programmes and funds.
* *Specialized agencies.* These are autonomous organizations working under the auspices of the UN. We mention here in particular the World Bank group and the IMF (International Monetary Fund). We mention next the ILO (International Labour Organization), the IMO (International Maritime Organization) and the ITU (International Telecommunications Union).
* *Divers substructures.* These are created for the management of programmes and funds, such as the UNEP, the United Nations Environmental

Table 6.1 The UN system

Programmes and funds	Commissions	Specialized agencies*

UNCTAD
United Nations Conference
   on Trade and Development
	Functional Commissions
	Social development
	Human rights
	Narcotic drugs
		IMF
		International
		   Monetary Fund

UNEP
United Nations Environment
   Programme
	Crime prevention and
	   criminal justice
	Science and technology
	   for development
		IBRD
		World Bank Group

UNDCP
United Nations Drug
   Control Programme
	Sustainable development
	The status of women
	Population and
	   development
		ICAO
		International Civil
		   Aviation
		   Organization

UNDP
United Nations
Development Programme
		IMO
		International
		   Maritime
		   Organization

UNFPA
United Nations Population
   Fund
	*Regional economic
	   commissions*
	Africa (ECA)
	Europe (ECE)
	Latin America and
	   the Caribbean
	   (ECLAC)
	Asia and the Pacific
		ITU
		International
		   Telecommunication
		   Union

UNHCR
Office of the United
   Nations High Commissioner
   for Refugees
	(ESCAP)
	Western Asia (ESCWA)
		ILO
		International
		   Labour
		   Organization

UNICEF
United Nations Children's
   Fund
	Other
	Sessional and standing
	   committees, expert,
	   ad hoc and related
	   bodies
		FAO
		Food and
		   Agriculture
		   Organization

WFP
World Food Programme
		UNESCO
		United Nations
		   Educational,
		   Scientific and
		   Cultural
		   Organization

		WHO World Health Organization

		WIPO
		World Intellectual
		   Property
		   Organization

		UNIDO
		United Nations
		   Industrial
		   Development
		   Organization

Source: United Nations website.

* Selection.

Programme and UNCTAD, the United Nations Conference on Trade
and Development.

- *Related organizations.* These are not formally part of the UN architecture
  but liaise with the UN (General Assembly). The most important here is
  the WTO (World Trade Organization).

In the following sections of this chapter we will describe only the
essential features of those parts of this total organizational architecture that
will be dealt with in detail in the following chapters, respectively WTO and
UNCTAD (Chapter 7), IMF and World Bank (Chapter 8), UNEP (Chapter
9), IMO (Chapter 10) and ILO (Chapter 11).[1]

6.2.1.5 Compliance

The UN system comprises the International Court of Justice. However, the
court can only handle cases that both parties (member and non-member
states) refer to it. It also has an advisory function to the various organs of
the UN in matters of international law. The court handles relatively few
cases. So most of the compliance of the member countries with UN decisions
is based on aspects such as self-interest and reputation.

6.3 The trade organizations

6.3.1 The World Trade Organization (WTO)[2]

6.3.1.1 Emergence

The origins of the WTO can be traced back to the Second World War
when the UN tried to set up a specialized organization for trade (the
International Trade Organization (ITO)). As the negotiations dragged
on, a number of countries decided to move ahead outside this UN
framework. They signed in 1947 the General Agreement of Tariffs and
Trade (GATT). Over time the limits to the (still provisional) GATT set-up
became visible and the need for a stronger legal basis and for a real
international organization became apparent. The WTO was created in
1995 following the Uruguay Round negotiations. The contracting parties
to the General Agreement became members of the World Trade
Organization. The WTO remained a freestanding organization however,
not related to the UN system. Compared with GATT the tasks of the
WTO were broadened to cover not only trade in (manufactured) goods,
but also in services.

6.3.1.2 Objectives and tasks

The WTO is charged with the establishment and surveillance of the rules of
trade between nations. The basic objective is to liberalize trade on a global
level. The legal form used is the agreement. The functions of WTO are
essentially a continuation of those of GATT. They concern:

- Setting of principles. The 'most favoured nation clause' specifies that trade concessions given by a country to a third country would immediately apply to all signatories to the agreement.
- Provision of a framework for multilateral negotiations on trade liberalizations (examples are the famous 'trade rounds').
- Surveillance of the system (trade policy review mechanism).
- Settlement of trade disputes between nations that have a conflicting interpretation of the rules (a case in point is antidumping).

6.3.1.3 Membership and power structure

Membership is widespread; all major countries and a large number of the other countries in the world have acquired membership (total of 142 as of mid-2001). Membership of the UN does not qualify a country for WTO membership; it has to show that it is capable of transforming all the rules of WTO in national law. The EU is a member alongside its member countries. After long-winded negotiations China has recently become a member.

The contracting parties have, in principle, equal positions ('one country, one vote'). However, there is not much voting; parties negotiate in groups and try to come to consensus.

6.3.1.4 Internal structure

The internal organization of the WTO is given in Figure 6.12. It distinguishes between:

- The Ministerial Conference represents the highest authority in WTO. It meets at least once every two years.
- The General Council is a top day-to-day decision-making body; that means that it is responsible for the regular execution of the various tasks of the WTO. It has delegated much of this task to various bodies and councils. First, to the trade policy review body and the dispute settlement body. Second, to the councils for respectively trade in goods, trade in services and for trade related aspects of intellectual property rights.
- Committees and working groups prepare meetings and work out agreements on a multitude of detailed subjects.
- The director general (head of the staff numbering some 600) has the tasks to prepare the meetings of the various conferences and councils.

The WTO has no executive body. So, notwithstanding its high profile, the WTO is only a small organization (its total budget is comparable to the budget for travel expenses of the World Bank!). Proposals for introducing such a body were never accepted due to lack of agreement between the EU and the USA and opposition of the LDCs.

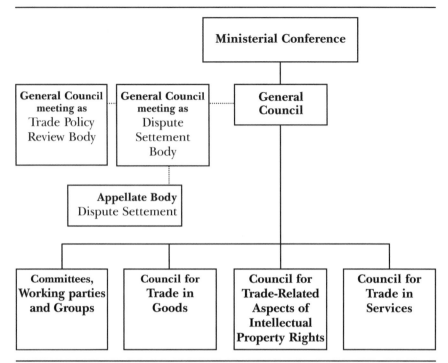

Figure 6.1 WTO structure.
Source: WTO website.

6.3.1.5 Compliance

The WTO has a strong position in compliance, compared with other global organizations. Member countries that have a dispute with another member country have to bring this before the WTO. The WTO Dispute Settlement Body exercises the authority of the General Council and all other councils and committees of the detailed agreements.[3] When a country has made an infringement to the rules it is asked to comply. When it does not, the country that has felt the negative consequences is authorized to retaliate with trade policy measures (such as special duties on import products).

6.3.2 United Nations Conference on Trade and Development

6.3.2.1 Emergence

In the course of time the group of developing countries became convinced of the fact that the major powers that dominated the international institutions, such as GATT/WTO and the IMF/IBRD group used this dominance to their own advantage. As a consequence, the LDCs experienced adverse developments of their trade and their terms of trade. They felt they could not follow their own preferences in matters of economic growth and societal choices. So they urged the creation of a negotiating platform where their interest would occupy the central place. This discussion was set in the framework of the need for a 'new international economic order'. One of the constituting ideas was the creation of regimes that would make it possible to discriminate positively in favour of development. In 1964 the UNCTAD was set up.

6.3.2.2 Objectives and tasks

The main objective of UNCTAD is to improve the development process of the LDCs. To that end it tries to improve the access of LDC products to the markets of developed countries, to improve the conditions for investment in LDCs and stabilize the prices on the markets of the main commodities.

6.3.2.3 Membership

All member states of the UN are members of UNCTAD. There are several groups of members. Two of them cover regional groupings of developing countries (formerly known as the group of 77). One regroups the most developed countries (more or less coinciding with OECD). A final group consists of countries in transition from a central planned economy to a market economy. As UNCTAD follows the UN principles, each member country has one vote. The numerical majority of the LDCs gives them much more voice in UNCTAD than in other international organizations, such as the IMF and IBRD.

6.3.2.4 Internal structure

UNCTAD has been set up as a permanent organ of the General Assembly of the UN. The tasks are distributed as follows:

* The Conference meets regularly (some ten times since its creation).
* The Secretary General supported by a permanent secretariat (some 700 strong) does all the operational work.
* The Commissions (recently reduced to five) meet once a year (viz. on trade, investment, enterprise, transnational corporations and science).

The results of the work of the UNCTAD come in several forms:

* Agreements: the most important ones are those that try to stabilize the markets for commodities (e.g. grain, sugar, tin).
* Codes of conduct: examples are the ones for transfer of technology and on multinational enterprises (direct investment).

- Generalized system of preferences (GSP), permitting the developed countries (or groups such as the EU) to grant preferential access to imports from the LDCs.

6.3.2.5 Compliance

UNCTAD has no means to make sure that countries comply with its agreements, codes of conduct, etc. However, by the very fact of its existence and the political importance of the issues it deals with, countries tend to comply.

6.4 The finance organizations

6.4.1 The International Monetary Fund (IMF)

6.4.1.1 Emergence

The IMF grew out of the post-war necessity to recast the financial system and notably to reform the international monetary system in the light of the payment difficulties of many countries. The fund has on several occasions been reformed so as to come up to the new exigencies of rapidly changed global economic relations. The capital of the fund has been contributed by the members, based on a quota system.

6.4.1.2 Objectives and tasks

The objectives of the fund are rather general: for instance, the promotion of the international monetary cooperation. To that end the fund executes a number of more specific tasks, such as:

- reduction of the dis-equilibrium in the balance of payments of member states; the main instrument here is the special drawing right;
- promotion of exchange rate stability and orderly exchange arrangements.

The organization has had to adapt to new realities and now has three new tasks:

- supervision of a cooperative system of orderly trade in national currencies;
- lending money to members in order to pursue adequate policies that sustain the fulfilling of the traditional tasks;
- provision of technical assistance to members to facilitate their compliance with international objectives, standards and norms.

With resources of almost $300 billion and its expanded mandate, the IMF is now probably the most powerful of all international organizations.

6.4.1.3 *Membership and power structure*

The membership of the fund has greatly increased over time. Since its modest beginnings with some thirty countries, the fund now covers almost all (some 180) sovereign states in the world. These members, however, do not carry equal weight in the organization; on the contrary, the major Western countries (in particular the US) have most of the contributions to the capital of the fund and as power is distributed on that basis they practically control the organization.[4] There is a clear need to bring these shares more in line with the actual weight in economic or population terms.

6.4.1.4 *Internal structure*[5]

The IMF has distributed the responsibilities for the execution of its tasks in the following way:

• The Board of Governors is the head of the organization. Each member appoints one governor. Each governor has one basic vote, but this vote is weighted more heavily according to the country's quota in the capital.
• The Executive Board is responsible for the operational aspects of the work of the IMF. It consists of a number of directors that are appointed by the largest member countries and a number elected by the other countries.
• The managing director heads the staff (some 3,000 at the end of 2001, mostly in Washington) and is responsible for the day-to-day management of the organization. The work is organized according to Table 6.2.

6.4.1.5 *Compliance*

The member states are obliged to keep the IMF informed about the value of their currency, to maintain the value of their currency and finally to pursue sound economic policies so as to create the fundamental conditions for stability.

Table 6.2 Department structure of the IMF

Area	*Functional*	*Special service*
Africa	International capital markets	Research
Asia and Pacific	Monetary and exchange affairs	IMF Institute
Europe I	Policy development and review	Statistics
Europe II	Fiscal affairs	Treasurer's
Middle East		Legal
Western hemisphere		

Source: Adapted from IMF website information.

The main process by which the IMF appraises its members' exchange rate policies and the situation on its balances of payments is within the framework of a comprehensive analysis of the general economic situation and the policy strategy of each member. It does this by:

• annual bilateral consultations with each member individually;
• multilateral surveillance twice a year in the framework of the IMF's world economic outlook;
• special precautionary arrangements including enhanced surveillance of countries that need to boost international confidence in their policies.

This surveillance and consultation system is operated in a continuous and candid way on behalf of the credibility of the policies of the organization as a whole and the individual members. It covers all factors that may have an influence on exchange rates or are possible causes of a financial crisis, such as the functioning of the financial sector. There is no formal way of coercion; much is done by two mechanisms: conditional financial help to and peer pressure from other members on the member country that needs to comply.

6.4.2 The International Bank for Reconstruction and Development (IBRD)

6.4.2.1 Emergence

One of the main problems facing the world economy in the 1940s was the reconstruction of the economies devastated by the war. It was felt that the provision of a sound financial system with balance of payments aid would not be sufficient to bring accelerated growth to these countries. Long-term finance would also be required. This would reinforce the capacity of countries to stand up to competition, which would in turn help the gradual liberalization of trade. After the quick recovery of the most developed countries the work of the IBRD shifted towards the support of the less developed countries (LDCs).

6.4.2.2 Objectives and tasks

The main objectives of the IBRD, colloquially called the World Bank, are to support the development process in the LDCs by the provision of:

• Loans (particularly the guaranteeing of loans) for development projects, such as infrastructure (for instance, a dam for irrigation) or industry (a local bank financing small and medium industries).
• Technical assistance. One of the main bottlenecks for development is often the lack of knowledge. This bottleneck is removed by the bank

financing the cost of expatriate and local experts who assess the feasibility of projects, including their impact on the rest of the economy of the country.

6.4.2.3 Membership and power structure

Only countries that are members of IMF can become a member of the IBRD. Originally, the number of members was limited, but over time new members have joined so that the membership now includes almost all sovereign countries. Voting in the World Bank is also on a weighted basis (with capital as the criterion), so like the IMF the World Bank is in practice controlled by the major Western countries.

6.4.2.4 Internal structure

The way the bank is organized bears much resemblance to the set-up of the fund (IMF).

- A Board of Governors (meeting once a year) sets the general policy.
- The Board of Executive Directors of the bank is responsible for the translation of this general policy in concrete terms. It consists of five people who are appointed by the largest shareholders and nineteen persons who are elected by the other shareholders.
- The president of the bank, elected by the executive directors, is responsible for the management of the operations of the bank. The staff of the organization is very large; they number about 8,000 at the headquarters in Washington and some 2,000 in the field.

Associated to the IBRD are several other organizations that together form the World Bank Group. The International Development Association (IDA) has been set up to provide loans to the least developed countries on softer terms. The International Finance Cooperation provides funds for the improvement of private enterprise. The Multilateral Investment Guarantee Agency (MIGA) is set up as a response to the global debt crisis to guarantee the investment in LDCs against risks such as political unrest, currency inconvertibility, etc.

6.4.2.5 Compliance

The World Bank provides finance to projects in developing countries. So the compliance issue is limited to the wish of every banker to get back his money by the results of the project. The most important point in this respect is the specific position of the bank; there are few alternatives so a country that knows it will need IBRD finance in future will be well advised to keep on side with the World Bank now.

6.5 Other UN-related organizations

6.5.1 United Nations Environment Programme (UNEP)[6]

5.5.1.1 Emergence

In the 1960s and 1970s the concerns about worldwide pollution and degradation of ecosystems grew very fast. Many of these problems are of a global nature and cannot be solved by individual countries or regional groups of countries. To cope with the increasing concern for a sustainable development worldwide, the UNEP was established in 1972.

6.5.1.2 Objectives and tasks

The role of UNEP is to support sustainable development through sound environmental practices everywhere. Activities include:

- assessment and protection of atmosphere and terrestrial ecosystems;
- promotion of environmental science and information;
- early warning of problems and emergency response capacity to deal with environmental disasters and emergencies.

6.5.1.3 Membership and power distribution

Most countries of the world are members.

6.5.1.4 Internal structure

The various roles of the organization are distributed as follows:

- The Governing Council is the supreme decision-making body of UNEP. This council has some sixty members and a limited number of them are members of the bureau. The governing council can meet in the form of a global ministerial environmental forum, in which delegates from NGOs can also participate.
- The executive director leads the work of the organization, supported by a staff numbering about 700.

The instruments of the UNEP are mostly conventions (or multilateral environmental agreements); after ratification these are binding on member states. Some of these foresee the use of a battery of instruments (see in this respect Chapter 9).

6.5.1.5 Compliance

In environmental matters self-enforcement is very important. A country can be taken to the International Court of Justice for failing to comply with a multilateral environmental agreement (MEA), but only with the defendants' permission. Even after a Court decision there is no mechanism to enforce compliance. The UNEP has a special unit that deals with possibilities for improving compliance by enhanced monitoring of and early negotiation with (potential) defectors. A set of guidelines is now being worked out.

6.5.2 International Maritime Organization (IMO)[7]

6.5.2.1 Emergence

The IMO was established in 1948 under the auspices of the UN. It came into force in 1958. Its initial concern was safety at sea. Gradually, other aspects came to the fore as well, such as the environment.

6.5.2.2 Objectives and tasks

The main tasks of the IMO are to serve as a custodian for a number of international conventions that organize the use of the seas by states and private interests. It also develops agreements between the parties involved on non-economic aspects of maritime transport and other maritime industries (fishery, etc.). These fall into three categories: marine safety, prevention of marine pollution, and organization of liability and compensation for countries that have suffered damage from pollution.

6.5.2.3 Membership

Currently, 160 states are members of IMO and two are associate members.

6.5.2.4 Internal structure

IMO is a technical organization and most of the work is carried out in a number of committees and subcommittees. A draft instrument (convention, code, protocol) is then produced which is submitted to a conference to which delegations of all member states in the UN system (including non-IMO members) are convened. The conference adopts a final text, which is then submitted to governments for ratification. It enters into force after a minimum number has ratified.

6.5.2.5 Compliance

The organization itself has no powers to enforce conventions. Implementation of the requirements of a convention is mandatory on countries which are party to it. Contracting governments enforce IMO conventions as far as their own ships are concerned; in some cases governments of port states do the enforcement. They set penalties for infringements. IMO codes and IMO recommendations are not binding; however, they play a very important role as in many cases countries do incorporate them in national law. Compliance is fostered by the IMO through the monitoring of the behaviour of states and the publication of the results.

6.5.3 *The International Labour Organization (ILO)*[8]

6.5.3.1 *Emergence*

The ILO was created in 1919 at the end of the First World War. The initial motivations were humanitarian (conditions of labour), political (avoid revolutions) and economic (fair competition conditions). The organization adopted a set of international labour conventions dealing with hours of work, night work for women and young persons, and maternity protection, etc. During the inter-war period the activities were rather limited, as many governments complained about the constraining nature of many of the standards adopted. After the Second World War, the ILO became a specialist organization of the UN.

6.5.3.2 *Objectives and tasks*

The ILO pursues mainly three objectives:

*   Promoting international labour standards on issues such as freedom of association, collective bargaining, abolition of forced labour, equal opportunities, and work conditions.
*   Providing technical assistance primarily in the fields of vocational training, labour law, industrial relations, occupational safety, social security, etc.
*   Promoting the development of independent employers and workers' organizations and of tri-partism and social dialogue.

6.5.3.3 *Membership*

Membership of the ILO is open to all members of the UN. All countries that were already members of the original ILO have automatically become members of the successor ILO.

6.5.3.4 *Internal structure*

The ILO accomplishes its work through three main bodies, all of which encompass the unique feature of the organization: its three partite structure (government, employers, workers).

*   The International Labour Conference. This conference meets once a year; each member state is usually represented by its cabinet minister responsible for labour affairs. Representative persons of both employers and workers' organizations complement the national delegations.

- The Governing Body (executive council) takes decisions on ILO's policy. It meets three times a year. It is composed of twenty-eight government members, fourteen employers and fourteen workers members.
- The International Labour Office is the permanent secretariat of the International Labour Organization. It is headed by the director general.

6.5.3.5 Compliance

The ILO frames conventions and recommendations. Each member has the right to file a complaint with the ILO if it is not satisfied with the effective observance of such a convention. The Governing Body (GB) may refer such a complaint to a commission of enquiry. This commission reports to the GB and its report is published. If the government of the defaulting state follows up the recommendations of the commission the procedure is closed. In case the government does not comply, the complaint may be brought before the International Court of Justice, whose decision is final. In practice the ILO, however, relies very heavily on technical assistance, on peer pressure and on persuasion to enhance compliance.

6.6 Specialist organizations of less than world coverage

6.6.1 Organization of Economic Cooperation and Development (OECD)

6.6.1.1 Emergence

The OECD has developed out of the former OEEC, the Organization for European Economic Cooperation created after the war to administer the aid of the US to European recovery. Its objectives were to stimulate trade and to coordinate a number of national policies. After the creation of the EU (or more precisely its forerunner the EEC) the OEEC extended its membership and redefined its role. It was relaunched in 1961 under its new name, the OECD.

6.6.1.2 Objectives and tasks

The objectives of the OECD are of a very general nature (Art. 1). The organization's aims are:

- Achievement of the highest possible growth for members and for the world at large
- Expansion of employment
- Improvement of living standards
- Maintenance of financial stability
- Extension of world trade and investment on a multilateral basis.

This has led the organization to deal with a very large number of subjects, for instance macroeconomics, sectoral economics (agriculture, industry, energy, transport, etc.), environment, etc.

6.6.1.3 Membership

With the recast of 1961 the number of members was increased in such a way that the organization regrouped the most developed countries in the world. Recently a number of 'tigers' were admitted too. It now covers Western and Central Europe (EU countries and the most developed accession countries), North America (US, Canada and Mexico) the Antipodes (Australia and New Zealand) and Asia (Japan and Korea). The commission of the EU takes part in the work via many working groups.

6.6.1.4 Internal structure

- The main authority is vested in the Council. All member states have one seat. The council meets regularly at the ministerial level for important issues; meetings are prepared at the level of permanent representatives.
- The secretariat is responsible for the preparation of the work of the Council and for the implementation of the decisions. Staff number approximately 2,300.
- The actual work is done in numerous working groups and committees; often formed of experts from the administrations of the member states.
- For very specific tasks the OECD has created agencies (e.g. the International Energy Agency).

6.6.1.5 Compliance

The OECD is essentially a study club. However, its activities may lead to the adoption of codes. The compliance with those codes is a matter for the members; the OECD will monitor this, but has no agreed ways to enforce them.

6.6.2 The G7/G8/G20[9]

6.6.2.1 Emergence

The G7/G8 summits of the heads of government of the most important economic powers have started off like single freestanding events. They were intended to cope with important specific problems that had been too difficult nuts to crack at the other levels of bilateral and multilateral decision-making. However, the summits soon became an annual series.

The G8 has often got the criticism that it is a club of rich and powerful and as such is not capable of acting in the interests of the developing world. To solve this problem a new forum, the G20, has recently been created. It groups, apart from the G8, also ten of the major developing countries (e.g. China, India, Brazil) and the Bretton Woods institutions (IMF/IBRD).

6.6.2.2 Objectives and tasks

The leaders of the G7/8 countries set guidelines for action that provide other international organizations with the necessary impulses to come to solutions. However, they have not dealt with all subjects discussed in the various chapters of this book to the same degree. In practice they devoted most of their attention to questions of macro-economic governance and finance. Their record in trade is limited and recent initiatives in this area have not been very successful.

The mandate of the G20 is very large and includes apart from macro-economic issues also urgent LDC problems such as sustainable development, poverty reduction and debt relief.

6.6.2.3 Membership

The G7 and now G8 consist of countries with a democratic political regime and a market based economy. The members are (by region) the US and Canada in the Americas, Germany, France, Italy and the UK in Europe, Japan in Asia and also, since its transition, Russia. China is a potential member. Given the transfer of many economic responsibilities from European nations to the EU, the presidency and the Commission of the EU are present at many activities of the G8. In economic terms the members of the G8 account for the bulk of the international transactions (trade, investment, etc.).

The G20 accounts for some 85 per cent of world GDP and 65 per cent of world population.

6.6.2.4 Internal structure

The G8 is a forum rather than an organization.

- It is a free-standing entity at the level of heads of government. This is unlike many other meetings of heads of government, which were added as the apex to existing organizations, with well-developed decision-making structures at ministerial, ambassador or other levels.[10]
- There is no formal organization, no headquarters, and no written constitution or procedures. This has its advantages, such as flexibility, but also its drawbacks, such as the pressure it puts on the apparatus of the host country. It need not thus be a surprise to see a growing pressure to develop an organization downwards, beginning with a permanent secretariat.
- Ministerial groups emerged in the 1980s. These ministers have their groups of personal representatives who meet to prepare meetings on the higher levels. The G7 ministers meet not only in this framework. Examples are the ministers of finance who meet in the margins of meetings of IBRD and IMF, and the ministers of trade who meet in the

margins of the WTO. With the broadening of the scope of subjects treated by the G8, other stand-alone and regular ministerial meetings have been introduced as well (such as environment, crime, etc.).

The G20 operates along similar lines as the G8.

6.6.2.5 Compliance

Summits are usually concluded with declarations. These are not legally binding. The G8 has no formal enforcement mechanism. Yet the compliance of international organizations and national governments with summit commitments has in general been very high. A large part of the explanation is to be found in the existence of strong national procedures for compliance with decisions of treasury ministries.

The structure of the G20 bears much resemblance to that of the G8 but its effectiveness in terms of compliance has still to be proven.

6.7 Regional organizations

6.7.1 Europe

At the moment the most relevant regional organization in Europe is the European Union (EU) (Molle 2001). The EU started off in 1958 with only six western European countries. In several rounds of enlargement of its membership it has integrated almost all countries in Western Europe and is about to accept ten central European countries. Others have applied for membership, but do not (yet) qualify.

The EU differs from the other regional organizations that we discuss in this section in mainly two respects. First, its aims go far beyond the integration of good and capital markets. Its final aim is political integration. In the economic field the EU aims at the highest stage of integration. It was started with the creation of a common market for all goods, services, labour and capital. Since then a fully-fledged economic union has been realized, which implies that common policies have been elaborated and implemented for such diverse areas as competition, transport, external trade, environment, occupational health and safety, etc. Particularly important are the so-called structural funds, destined to aid disadvantaged regions and social groups. Finally, the EU has accomplished monetary union, which implies a common currency.

Second, the EU has set up an original governance system that is called supranational. It goes far beyond the structure of the classical international organization, but falls short of a federal structure. One of its main features is that much of the EU law is directly applicable in member states. Another important feature is that the EU Commission (contrary to a secretary general) has the right of initiative for new legislation and has considerable executive powers (for instance, in competition matters). A third important feature of the EU is its system of voting. The main decision-making body is the Council of Ministers where decisions on very important issues are taken by consensus but where all other business is done by qualified majority voting; each member country having a number of votes which is grossly in proportion to its population size. A final important feature is the role of the European Parliament, an institution that is absent in the decision-making machineries of practically all other international organizations.

6.7.2 North America

The North American Free Trade Agreement (NAFTA) came into effect in 1994. Members are the USA, Canada and Mexico. NAFTA was preceded by a customs union between the US and Canada. The treaty has become possible for several reasons. The US changed their traditionally hostile attitude towards regional integration in view of the successes of the EU and the slow progress in the WTO. Mexico had prepared the ground for external liberalization by an internal liberalization programme, that it wanted to be locked in by NAFTA. All three members thought there were big net benefits to be had from the specialization between highly- and medium-developed economies.

The objective is to create a free trade agreement; there is as yet no common external tariff, neither is there a common external policy. NAFTA covers manufacturing and most commercial services. It has, moreover, provisions for investment (that stood as a model for those in the MAI, see Chapter 11) for competition and intellectual property. There are side agreements on labour and environment.

The regime is not supported by much of an organization. Compliance is monitored by the members. Rules about dispute settlement have been agreed upon for instance concerning direct investment.

6.7.3 South America

The two largest economies in the region, Argentina and Brazil, concluded a bilateral trade agreement in 1986. In 1991 followed the treaty on the MERCOSUR, to which the two neighbouring countries, Uruguay and Paraguay, also became signatories. Their accession was only logical given their very close economic ties to the two main member countries (Teubal, 1998).

The primary objective is to create a common market. This has not been easy. The creation of a common tariff has been extremely long-winded. The same is true for the reduction of the internal protective measures that has been victim of the vicissitudes of powerful pressure groups influencing governments. Moreover, the whole process has suffered from monetary unrest exacerbated in recent years by the virtual collapse of the Argentine economy. Mercosur also foresaw the coordination of major policies. However, not much has been realized in these matters as yet.

The governance structure of Mercosur is simple (see www.mercosur. org.uy). The top decision-making body is the council of ministers. They decide on the questions concerning the common market and coordinate other policies such as macro-industrial, etc. An expert group on common market issues does the technical preparatory work for the council. This light structure is completed with a secretary general, a joint parliamentary committee and an economic and social consultative body.

There are a number of other regional cooperation schemes in Latin America, such as CARICOM (in the Caribbean) and the Andean pact. We will not go further into them given the limited size of the economies and/or the limited objectives and results of the agreements.

6.7.4 Asia[11]

The major organization in the region is the Association of Southeast Asian Nations (ASEAN). The group now numbers ten countries in the region, among them Indonesia, the Philippines, Singapore and Thailand.

The initial objective was relatively modest: the creation of a preferential trade area. More recently the ambitions have been stepped up to the creation of a free trade area (AFTA; Asian Free Trade Area) and even a customs union, including rules for FDI (Simatupang, 1998; Chirathivat *et al.*, 1999). AFTA has had limited progress on the road to the realization of its ambitions (Menon, 2000). It has increased its membership from the original five to ten now. It has decreased tariff barriers among the original members to less than 5 per cent, for a range covering more than 90 per cent of trade. Further progress in widening its geographic scope is unlikely as present members are very afraid that the greater diversity it entails will decrease its effectiveness. The coverage is far from complete (excluding agriculture, services and investment). The time schedule for reduction of trade barriers was far from ambitious and has not been realized to a large extent. The reasons for this lack of progress in extending its reach are to be found in the fear of unequal benefits (more to rich and less to poor), indeed a factor that we found to be important in explaining regime change (see Section 5.5).

The governance structure of ASEAN is essentially based on inter-governmentalism. Power is vested in ministerial meetings. The supreme decision-making authority is vested in the heads of government meeting; colloquially called ASEAN summits. The organization has for some time now been supported by a secretariat in Jakarta. An important feature of ASEAN is the consensus style of decision-making. It is also called the ASEAN way and relies very heavily on a personal approach of consultations. This stands in contrast to the more formal and legalistic way favoured by Western countries (Davidson, 2002).

Next to ASEAN exists the SAARC, the South Asian Association for Regional Cooperation. It covers countries on and around the Indian sub-continent. It is not a real economic integration area in the sense that its objectives fall even short of a preferential trade area. The history of the region has shown many conflicts between the major member countries that have precluded any major progress. So we will not deal with it further, notwithstanding its large size in population terms.

6.7.5 Africa

The African continent has seen a large number of regional integration initiatives over the past decades. Many of these overlap, due to the multi-plicity of objectives and the lack of coordination between member states. Most were short-lived; many others that did survive failed to produce any material results. Of the ones that do function at the moment we cite but two:

1   The Southern African Development Community (SADC) was created in 1992 and now has fourteen member states (Angola, Botswana, Congo, Lesotho, Malawi, Mauritius, Mozambique, Namibia, Seychelles, South Africa, Swaziland, Tanzania, Zambia and Zimbabwe). SADC is the suc-cessor of the SADCC, the Southern African Development Coordination Conference, established in 1980 by the so-called frontline states. The objective then was to become more independent of SA (apartheid). The main objectives of SADC are poverty alleviation through increased regional cooperation, and equitable and sustainable growth and develop-ment, based on democratic principles. SADC does not try to follow any established model of integration, but wants to seize feasible oppor-tunities for cooperation.

2   The Economic Community of West African States (ECOWAS), estab-lished in 1975, has sixteen members (of which the most important ones are Nigeria and Côte d'Ivoire). The treaty sets as its objective the creation of a common market and a monetary union. Moreover, agree-ments have been made concerning the coordination of a whole series of policies. The tool kit of the organization has been complemented with a compensation mechanism helping weak partners who would lose government revenue due to tariff cuts. Some progress has been made on the trade front, but work on other objectives remains to be done. The causes for this state of affairs are manifold and range from the differences between countries in power, in culture (language), adminis-trative practices, participation in other integration schemes (for instance the franc CFA zone), economic structure, transport, etc.

Recently a pan-African initiative has been launched called NEPAD (New Partnership for African Development). One of its objectives is the economic integration of the continent in a way that is consistent with global integration. Its ambitions are very high; they want to create conditions for the eradication of poverty and to stop the marginalization of the African continent. The future will show in how far this initiative will fare better than the many similar ones that have been taken in the past.

6.8 Representation of civil society and business

6.8.1 *The role of third parties in intergovernmental organizations*

The previous sections have made clear that international organizations are constructs where national governments work together. This comes about because they have:

- The task to provide certain public goods and can only do that by organizing collectively what they can no longer do effectively individually (see Chapter 3).
- The legitimacy to regulate and the power to make actors comply with the rules.

The positions that governments take in the process of the creation of organizations (systemic) and in the work of those organizations (operational) are motivated by a multitude of actors. Most of them act on a national level. So much of the actual dealings are organized on the national level and governments tend to take these into account. Sometimes this includes the taking into account of the views of experts and of interest groups by including them in national delegations or at least associating them with national government delegations. Only in one case (that of ILO) has this logic been pursued to its final consequence by not only providing for a formal tripartite constitution of national delegations, but also of the operations of the international organization.

This traditional mode of international cooperation is challenged by the same factors that have driven globalization. Many interests are of a specialist nature and are most forcefully articulated by special interest groups. Moreover, the cost of communication and organization has decreased dramatically over the past period, so the capacity of non-governmental organizations to articulate such wishes directly on the international scale has grown considerably. For that reason we detail hereafter the operations of the two most important categories of actors influencing international institutions.

The strength of the organized business interest in the world is decreasing the more one moves from the national to the global level. This is in line with the theory of representation of interest, or with collective action (Olson, 1965; van Schendelen, 2002). The more diffuse the gain to be obtained and the higher the cost of organization, the lower will be the inclination of business to get organized and to defend their interest collectively.

Within national states the various business interests are well organized on different criteria, by branch, by size, by type (energy users), etc. Moreover, many corporations have themselves direct access to government and others.

On the regional level we take the example of the European Union. Here, the representation of business with the European Commission now more or less resembles the situation that prevails in individual member states. There is an umbrella organization (UNICE) and a very wide spectrum of branch organizations. There are also informal groups, such as the Round Table of Industrialists. Moreover, it is clear that EU policy-makers listen even to the voice of individual enterprises (such as Philips on the internal market).

On the level of the industrialized world (OECD), the regulatory powers are much less developed than on the national or regional level. However, it is an important platform for international regime development as it has built up credibility with a number of codes for economic issues. An important example of this sort of work is the guidelines for multinational enterprises (see Box 6.1). In cases where little chance exists that a worldwide solution can be found, business tends to opt for a second-best solution. At

---

Box 6.1 **The OECD Guidelines for Multinational Enterprises**

The guidelines are:

- Recommendations addressed by governments to multinational enterprises operating in or from adhering countries; in effect they are the only comprehensive, multilaterally endorsed code for multinational enterprises.
- Voluntary principles covering a broad range of issues in business ethics, including information disclosure, employment and industrial relations, environment, corruption, consumer interest, competition and taxation.
- Expressions of the shared values of governments of countries that are the source of most of the world's direct investment flows, and home to most multinational organizations.

They are:

- Designed to prevent misunderstandings and build an atmosphere of confidence and predictability between business, labour, governments and society as a whole.
- Supported by OECD governments (as well as a number of non-member countries), business and labour organizations, as well as several NGOs.

Source: Adapted from OECD 2001.

the level of the OECD functions the Business and Industry Advisory Committee (BIAC). It is involved in all major discussions regarding business (it is the OECD variant of UNICE).

On the world level, the representation of business with the most important international organizations is extremely weak. There are some specific cases where the high involvement of the public sector has actually led to a worldwide organization of business (see, for instance, IATA, Chapter 10). However, for most sectors of activity these conditions do not hold. The International Chamber of Commerce (ICC) is an organization representing mainly large multinationals. This organization was already active at the end of the 1940s in issuing an international code of the fair treatment of foreign investments, containing suggestions for host governments. This was followed in the 1970s by an ICC guideline for international investment. This document contained recommendations for both enterprise and governments. The ICC has made other recommendations in related fields on corruption, on environment, etc.

However, most of the work is still done in a two-tier system. Business communicates with the governments of the member countries of these international organizations on a national basis. In all cases national governments try to understand the opinion of the business community on the stand they can best take in the negotiations. In many cases representatives of the business community are actually members of the official delegation; this is the case of the WTO, for instance. This means that there is a national arbitration in a multinational negotiation. In the case of the IMF and WB this is not the case; here the financial sector tends to meet in the margin of the meetings of the institutions. This does not have the structure of an organization that is involved in the articulation of positions and in lobbying, but rather that of a loose network for passing information.

An international complement to this multinational set-up has been found there where the interests of business tend to converge best. The business communities of both the US and the EU have realized that the diffuse structure could not be very effective and hence have joined forces by creating the Trans Atlantic Business Dialogue (TABD). An example of its activity is its action to influence the two most important players in the WTO with proposals for reform. The emphasis is on regulatory convergence. Within this context a large range of issues have been tackled since its creation in 1995. The business interest tend to come rather quickly to common standpoints, however, the progress in implementation has been felt to be slow.

6.8.3 NGO representation

Non-governmental organizations are usually organized around a single issue. They organize interest without aspiring to be representative of all those who are supposed to share this interest. They play an increasingly important role by influencing the work of international (intergovern-mental) organizations (Florini, 2000). They have existed for a long time, as witnessed, for instance, by the antislavery movement in the nineteenth century. In recent times their number and influence has surged. NGO activity on the international level has been greatly stimulated by the Internet, which has facilitated both networking and coalition building among national and international groups by offering a low cost formula for exchange of information.

The subjects that NGOs deal with vary over the whole range of public goods. Paramount among them is environmental protection. The activities of NGOs in this field are mostly directed at symbolic issues that are likely to attract much attention from the media. They tend to leave much of the technical issues aside. Another major issue is labour. Here the well-organized labour movement (trade unions) is notably concerned with issues related to labour standards (see Chapter 11). A third major issue is development; many NGO are actively involved in projects to stimulate the welfare of the LDCs. In this area they play an increasingly important role due to the limits of intergovernmental organizations (Stiles, 2000). Many of the NGOs tend to rally the cause of the antiglobalist, blaming the present (lack of) international government for many of the problems.

The representation of NGOs is not so much in the daily work of international organizations, although many NGOs have obtained consultative status with these organizations. For that reason it is not so easy to order their work by the layers of international organization that we used in the previous section. NGOs' influence comes through their capacity to convince policy-makers at all levels and to mobilize massive support for their issues by seeking coverage by the media. It is this public support that influences national governments both domestically and internationally to opt for certain institutional change.[12]

6.9 Summary and conclusions

- The global system is a patchwork of organizations that differ on a whole range of features, such as membership, scope, voting rules, governance structures, etc.
- With respect to power distribution, there is a notable difference between the UN-oriented organizations, where the rule is 'one country, one vote', and the finance organizations, often characterized as 'one dollar, one vote'.
- Governance structures of international organizations mostly rely on compliance by reputation and peer pressure. The notable exception is the WTO, which has a dispute settlement procedure.
- All of the main global problems are addressed by at least one international organization. For instance, the WTO and the UNCTAD want to enhance more sustainable and equitable growth by trade regimes;

the IMF and the G8 strive for less volatility on financial markets. There seems to be considerable uncertainty as to the borderlines between organizations; in other words, there is much overlap.

- The core of the global system is formed by intergovernmental organizations. They are complemented by increasingly influential private organizations representing the interests of civil society and business.
- Next to the organizations on the global level exist a number of organizations at the regional level. However, the degree to which they have developed differs much from one continent to another. Europe is most integrated; Africa is least integrated.

Part III

Solving problems in practice

The global regimes approach

7   Trade in goods and services

7.1 Introduction

Trade has been attracting the attention of economists for a considerable time. Indeed, trade issues were already paramount in the writings of the major classical economists and have dominated the literature on international economic relations since. This need not surprise us as we are at the heart of the economy. Matters such as accessing goods that could not be produced locally, the reasons for international specialization and the benefits countries could obtain by trading have intrigued generations of economists. In line with the general topic of this book we will focus on a different area than that of most of the literature. The aim of this chapter is to show what regime will best enhance the benefits of international trade.

The structure of this chapter is as follows. First, we will describe the problem that has arisen in trade matters, the occurrence of much protection. In the following sections we will describe that it is in the interest of all to do away with protection; indeed, a stable free trade regime is a collective good. We pursue the demonstration by describing the organizations that provide that collective good and the instruments they use to safeguard it. Finally, we will round off the discussion of this chapter by making an evaluation of the present regime and we will provide some ideas for improvement.

7.2 Where is the problem?

7.2.1 Motives for obstacles to trade in goods

In the past, all governments have been subject to pressures that plead for protection, mostly from domestic producers which sought shelter against foreign competition. Most governments have given in to such pressures, so obstacles to trade in international production have become the norm. Protection against third countries is mostly done by import restrictions. From the extensive literature we have distilled the following arguments for such measures:

- *Strategic independence.* In times of war and supply shortages, a country should not depend on unreliable sources in other countries as far as strategic goods are concerned.
- *Nurturing so-called 'infant industries'.* The idea is that young companies and sectors which are not yet competitive should be sheltered in infancy in order for them to develop into adult companies holding their own in international competition.
- *Defence against dumping.* The healthy industrial structure of an economy may be spoiled when foreign goods are dumped on the market at prices below the cost in the country of origin. Even if the action is temporary, the economy may be weakened beyond its capacity to recover.
- *Defence against social dumping.* If wages in the exporting country do not match productivity, labour is supposed to be exploited; importation from such a country is held by some to uphold such practices and is therefore not permissible.
- *Boosting employment.* If the production factors are not fully occupied, protection can turn local demand towards domestic goods, so that more labour is put to work and social costs are avoided.
- *Diversification of the economic structure.* Countries specializing in one or a few products tend to be very vulnerable; problems of marketing such products lead to instant loss of virtually all income from abroad. This argument applies to small developing countries rather than to large industrialized states.
- *Easing balance of payment problems.* Import restrictions reduce the amount to be paid abroad, which helps to avoid adjustments of the industrial structure and accompanying social costs and societal friction (caused by wage reduction, restrictive policies, and so on).

National governments are sovereign in their setting of the rules for international trade. Some of the motives for protectionist measures cited here have some basis in economics, such as the infant industry. However, often obstacles will go against the interest of the economy as they are introduced to protect less efficient industries from going bankrupt or to permit rent seeking by powerful national producers, sometimes national monopolies.

7.2.2 Categories of obstacles to free trade in goods

Obstacles or trade-impeding factors fall into two categories, tariffs and so called 'non-tariff barriers' (NTBs). They can be described as follows:

- Tariffs, or customs duties or import duties are sums levied on imports of goods, making the goods more expensive on the internal market. Such levies may be based on value or quantity. Levies of similar effect are import levies disguised as administrative costs, storage costs or test costs imposed by the customs.

- Quantitative restrictions (QR) are ceilings put on the volume of imports of a certain good allowed into a country in a certain period (quota), sometimes expressed in money values. A special type is the so-called 'tariff quota', which is the maximum quantity, which may be imported at a certain tariff, all quantities beyond that coming under a higher tariff.
- Currency restrictions mean that no foreign currency is made available to enable importers to pay for goods bought abroad.
- Other non-tariff impediments are all those measures or situations (such as fiscal treatment, legal regulations, safety norms, state monopolies or public tenders), which ensure a country's own products' preferential treatment over foreign products on the domestic market.

7.2.3 Motives for obstacles in trade in services

Traditionally the markets for services are segmented. Many reasons are given to justify such obstacles to free trade in services; among them are both consumer and producer interests.

Most of the obstacles are allegedly drawn up to protect *consumers*. A few examples from different sectors may illustrate this:

- In banking and insurance, regulation serves to limit the risk of insolvency through surveillance of private operators by (semi-) public organizations (central banks, among others). Since foreign suppliers are hard to control, access to the national market is barred to them.
- In air transport, the safety of the passenger is the main concern. Standards are accompanied by mutual import controls in the form of landing rights.
- In communication and energy (electricity), services are regulated to protect consumers from unfair pricing by a natural monopolist.
- In medical services, the interests of the patient are protected by the enforcement of standards for the qualifications of personnel (medical doctors and so on).

Although the arguments for consumer protection are valid, they do not necessarily have to lead to trade protection; indeed, other policy measures can be devised with the same effect for the safety and health of consumers while leaving international competition free. However, even if consumer protection is the official reason for this protectionist regulation, in practice the reason is often that domestic firms want to be sheltered from international competition.

Another set of motives concern the protection of national *producers*:

- strategic importance: an example is maritime transport, where international trade is restricted by a complex system of cargo reservation; a national merchant navy is thought to be necessary in times of war to safeguard the provision of the country with essential goods (see Chapter 11);

- economic policy: the control of macro-economic policy (through the banking system);
- enhancing national prestige (civil aviation);
- control of key technologies (telecommunication);
- safeguarding cultural values (movies, television).

7.2.4 Obstacles to trade in services

The forms in which the free trade in services is impeded cover a wide spectrum. Many of them are fairly comparable to those that hinder goods trade. However, as the value of a border-crossing service is harder to control than that of a good, tariffs are seldom practised, and restrictions on the trade in services are mostly of the non-tariff type. Moreover, because the provision of some types of service across the border involves direct investments, a set of restrictions to entry of markets is relevant too.

Trade in services can be hampered by the following instruments:

- quantitative restriction, notably on domestic consumption (for instance, advertising, air transport); shares of markets reserved for home producers (for example, for movies);
- subsidies (for instance, in construction);
- government procurement (for instance, construction, data processing);
- currency controls on transfers to foreign countries for services provided;
- restrictions on the qualifications of manpower required to perform certain services (legal, medical);
- technical requirements for capital goods (transport, for example);
- customs' valuation problems for goods required to perform services (for instance, plumbers' tools);
- entry restrictions on a profession or restrictions on setting up in business. These can take the form of restrictions on the right of foreign firms to set up or take over subsidiary companies, the exclusion of foreign firms from certain types of activity, etc. They can also take the form of restrictions on migration.

7.2.5 A tangle of protection

The reasons given in the previous sections have led many governments to introduce measures of a protectionist nature. Under the influence of their local beneficiaries such measures tend to become ever more detailed, specific and complicated. They tend, moreover, to discriminate among various trade partners. The effect of this tendency has been that over the course of years a whole tangle of trade protection has evolved.

7.3 Main public good[1]

7.3.1 *Definition and principles*

The theory of international trade is very clear about the choice of the best regimes; it teaches that protection has important negative effects on prosperity and that the best way to avoid these negative effects is for all countries to adopt free trade. Only in specific cases can other principles be optimal (see, for instance, Grimwade 2000). Free trade leads to such beneficial results as it stimulates a better allocation of production factors: capital and labour are used for those activities where they have the highest output. Moreover, free trade permits producers to use scale economies as much as possible, while the keener competition it engenders leads to cost reductions and innovations.

However, once a tangle of protectionist measures is in place, a change-over to free trade is not something that is going to happen by itself. On the contrary, we can show with a simple example of a two-country game that it is likely that a stalemate situation of all countries maintaining protection will install itself (see Box 7.1). If all governments give in to pressures of groups that ask for protection, the group as a whole suffers collectively, as the benefits of free trade are foregone for everybody. Thus in trade matters the collective good of free trade can be provided only by collective action to install a regime that fosters liberalization and maintains fair trade. This will permit investors to have trust, that individual protectionist actions by governments will not undo the conditions they assumed to exist while making their decisions.

Free trade is called a collective good as it may have more the character of a club good than of a public good (see Chapter 4). Indeed, there exists some potential for exclusion, so the formation of clubs is feasible.[2] This expresses itself mostly as regional free trade arrangements. However, as most benefits can be obtained by a wide-ranging worldwide liberalization, one can in practice speak of a public good.

The next question is how to arrive at such a regime. Critical in this respect is the transition of protection to free trade. Given the situation that has evolved historically, all governments will consider their tariffs as bargaining chips that can be traded against similar chips of other countries. Liberalization can be achieved when the various governments involved can be convinced of the priority they should give to the long-term general interest over the immediate sectoral or individual interest. Now each change in trade regime has redistributive effects; it benefits some while hurting others. The best way to bring forward a change in such a situation is to mobilize the most important beneficiaries of the opening up. This can be done by exchanging access of foreign producers to the home market for access of home exporters to the markets of the partner country. Each government will thereby have to overcome the opposition of import-competing activities, but it will be able to build on the interest of potential exporters. If everybody behaves in this way

***Box 7.1* How a trade game leads to generalization of protectionism**

The standard theoretic model that characterizes best the international trade game is based on the following assumptions:

- There are two actors, states A and B, who are unitary rational state actors that seek to maximize national income.
- Each state has one of two acts available to them: C cooperate or D defect. To cooperate means to contribute to the public good by not imposing a tariff. To defect means not to contribute and imposing tariffs.
- The game is non-cooperative, which means that binding agreements are not allowed. Moreover, each player selects only one act and the two players choose simultaneously.

Now four different outcomes can theoretically result:

- CC: generalized free trade
- DD: generalized protection
- CD: country A being exploited by country B
- DC: country B being exploited by A.

We assume that both players order their preferences for the outcome of the game in the same way. For country A this is: DC > CC > DD > CD. This is consistent with the fact that each country individually has an interest in having high tariffs on its imports while benefiting from the low tariffs on the partner country's imports (DC for A). It is also consistent with international trade theory that puts free trade (CC) over protectionism (DD).[3]

By choosing C, a country runs the risk of ending up in the situation of CD. In order to avoid that risk, both countries will choose D. So the rational behaviour of individuals leads to a sub-optimal situation for the group where the public good is not provided.

Source: Adapted from Carlson, 2000.

the allocation of production factors improves, and welfare increases for everybody (static gains). Moreover, the change in competition will drive towards further innovation and technological progress, which leads to dynamic gains for the participating economies. Once a certain level of free trade is established, one may work on the maintenance of the rules of the system and the further reinforcement of the deals.

The question now is how this cooperation will be achieved. On the basis of the theoretical notions developed in Chapters 4 and 5, we will develop in the following sections the logic that will be the foundation for the international regime building that we will explain in Section 7.4.

7.3.2 *The basic principle of the regime: the most favoured nation rule*

The parties involved in trade liberalization are confronted with the problem of how to achieve mutual advantages. Imagine that the first round of discussions is between two countries that assume they have something valuable to offer to one another. Country A has an advantage in the production of good X, country B in the production of good Y. Imagine further, that both are of about equal importance and that both countries see further specialization along their comparative advantage as a net benefit. The first option that comes to mind is that both countries agree on a tariff cut of both good X and Y originating from the partner country of say 15 per cent. This is, however, not a viable solution when there are third countries that produce goods X and Y. Suppose country A, after having negotiated the deal with B, offers to country C a tariff cut of 20 per cent for good Y in exchange of a tariff cut of 15 per cent of their part for good X. It means that the concession given to country B has become worthless for country B as they will be outcompeted on the market of A by producers from C. On the other hand, the access of A producers to the market of B for good Y remains intact.

The solution to this problem is to be found in the mutual award of the most favoured nation (MFN) status. It implies that country A and B promise each other that they will not give better deals to any other partner.

7.3.3 *The need for and the mechanics of multilateral liberalization*

The putting into effect of the MFN option in bilateral deals is besieged with problems. These come about because in general there are many suppliers of many different goods. Trade negotiators are confronted with considerable uncertainty about the intentions of all other actors. In such situations governments have an interest in pursuing Multilateral Trade Negotiations (MTN) (McCalman, 2002). We cite two reasons for this preference:

1   *Hindrance of previous deals.* If after the game described in the previous section country A wants to come to a deal with country D on good Z, there does not seem to be a conflict. However, when countries A and D also involve either good X or good Y in their deals a problem arises. If A and D want to strive for a very significant liberalization, they are limited by earlier agreements, which implies that between A and D tariffs cannot be reduced below the level agreed on between A and B initially. The more deals country A has already entered into, the less it can offer in terms of access to its markets to new trade partners.
2   *Package deals.* Possibilities for trade-offs between different negotiation items and issue linkage increase with the increase in the number of participants.

The question now arises as to how far the results of the multilateral trade negotiation (MTN) are indeed a credible commitment; that is, what mechanisms can be devised to make individual countries comply with the mutual international agreement they have subscribed to. This is important in the sense that each country will be tempted to breach the rules agreed to in individual cases while still benefiting from the general liberalization. The solution to this problem is (in the absence of an international authority with coercive powers) punishment by members. In terms of tariff cuts the situation may arise that country A, which had agreed to cut its tariffs (just like all its partners) by 20 per cent, does not do so. Then country B can immediately respond by not giving the promised tariff cut to country A either. Also, if all countries do that, country A will be virtually excluded from the advantages of liberalization.

This capacity of retaliation implies that in principle the system is self-policing. This adds to the credibility of the commitment. It is the more effective the more countries participate in the agreement. In the following sections we will see, however, that the application of this theoretical system in practice poses lots of problems.

7.3.4 What results can MTN achieve?

Before the negotiation starts, every country will establish its objective function, in other words it makes its calculations about the possible benefits and cost of the results. Countries that will have much to win from liberalization will try to obtain considerable tariff cuts over a wide range of products. Countries that consider that they have little to win or much to lose on certain specific products will ask for lower tariff cuts and for exceptions for these specific products. The outcome of this game is determined by the objective function of the partner that has the lowest gains from trade (country Z).[4] This can be shown easily. Suppose the group decides on a liberalization that goes beyond the point where the benefits and cost of country Z level out, country Z will simply not live up to the commitment. Retaliation by other members will not be effective, as the cost involved would not match the cost of the foregone liberalization for country Z. Thus the member with the lowest incentive to liberalize will determine the outcome of the negotiations.

This fact has an important consequence for the game that will be played. It means that the countries that have a large interest in pushing liberalization will also have an interest in limiting the group of negotiating partners to those that are keen to safeguard similar interests. However, the restriction of the participants runs counter to the results of the previous section where we saw that countries had an interest in making the agreement as comprehensive as possible. So a balance has to be struck between these two elements. A likely outcome of this is that those countries that have a big interest will form a core group of negotiators and then see how many others will be inclined to join the proposed deal. If only a few of the latter group follow the core group, an unsatisfactory deal in terms of geographical coverage will result.

7.3.5 Ways to improve the results

What can be done to improve the results? Evidently establishing a higher tariff reduction than would result from the MTN initially would imply rebalancing the cost–benefit situation for the countries that are hesitant or unwilling. Often this will imply the accommodation of some special situation of protection related to a special interest group. Now the granting of such derogation may come at a small cost to the core group, while it would permit to reap large benefits for all. So a likely outcome is that a general deal is made on a higher ambition level (e.g. overall tariff cuts) than would result from a game as described in the previous section, with a series of exceptions for special cases for products and countries.

The outcome of such a deal may be optimized by:

- Stipulating that the derogation has *a temporary* character and will expire automatically after some pre-fixed period, sufficient for the country that has obtained the derogation to restructure its economy.
- Accepting discrimination: when the country that has asked for a derogation fears particularly the competition from some very strong trade partners, it might make its protection measure specific to this partner only.
- Determining clearly the quantitative size of the specific case at hand; in such a way one can avoid the occurrence of further distortions.
- Specifying the instruments that may be used to effect the agreed protection, e.g. a higher tariff or a quantitative restriction.
- Pushing the liberalization a little bit further, as the core group can indeed claim that it needs some extra benefits to compensate for the loss incurred in the derogation.
- Making side payments. By providing advantages on other scores (e.g. development aid) the benefit–cost ratio of hesitating countries can be improved.

So the conclusion is that trade negotiations will involve the MFN rule, that they will be done in a multilateral way, and that they will consist of a basic text on the key point (tariff reduction) accompanied by a set of special provisions.

7.4 Organizations involved in the provision of the public good

7.4.1 Categories of players

In matters of international trade, private firms are the most important actors. However, the public authorities set the conditions and the rules.

Next to these two principal actors there is the civil society that has a stake in the outcome of the process. We can describe the roles of the various groups of players somewhat more in detail as follows.

Multinational firms (MNFs): These have developed in line with globalization (see Chapter 2) and do account for a very large share of international trade. Of course, to MNFs the conditions under which international trade is handled are of vital importance; these conditions determine to a large extent the possibilities for specialization and hence the profitability of their individual operations. Only the most important MNF can hope to influence international negotiations directly, others have to use collective action to have themselves heard. So, many specialist groups of interested private sector players have developed. Cases in point are farmers in developed areas, such as the EU or the US (against imports), producers of primary products in developing countries (in favour of exports), etc.[5] Often the interests of these different subgroups are conflicting. But they all try to influence trade rules in their favour and to get to that result they display very active lobbying. The more encompassing the lobby groups are, the more they are in favour of the application of a limited set of clear transparent rules that favour free trade. A representative of the latter case is the International Chamber of Commerce.

National governments: Since time immemorial, governments have influenced international trade mainly for tax, security and industrial policy reasons (see Section 7.2). They have regulated trade with very elaborate sets of instruments. Some have nationalized a part or even the total of their international trade. At present there are only very few countries left that have state controlled trade. But all governments keep a keen interest in international trade matters and it is they who are the players in international negotiations on trade matters.

Non-governmental organizations (NGOs): These are, in general, entities with voluntary membership that defend causes that are not directly economic, such as labour standards, environmental protection, food safety, consumer protection and fair trading (anticorruption). Often they are single-issue groups, such as environmentalists. They have become very powerful in mobilizing public opinions and on that basis have been able to raise considerable funds to make their views heard by decision-makers. Recently, many of these groups with different claims have bundled their activities in an antiglobalization (or socioglobalization) movement, using modern facilities, such as the Internet and media coverage of conflicts, for increasing their operational effectiveness.

7.4.2 The main international organizations

The institutional set-up that has to deal with the problems cited above has developed fairly well over the past decades. Intergovernmental organizations are the main components. So the other stakeholders mentioned in the previous section, notably firms and NGOs, have no direct say in the dealings of these organizations. They have to turn to national governments or to the permanent instances of these organizations to be heard and to try to have their interest represented (see, for the resulting two level games, Section 4.6). The following organizations deal with trade (see Chapter 6 for more details).

WTO[6] (formerly GATT) plays the central role in trade liberalization. Its coming into existence cannot be explained by the factor interest (see Section 5.3), given the interest of individual countries in protection. It is the particular configuration of power that prevailed after the Second World War (the US could impose their view on the other players) that is the main explanation for its emergence. Moreover, the factor 'awareness' also played a role as the crisis of the 1930s had taught the lesson that an international regime for trade was needed in order to avoid a rebirth of the problems that had led to the Second World War. We will go into more detail about the workings of the WTO in the following sections of this chapter.

The *G8* has an occasional involvement in matters of trade, but this is very limited. The G8 analyses problems, makes suggestions and brings these to the agenda of the WTO. It tries to influence the negotiation position of the major participants in such a way as to improve the chances of coming to an agreement. This latter role was successful on some occasions in the 1980s. However, in recent years the G8 has not been able to provide such leadership as members could not agree on basic issues.

The *OECD* has played a limited but important role. The organization has always been helpful in making analyses of important trends and in coordinating the positions of the industrialized countries.

UNCTAD has been created because of conflicts between rich and poor countries over the organization of trade. UNCTAD has tried in many ways to put into practice more interventionist approaches to improve the trade position of the LDCs. It has dealt notably with a set of commodity agreements. Its successes have been limited and now its role is more in information and analysis than in regime setting.

Specialist sectoral organizations, such as the IMO and IATA, are discussed in Chapter 10.

Finally, we draw attention to a whole series of regional trade arrangements (see Section 6.7). The issue of regionalism has for a long time been the subject of considerable controversy (see Box 7.2). A hybrid version of regionalization has developed within the framework of the WTO, where regional groups (e.g. Africa) coordinate their positions.

7.4.3 Objectives of the WTO

The WTO pursues a double objective which is to further:

- trade liberalization; in other words the dismantling of protection of all forms;

Box 7.2 **The controversy of regionalism and multilateralism**

Regional integration consists of two elements. First, the abolition of trade barriers between neighbouring partner countries. Second, the creation of some form of common external protection towards third countries. Important examples of regional schemes for trade liberalization are the European Union, NAFTA and Mercosur. Many other less successful attempts have been made. Most notably, initiatives that were based on import substitution have failed to develop. Trade liberalization on a regional basis has been a controversial issue for a long time (Blackhurst and Henderson, 1993).

Advocates of regionalism bring forward the argument that it is an expedient way to liberalize trade. Geographically contiguous countries tend to have a higher propensity to trade with each other than countries that need to bridge considerable distances; so important trade flows tend to be liberalized. Under some conditions that are relatively easy to satisfy, such trade liberalization (both by way of free trade areas and customs unions) has positive welfare effects (see Molle, 2001, and Panagariya and Krishna, 2002). Moreover, groups of countries that have similar objectives in trade matters and tend to have similar levels of development are more likely to achieve effective deals for full free trade than countries with different types of economies and cultures.

Opponents to regionalism point to the fact that it violates the basic principle of non-discrimination. Indeed, under regionalism trade advantages are only given to partners in the scheme, not to everybody. They consider, moreover, that regionalism erodes the effectiveness of deals on a global level.

The outcome of this controversy has been uncertain for some time. However, the GATT/WTO has finally accommodated regionalism (Article XXIV) under pressure from important political bodies, such as the EU. Regionalism was accepted as a sort of second-best option. As world trade liberalization proved to be a long-winded process, regional integration provided a comfortable half-way house. However, this exception to the basic rule of most favoured nation (see Section 7.5.1) can only be accepted on two conditions:

(1) no increase in protection of the new group towards third parties; and
(2) no sectoralism; a free trade area should cover substantially all trade between members.

- elimination of discrimination; in other words equal treatment for producers irrespective of the country of their location.

In practice, the WTO has had to accept limitations to its coverage on three scores:

- *Sectors.* For a long time, agriculture, textiles, clothing and services have been almost exempt from liberalization. All three sectors have recently been brought under the working of the WTO rules.[7] There are, however, a few exceptions such as maritime and air transport that remain outside the domain of WTO (see Chapter 10). In order to avoid new trade barriers emerging, the WTO has installed a moratorium on E-commerce, implying that no customs duties or other barriers are to be imposed (see Chapter 10).
- *Areas.* GATT has started with a limited number of signatories. Over time it has gradually increased its coverage. At the moment most countries in the world are members of the WTO; although a number of the more important ones have actually stayed outside for a long time (for instance, China). Consequently, the principle of non-discrimination did until recently not acquire universal application. Regional integration schemes were considered compatible as long as the average protection of the group did not increase (see Box 7.2). Moreover, it has been accepted that developed countries could give preferences to less developed countries to foster their trade (see Box 7.3).

Box 7.3 Coping with the asymmetry between developed and less developed countries

The GATT/WTO organizes a large diversity of countries. On the one hand, we find big countries that have very highly developed and diversified economies. On the other hand, we find small countries that are among the poorest in the world and have little human and other resources. The former are generally capable of adapting their production structures to new conditions without too much difficulty. The latter, on the contrary, are often caught in situations from which it is difficult to escape without external help.

In bargaining terms, power is very important to obtain advantages. Now, power is very unequally distributed over developed countries and LDCs. So it is very unlikely that the latter will be able to strike advantageous deals in multilateral negotiations. An accelerated development of the LDCs is in everybody's interest. Trade is more effective than aid to foster growth in LDCs. So developed countries need to offer LDCs facilities for entering their markets. The most appropriate instrument in this respect is the special and differential (S&D) treatment of LDCs.

S&D provisions within WTO agreements can be grouped into three categories, allowing developing countries:

- greater flexibility with regard to rules and disciplines governing trade measures;
- longer transition periods for the implementation of WTO agreements;
- technical assistance to help in the implementation of commitments.

Moreover, there are S&D provisions that are being applied to developed countries. These concern particularly:

- preferential treatment for LDC exports to developed countries' markets, which may imply lower tariff rates for LDC imports than MFN;
- priority to the removal of trade barriers that affect particularly goods of interest to LDCs;
- implementation of agreements that permit trade protection in a way that does least harm to the LDCs.

The last two categories of provisions are so called 'best endeavour' clauses; they do not impose any specific action on the developed countries and their importance and effect are difficult to measure.

The preferential treatment of LDC imports in developed countries is more concrete and has been practised for some time. In essence, this means applying a lower tariff for goods originating from LDCs than to goods originating from other countries. Although preferential treatment breaks two principles of GATT: non-discrimination and reciprocity, it has been accepted to solve the conflict between objectives and means. Both the US and the EU have set up a Generalized System of Preferences (GSP). Their putting into operation has given rise to problems regarding the selection of countries and products[9] and the margin of preference for different categories of LDC according to their relative level of poverty. In the past, GSPs were of limited relevance as many of the products of LDCs were hurt by other measures (notably the multifibre agreement and the agricultural policy of the most-developed countries, such as the US, the EU and Japan). Recently, the GSPs have lost much of their relevance as tariffs have been considerably lowered so that the effective preference is, in many cases, no longer substantial.

Other packages can in this respect be devised, such as the recent 'everything but arms' initiative of the EU, which grants least-developed countries duty-free access to the EU market for all products except arms. Although the effect of this initiative may be limited due to access constraints in the EU (transition periods for sensitive agricultural products) and supply constraints in the LDCs, it is an important step in the recognition of the special problem of LDCs.

- *Instruments.* There have for a long time been exceptions as to quota[8] and other non-tariff barriers, whereas the WTO has not really been able to come to grips with the aspect of disguised export subsidies, etc. Moreover, the WTO has accepted all sorts of safeguards against negative effects of specific trade measures and loopholes through which trade can be limited in case a member country feels its vital interests are at stake.

So, the far-reaching objective to realize free trade for all goods and services for all countries in the world is still some way off.

7.5 Governance

7.5.1 Basic principles of operation

Fundamental to the GATT/WTO is the recognition of the signatories/ members that trade is a matter of common interest and that changes in national trade regimes can only be made after negotiation with trade partners.

The basic set-up of the WTO rests on the principle of non-discrimination between:

- *Different trade partners.* This principle has been given its legal form in the most favoured nation clause. It reads as follows: '. . . any advantage, favour, privilege or immunity granted by any contracting party to any product originating in, or destined for any country shall be accorded immediately and unconditionally to the like product originating in or destined for the territories of all other contracting partners' (Article I of GATT). In closely looking at this phrase two aspects stand out as particularly important. The first is the rule with respect to members: if you favour one, you favour all. The second is the rule with respect to procedure: there is no negotiating, the MFN is, in principle, unconditional and takes effect immediately (see further Horn and Mavroidis, 2001).
- *Imported and home products.* This principle is laid down in the National Treatment Provision (Article III of GATT) that requires 'like or directly competitive or substitutable' foreign products not to be treated less favourably on the domestic market once they have been imported.

7.5.2 Platform for negotiating

The WTO is essentially a permanent forum for negotiations. These concern, in the first place, the way in which the objectives of the organization should be reached that is the liberalization of trade. Next, they also concern the rules by which the organization will work and the acceptance of new members of the organization.

Devising an effective formula for negotiations on trade liberalisation has been a first task of GATT. Fundamental in this respect has been the concept of reciprocity. It means that a country that is prepared to make concessions in matters of liberalizing its trade can demand that its partners offer similar cuts in protection. These can be in the same issue (for instance, mutual liberalization of car trade), but may also be cross-issue (for instance, tariff reduction in cars by country A against quota reduction in textiles by country B). In negotiation terms this is difficult as it involves barter (one exchanges something for something different). There is no common denominator that could facilitate the functioning of such a 'market'. Hence negotiations on series of specific issues tend to become very long-winded and may achieve little. In this case multi-issue negotiations can be a way out as they permit a settlement involving concessions on the items that for each country imply the lowest perceived cost.

Several aspects of the multilateral negotiating rounds are very important from the point of view of transaction cost analysis and game theory (see Chapter 4 for a theoretical foundation).

- *Commitment of parties*. Parties may not change their trade conditions unilaterally. This prevents countries from raising stakes before negotiations in order to obtain better deals.
- *Reference to principles*. The adoption of the free trade, most favoured nation and non-discrimination principles improves the efficiency of the negotiations. For instance, because it removes the fear that striking an initial deal is disadvantageous as someone else may get a better deal.
- *Comprehensive bargaining*. This opens up possibilities for coalitions that permit package deals that offer a better final outcome for everyone. Multi-industry bargaining permits the breaking of powerful special interest of industries that are seeking to maintain protection from imports; they can now be overturned by coalitions of parties having an interest in the broader deal of mutual liberalization.
- *Reciprocity of concessions*. These tend to mobilize in all countries those who have an interest in exporting. In order to facilitate the coming together of such interests over a large range of products, the WTO has staged negotiations on a basis of a linear cut in all tariffs for a group of products.
- *Core groups*. Although the organization has a multilateral set-up, initial negotiations are often conducted between the two major members (US–EU) or a small group of members. The results are then submitted for approval to the whole organization to become applicable to all members.
- *Focal points*. The terms at which a cooperative solution can be identified in an indeterminate bargaining situation.

Almost every decade saw a major multilateral trade negotiation round. Such rounds demanded much preparation and most of them took several years to conclude. After the first round (Geneva) in 1947, the Dillon and Kennedy rounds of the 1960s made a big step forward and so did the Tokyo round in the 1970s and the Uruguay round in the late 1980s/early 1990s. Together, these rounds have resulted in substantial reductions in tariffs and quantitative restrictions and in improvement of the conditions for fair trade. At the moment the tariffs for industrial products in developed countries are very low, in many cases even zero.

7.5.3 Dispute settlement and enforcement mechanisms

The problem of many international agreements is that there is little power with the organization that patronizes the agreement to force the signatories to comply with it. The members of the organization (signatories to an agreement) are sovereign states and the only way they can be made to comply is by threatening them with some sort of sanction that would harm their interest. Such a sanction may be to be expelled from the organization, which implies the exclusion of the non-complying partner from the benefits of membership (club good). However, many problems will be too small to justify such a drastic measure. On the other hand, if non-compliance goes unpunished it may incite others to go along the same path with the risk of erosion of the whole deal. So other, less drastic forms have been devised.

The situation of GATT/WTO in matters of compliance has evolved over time. At the beginning of GATT, no effective enforcement procedure was set up, as nobody thought that the organization would be long-lived. However, over time a simple yet effective procedure has been worked out. It consists of three elements:

- Transparency of national trade measures and international agreements; so that breaches of an agreement can be easily detected;
- Mechanism for dispute settlement that provides for a standard procedure to be followed in case of litigation;
- Measures for compliance, such as the right of retaliation. In case an agreement is not respected and harm is done, the GATT/WTO rules permit the country that has suffered to impose countervailing tariffs on imports from the infringing country, to an extent that is substantially equivalent in its effects to the measures of the infringing country.

The GATT/WTO situation in matters of compliance is quite exceptional; no other international organization has developed so far. Most rely on less effective measures such as self-interest and reputation. The emergence of these features of the world trade regime can be explained by a number of factors that we have seen in theoretical terms in Chapter 5. First, there is the interest that all countries have with a smoothly functioning trade system; and a compliance mechanism is essential to such a system. Next, countries know that they are in a repeated game: even if an individual member may lose out in one case, they may benefit in the settlement of the next case. Finally, there is the locking-in aspect. The 'loss' of a case of a particular pressure group can be blamed on international obligations in the GATT/WTO. It may lead to the adoption of an efficient policy package that would otherwise not have been possible given the internal distribution of political power.

The core part of this compliance is the dispute settlement procedure. We have seen how important this is in order to cope with the problems of incomplete contracts, moral hazard and opportunism. The GATT/WTO has set up and improved over the years such a dispute settlement procedure (DSP). It has worked relatively well in those cases where it has been applied. The workings of the WTO dispute settlement procedure are given in a schematized form in Box 7.4.

The WTO/DSP has clear advantages, but also has considerable weaknesses. These can be listed as follows:

- *Government filter.* Business interests are taken up by governments, the only actors having legal status in the WTO. Due to issue-linking, governments may not bring up some important cases, even if they would have improved the efficiency of global allocation.

- *Delays.* In the past, a long time elapsed between the moment a matter was brought up by the complaining party and the implementation of the WTO decisions by the infringing party. Recently, the situation has been improved by setting a maximum to the duration of each of the stages of the DSP. However, the total duration is still long and considerable damage can be done in that period.

- *No coercion.* There is no instrument other than national retaliation and international opprobrium. The latter is generally not very effective, particularly when the infringing party has a strong national interest. Punitive action by third countries would imply a very effective instrument but this has explicitly been ruled out.

- *Retaliation hits wrong groups.* The exporters of the infringing country have to bear the cost of the protection of the interest group that causes the infringement. Consumers of that good in the importing country will also be damaged as they have now less choice at a higher price. Often the country that retaliates hits also domestic groups, mostly the importers of the products that are subject to retaliation.

- *Asymmetry of country sizes.* The members of the WTO are of very different size. If one of the major countries is responsible for an infringement, a small country has little power to effectively respond. This applies both to its capacity in institutional terms (diplomacy, legal council, etc.) and to the credibility of its retaliation. Moreover, small developing countries often fear that they will lose out on non-trade issues (financial aid).

The *conclusion* of this section may be that the WTO/DSP has the advantage of existing, but that it is still weak, and therefore deals only partially with the problem of transaction cost in international trade matters.

Box 7.4 **The WTO dispute settlement procedure (schematized)**

Step 1: A dispute arises

A member believes that he has a problem because another member infringes the rules or violates the result of negotiations. The parties concerned have to enter into bilateral talks in order to see whether they can solve the problem. The director general of the WTO may be asked to act as an intermediary.

Step 2: The conflict persists; request for a panel

If no solution can be found, the complaining party may request that the WTO set up a panel. Such a panel typically consists of international experts in trade matters that are no party to the conflict. The terms of reference for the panel are set up.

Step 3: The panel at work

The panel examines the facts, meets with the interested parties, draws its conclusions and presents these to the interested parties and the Dispute Settlement Board.

Step 4: Decision-taking and or Appellate Body

The dispute settlement body reviews the panel report and takes a decision. In the past, the report had to be accepted by the general council of GATT, which gave the infringing country a veto to decisions. Under the WTO this is no longer the case. If a party cannot accept the decision, it may refer to the Appellate Body. This appeal may be asked, however, only on arguments related to law or legal interpretation. The decision of the Appellate Body is, in practice, final.[10]

Step 5: Implementation

The parties must implement the decision of the WTO within a reasonable time period. If the infringing party does not comply, the complaining party may ask permission to retaliate; that is, to use trade protection measures against products from the infringing party. This need not be in the same sector. In order to end the conflict, the offending party may also make proposals for advantages in other areas (compensation in trade) or even in financial terms.

7.5.4 *Accepting exceptions and safeguards*

The commitment to the regime that the GATT/WTO has installed is sometimes put under severe strain. Countries that are feeling the effect of high external competition may be under such heavy pressure from internal forces that they will feel compelled to give in. This will notably be the case if they feel that the damage to their industry is done by the unfair trade practices of other countries. Now, the dispute settlement can be very long-winded and as the outcome is uncertain, governments may want to return to protective measures. If the GATT/WTO was not able to provide for such a possibility, countries might be inclined to leave the organization altogether, foregoing the benefits, but avoiding the immediate cost. This would weaken the world system and, therefore, be better avoided.

In order to deal with such problems, GATT/WTO has installed a system of escape clauses. These are temporary exceptions to the obligations of members, which are accepted in order to save the long-term survival of the regime. However, the permit to use safeguards can only be awarded in case it specifies conditions, defines temporariness and organizes surveillance.

The need for such exceptions and safeguards come from the fact that the world institutional order is incomplete. It cannot cope with a certain number of problems in the way a national state or even a cooperation scheme, such as the EU, can provide. Here, allocational efficiency can be pushed farther because the negative effects for certain groups can be taken away or at least alleviated by measures of cohesion (social and or regional) policies. As such, a first-best policy setting is not available on the global level, second-best solutions must be found of the type cited here.

7.6 Evaluation of the past and options for the future

7.6.1 *Major achievements*

The primary objective of the WTO is to liberalize trade. It has been very successful in pursuing this objective. This is visible on three scores:

- *Instruments:* Tariffs have been cut to very low levels now, whereas the ban on non-tariff barriers (NTBs) has done away with many quota, voluntary export restraints, etc.
- *Geography:* The number of countries that take part in the WTO has increased continuously. So the WTO rules cover an increasing share of all transactions.
- *Products:* The initial accent has been on manufacturing. Recently, other sectors have been integrated as well. Although progress has still to be made, sectors such as services and agriculture are now subjected to WTO rules.

Another positive aspect that should be mentioned is the creation of reinforced regimes in terms of:

- *Fair trade:* The WTO has set rules in order to take away distortions emanating from other sources such as export subsidies, dumping, etc.
- *Dispute settlement:* The device to cope with disputes has been working well generally and has permitted quite a few problems to be solved.

A puzzling situation now occurs. Most observers have up till now considered the trade liberalization record as positive. Yet in a large econometric exercise the effect of GATT/WTO membership on trade flows could not be established. On the contrary, many observers do not rate the effect of the GSPs very highly (see, for instance, Box 7.3). Yet the GSP showed up as highly relevant in this exercise (Rose, 2002). One thing is clear: further research is needed.

7.6.2 Inadequacies and challenges

The first major challenge of the WTO is to continue work on its primary task, which is the further liberalization of trade. There are quite a few areas where progress has not been sufficient (services, agriculture). Market access is the criterion here.

The second major challenge is to come to grips with the development aspect of trade. This will be reinforced by the growing importance of LDCs in the world trading system (among others by the accession of China as a member). Developing countries are disappointed with the limited positive effects for them of the previous rounds. Concessions made in the Uruguay round in matters of agriculture concerned traditional products that developed countries have to import anyway. Little progress was made on the score of temperate products where the most developed countries continue to practise import protection and export promotion. A similar reasoning applies to textiles and clothing, where the implementation of the agreement is long-winded. LDCs are, moreover, very concerned about the burden that certain WTO agreements put on their administrative and financial resources and the constraint they may constitute on development. This means that WTO rules may lead to inferior outcomes for low-income countries.[11]

This has a number of consequences that are relevant from the point of view of regime building.

Negotiations in the past have often been initiated by a small group of major trading nations. Other countries have been associated only at a late stage to the outcome of these dealings. This has been efficient from a transaction cost point of view, but unfair from a distributional point of view. Future negotiations will be more complicated because LDCs will have to be involved in earlier stages so that they can defend their interests better.

The remaining barriers to imports originating from the LDCs are still very significant. They include agriculture and labour intensive manufactured products, such as clothing. It is of the utmost importance to stimulate duty-free and quota-free market access for all products from LDCs. How-ever, getting to an agreement on these issues will be difficult as the remaining trade barriers are defended by single-issue pressure groups, whereas the general interest for such measures in highly developed countries is difficult to organize.

Effective support should be given to the development and the imple-mentation of WTO rules by the most vulnerable countries (technical and financial cooperation). Here, both international organizations, such as the World Bank and major trading partners have their role to play (IBRD, 2001b).

The third major challenge is to come to grips with the so-called 'trade and' agenda (see Hoekman and Kostecki, 2001, Chapter 13). Most of these issues span over the competence of WTO into other fields. Many of the subjects have been brought forward by NGOs that do not fall under the heading of the market access goal of the WTO, such as environmental protection. The 1996 ministerial conference of Singapore put four subjects on the agenda: investment, competition, public procurement and trade procedures.[12] The 2001 WTO ministerial conference at Dohar took a very cautious route in matters of the extension of the role of the WTO; it demanded that working groups investigate the issue further to clarify the principles and possibilities. However, a commitment was made to enter into negotiations on the relationship between multilateral environmental agreements and WTO rules. In a mature, coherent institutional system such relations would be set according to some basic rules and organizational procedures. The diversity of forms that prevails among the existing independent international institutions (such as the IBRD, ILO, UN, etc.) now precludes such efficient coordination.

7.6.3 Proposals for improvement

A number of proposals have been made to improve the scope of the WTO. These form part of the 'trade and' agenda mentioned in the previous section and relate notably to the following areas:

- *Investment.* There is a very close relationship between trade and direct investment (see Box 2.1 and Chapter 10). Moreover, the method of integration that WTO has used in the past could very well be applic-able to this area as well.
- *Competition.* Here again there is a close relationship (see Chapter 10) and a possibility that the WTO framework could accommodate this. However, in the immediate future it does not seem desirable to charge WTO with this for two reasons. First, many countries have no experi-ence with this sort of policy nationally. Second, the international welfare distributional effects are highly uncertain.[13]

- *Environment*. The protection of the environment is certainly a global public good (see Chapter 9). Trade and environmental issues are interlinked in many ways (see, for example, Batabyal and Beladi, 2001).[14] Yet there are good reasons not to charge WTO with the environment problem. First, the relation between trade and environment is not as strong as in the two previous cases. Second, it is unlikely that the WTO rule-based approach (MFN, reciprocity in bargains) would work in this area.
- *Labour standards*. There is much controversy about the role of labour standards and how to enforce them. Trade policy measures are, however, an inefficient tool for promoting them. LDCs are particularly afraid of the misuse of such policies. Again, the WTO governance mechanisms do not seem adequate for dealing with such issues.

For the reasons mentioned it is very unlikely that the WTO competence in any of these matters will be extended in the foreseeable future. So the locus for regime building for these issues (the two latter ones anyway) is likely to be outside GATT/WTO.[15]

Moreover, there are suggestions to improve the governance of the WTO. These relate to two subjects:

- Improve the decision-making process by moving away from consensus. The proposal to create an executive board has been strongly opposed by LDCs, who fear that this would strengthen the dominance of the already powerful.
- Give voice to NGOs by accepting them as partners in the negotiation process, even in the dispute settlement case. However, the issue of accountability precludes accepting this option to the full; the better alternative is to associate them more closely in preliminary stages such as fact finding and proposal formulation.

7.7 Summary and conclusions

- Free trade does provide economic advantages. However, under the influence of powerful interest groups, protection tends to override these advantages and become widespread.
- Progressive trade liberalization has become recognized as a global public good.
- GATT/WTO has over the past half a century provided the organizational framework for the development of the global trade regime. It has gradually increased its coverage as to member countries, subjects (products) and instruments.
- In matters of governance the WTO has two salient features: first, the

dispute settlement procedure and, second, the authorization for offended partners to retaliate against the offender.

- The WTO is confronted with two main challenges. The first is to come to grips with a considerable 'trade and' agenda (concerning subjects such as social and environmental sustainability). The second is to make sure that trade sustains economic development; to that end one needs to give more voice to the LDCs and make sure that the trade regime will lead to a better sharing of its fruits.

8 Finance

8.1 Introduction

The objective of this chapter is to expose the advantages of the creation and operation of an international regime for financial markets. We describe in the first section how world capital markets are inherently unstable and even tend to create major crises. These crises lead via a loss of confidence to a loss of investment opportunities and finally to a loss of growth. The cost implied can be avoided by creating a regime that improves the conditions for financial stability. We describe the basic characteristics that such a regime must have in order to be effective, the organizations that have to give substance to the regime and the instruments that can best be used. We round off this chapter with an evaluation of the regime in place and some ideas for improvement in the future.

Stability in capital markets is not the only public good that we may distinguish in financial matters. Traditionally, we also have the problem of the instability of the currency markets and hence the volatility of exchange rates. We will deal with this subject in an annex. More recently the idea has arisen that the provision of sufficient capital flows to less developed countries can also be considered a major objective for regime development as it improves the equitable distribution of wealth in the world. We will touch on this aspect in the final sections of this chapter.

8.2 The main problems

8.2.1 Capital mobility and controls

In the period characterized by the Bretton Woods system of fixed exchange rates (see Chapter 2), most transactions involving foreign exchange and or short-term capital had a direct relation with the real sector of the economy. In this period restrictions on international capital movements were widespread. In the past decades two major developments have changed that picture. First, the introduction of floating exchange rates; many international flows are now reactions to real or expected changes in the external value of currencies. Next, the gradual removal of restrictions on international capital movements; a tendency led by the most developed countries that was quickly followed by other countries, including some developing countries. The trend towards the liberalization of international capital movements has been set in as a corollary to the liberalization of national capital markets.

There are several reasons for the liberalization of capital markets, in other words for the abolition of capital controls. First, liberalization leads to better allocation of resources. Second, the technical enforcement of capital controls has proved to be very difficult and modern means of telecommunication have increased the capacity of traders to circumvent such controls. Third, capital controls proved rather ineffective in the long run anyway. Finally, they often seemed counterproductive in the sense that they slowed down the necessary adaptation of the economy.

8.2.2 Increased risk

As a consequence of liberalization, international flows of capital have increased tremendously. Moreover, their composition has changed. A large segment of the present-day transactions are portfolio investments instead of trade or direct investment-related operations. In order to facilitate these flows a whole generation of new financial intermediaries have emerged.

This new configuration has created a number of extra risks. They have emerged from the increase in:

- *Volume*. Short-term portfolio flows have increased dramatically. A large portion of these flows goes to emerging economies which have a financial sector that is functioning under an inadequate regulatory and supervisory regime. Unfortunately, there seems to be a negative correlation between the proportion of short-term capital (so risk) and the quality of the macro-economic and regulatory environment. Short-term financial flows tend to be very volatile and large outflows may very quickly become a source of instability for both the private and the public sector; that may even lead to a collapse of the national financial system (Griffith Jones *et al.*, 2001a).
- *Transmission*. In the modern world of financial integration, the risks of contagion are much larger than they were in the past. Some of this contagion is regional (for instance, through trade channels), some is global and affects the lenders that often come from the major developed countries.
- *Sophistication*. Financial markets have developed a very wide array of products that are adapted to the specific circumstances of particular groups of clients. Some of these products become very popular in the short term and the regulators have only little time to get to grips with the systemic problems that the use of such products may imply. Corporate chief financial officers have difficulty to see through the intricacies of such products. At the level of major banks, this problem also exists, as witnessed by the collapse of some of them.

These extra risk factors make the supervision and control of financial operations much more difficult than before. Hence systemic risks have increased.

8.2.3 Considerable market imperfections

Markets do not always function well for a variety of reasons:

- *Information and interpretation*. With the wide range of products now internationally available, there is a very high need to acquire good information so as to judge correctly the real facts and adjust accordingly. However, this is not always easy to realize. Market intermediaries that could help to provide this information have difficulty in coping with the theoretical intricacies and cultural variety and are not always neutral players. Moreover, similarities in situations are often taken as indicators of the same type of problems, which is not always the case. Scientific progress is made (e.g. Burkart and Coudert, 2002) and one should hope that markets integrate the results of these efforts instead of reacting to superficial similarities.
- *Moral hazard*. A debtor may accumulate excessive debt with the intention to force his creditors to accept that he cannot pay back on normal terms; in so doing he may hope to get a more advantageous deal. Moreover, lenders may go along with such a strategy as they may count on a bail-out by public organizations and/or international institutions that will pay for the debtor in question. This may even lead to a coalition of lenders and borrowers at the cost of the public organizations.
- *Adverse selection*. While most countries will want to have their finances in order and adapt to market signals, a limited number of countries may be willing to borrow even in cases where interest rates go up drastically. That would mean that only bad borrowers remain. They need it so badly that they are willing to take the capital almost at any price. As at such high rates good borrowers refrain from lending, only bad borrowers would remain. In such a situation lenders may shy away so that capital supply dries up.
- *Multiple equilibria*. Asset prices are based firstly on the expectations of future returns and secondly on the presumption of the stability of the institutional system. Now, if real estate prices are high, credit is adequate and economic activity sustains rents, there is a high level equilibrium. However, a slack in demand causing revenues of real estate to decrease may lead banks to review their lending. This may lead real estate investors to liquidate their assets quicker than foreseen, causing a loss. Such a change can bring the whole system to a lower equilibrium of prices, credit and economic activity. Herd behaviour is a powerful factor to explain why equilibrium at one level may be turned in for another one at a different level.

8.2.4 *Latent problems: financial instability*

The effective functioning of the market economy depends on a number of conditions. One of them is monetary and financial stability that provides the environment for rational decision-making on savings and investments. The attention often goes to the opposite end: the absence of financial stability. Financial instability is defined as, 'a situation in which economic performance is potentially impaired by fluctuations in price of financial assets or in the ability of financial intermediaries too meet their contractual obligations' (Crockett, 1996).

There are several reasons for the inherent instability of the international financial system:

- *Wrong fundamentals.* Governments are continuously tempted for internal policy reasons to pursue an expansionary monetary and budgetary policy too far. Such excessive spending can lead to unsustainable public debts and to external borrowing beyond the financial capacity of the country.
- *International spill-overs.* The markets for exchange and for capital have become global markets under the influence of liberalization and new technology (telecommunications). Over the past decade this trend has accelerated (Irwin and Vines, 2001). More and more trading takes place between actors in different countries. This leads to a dense international network of interlocking claims and liabilities (Sell, 2001). So the degree of spill-over and contagion has increased too.
- *Market failures.* We mentioned in the previous section the lack of quality of information and the poor performance of rating agencies. So markets may react in a rather erratic way. Moreover, the gradual adaptation of the price of finance to changed circumstances often does not take place. This means that one gets a rather violent reaction once the retarded movement of adaptation starts.
- *Race to the bottom.* Banks and other financial service providers tend to go for high margin market niches. This is part of the dynamics of the markets. However, high margins tend to go hand in hand with high risks. Now there is a lack of transparency as to the size and character of the total exposure of major players. So the sort of buffers needed is not always clearly understood. It means that the internal control of international financial providers is a problem.
- *Lack of insight with prudential control.* The control of public organizations on the exposure of market players has weaknesses as well. One is derived from the lack of basic information (see previous point). Another one is the consequence of the increasing sophistication; the authorities of countries with small resources have much difficulty in coping with these intricacies.

8.2.5 Acute problems: financial crises

Financial instability can lead to negative effects on the economy as a whole. For that reason, it is considered as a public bad. The main problem of financial instability is that it may deteriorate into a financial crisis.

The definition of a financial crisis has two dimensions:

- *Function default*. Episodes of disruption of financial markets (they cease to function in a normal way) in which adverse selection and moral hazard problems become much worse, so that financial markets are unable to channel funds efficiently to those who have the most productive investment opportunities (Mishkin, 1992).
- *Effect on actors*. Episodes of financial market volatility marked by significant problems of illiquidity and insolvency among financial market participants (incapacity of financial institutions to meet obligations) and or by official intervention to contain their consequences (e.g. Bordo *et al.*, 2001).

We distinguish several types of crisis:

- Banking crisis, characterized by financial distress resulting in the erosion of most or all of aggregate banking system capital.
- Currency crisis, characterized by a forced change in parity, abandonment of a pegged exchange rate and or international rescue operation.
- Twin crisis, characterized by the combined occurrence of elements of both a currency and a banking crisis.

The anatomy of international financial crisis is now fairly well understood. The process (see Figure 8.1) often starts in one segment of the economy and then spreads out to other parts. We describe hereafter a rather typical scenario of a crisis that has its origin in a real problem. However, some crises occur as for one reason or another the multiple equilibriums described in the previous section starts to be questioned. They may then be of the self-fulfilling type. The major features of such a crisis are described in Box 8.1.

The origin of a crisis is very often when some favourable event leads to the bidding up of asset prices. Price increases lead to further buying as more actors enter the market to take part in the bonanza. Paper profits induce speculators to engage in further operations, often financed with borrowed capital. This herd behaviour, based on expectations of other members of the herd, leads to deviation of asset prices from fundamentals. When an external event occurs that reveals that many assets are largely overvalued, some asset holders will start to sell or will be obliged to sell. Then the bubble bursts: lack of demand leads to a sharp decrease in asset prices (real estate, equity, etc.). The country that finds itself in trouble will

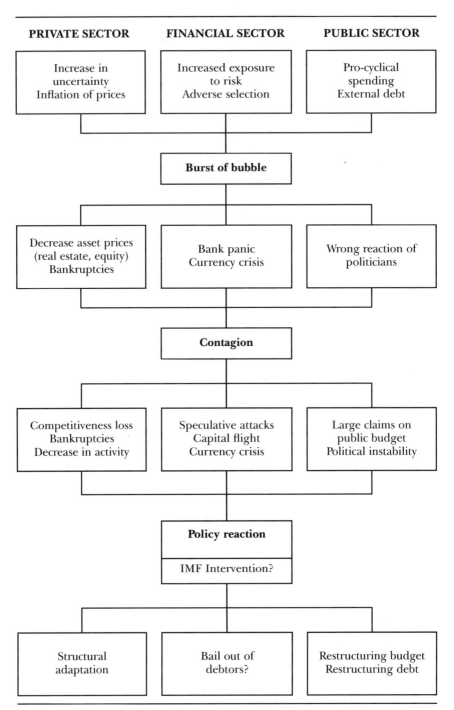

Figure 8.1 The anatomy of a financial crisis.

then often be subject to a bank and currency crisis. Speculation will set in; foreign and domestic depositors suddenly shift their funds into a foreign currency. This speculation will often oblige the country to devalue its currency.

The next stage is the spreading out. The collapse of one market is likely to have wide ramifications in other parts of the international economy. It may have a disastrous effect on those whose portfolios were financed with borrowed capital, including financial intermediaries. The incapacity of one organization to pay its debts often provokes the collapse of others that were its creditors, leading to waves of bankruptcies. If the public loses confidence in financial institutions that have become vulnerable because of important losses, they may be tempted to withdraw their deposits. They thus aggravate the situation because in this way organizations that are in principle sound will risk falling victim to the crisis.

Financial crises tend to spread rapidly from one country to another. The cause of this contagion is to be found in many of the factors that we cited as causes of instability in the previous section[1] (Hernadez and Valdes, 2001):

- *Trade*. Growing internationalization of goods markets. Countries that export the same goods as the countries that have devalued will face a loss of competitiveness; they too may be tempted to devalue to compensate.
- *Financial links*. Growing internationalization of capital markets, increased sophistication of the products and the high speed by which information travels and operations can be effectuated lead to intricate and extensive international interrelations. International fund managers facing losses may be obliged to divest to keep to preset rules (balance of the portfolio, risk exposure).
- *Neighbourhood*. Herd behaviour and market failures mean that similar countries can come under attack (see Box 8.1).

The third stage is the reaction of the public authorities. The lack of confidence in the possibilities of realizing business opportunities will lead to a slow down of economic growth; possibly even to a decline of the GDP. This negative effect on the economy is often aggravated as the crisis limits the capacity of many firms to issue bonds and raise money in share capital. Public authorities will intervene in order to restore confidence and stability and to cushion as much as possible the negative effects on the economy. Now the problem is that the capacity of governments to do so is very unequal. Weak countries will have to go through a very costly and problematic adaptation process. Their budget situation does not permit them to spend more, on the contrary the crisis will force them to cut public spending drastically, aggravating thereby the slow down of the economy. Most of the wealthier states tend to stay aloof and covered. The resilience of their systems is in general much higher, whereas the financial intermediaries located within their borders often benefit from international bail-outs.

The empirical studies into contagion tend to highlight specific factors of the three-stage model we described here. They tend to find strong neighbourhood effects, while trade links and similarity in pre-crisis growth also explain part of contagion. A favourable situation with respect to debt composition and exchange rate flexibility tends to limit contagion (De Gregorio and Valdes, 2001; Hernandez and Valdes, 2001).

The likelihood of a crisis to occur increases with the time that has elapsed since the last crisis. Many new players and new products come to the

---

Box 8.1 Crises: the role of psychology and contagion

The origin of a crisis may be rather trivial. It can start with the emergence of some underlying weakness. This may have all sorts of character: a balance of payment problem, some political unrest, etc. These are, as one knows very common problems and mostly their existence does not give rise to a real crisis. However, if for one reason or another a risk starts that is assumed to be potentially dangerous, such as a bankruptcy, a small reaction by one party may actually spark off a crisis.[2] Such events may provoke a chain reaction.

Contagion is due to a combination of psychological factors and system characteristics. A specific aspect of the latter point is information. As foreign lenders are often in a poor position to judge the quality of their assets in far away countries and the robustness of specific financial intermediaries, they tend to react on the basis of superficial similarities between countries. Financial institutions in countries for whom the fundamentals are good may thus come under attack because their situation with respect to exposure to shocks or institutional characteristics bears some resemblance to those in countries that have proven vulnerable. A problem in one segment of the system may induce depositors to withdraw their funds from banks that are sound. These banks may get into problems because they cannot cope with such sudden explosions of withdrawal. So the sound parts become infected as well. Bank cross-holding may comply others to re-interpret their total position and pull out as well.

Policy reactions based on the (mis-)interpretation of the crisis in terms of wrong fundamentals will imply a contraction of budget and credit. Markets will interpret this as if there is indeed something wrong and will adapt accordingly. An additional problem that may occur in these cases is that countries that are subject to such a crisis consider that they are unjustly under attack. As international help has mostly occurred only in fairly bad cases where the fundamentals were substantially wrong, such help leads to a stigma. In order to avoid such a stigma, countries have been tempted to postpone asking for international help.[3]

market, awareness of risks tends to decrease and major private and public players tend to be uncertain about the way the lessons learned in the past have to be applied to circumstances that are perceived as new.

8.2.6 Cost of crisis

The cost of financial crises can be very high. However, they are quite different for different players.

Developing countries, in general, pay a very high price. In the last three decades the cost of a currency crisis and of a banking crisis were on average some 6 per cent of GDP of the country concerned. The cost of twin crises was much higher; most of them occasioned a fall in the range between 10 and 20 per cent of GDP (e.g. Bordo *et al.*, 2001). However, in some cases much higher losses were incurred, going up to 40 per cent of GDP (BIS, 1997; IBRD, 2000: 36). In the Asian economies the crises did not only imply a loss of income and jobs for workers in the export sectors, but also a significant rise of the proportion of people living below the poverty line (Chu and Hill, 2001). Theoretically, the cost of such crises could have been much reduced had countries adopted flexible exchange rates (Osakwe and Schembri, 2002). However, the adoption of this regime has other problematic sides (see Annex 8.1) and is a reason why many countries have not had recourse to this option.

The cost of the crises to the international community are much more controversial. We can make a distinction here between the cost of the crisis itself and the cost of the remedies for getting out of the crisis. With respect to the former we see that there is some fall back in growth rates, but it is difficult to say in how far these are directly related to the crisis. With respect to the latter, recent evidence suggests (Jeanne and Zettelmeyer, 2001) that the cost to the global taxpayer of the major bail-outs of the past (where the IMF has given loans to countries in difficulty) has been very small, as almost all loans have been paid back over time.

This leads to the conclusion that the real cost has been fully borne by the countries that got deepest into difficulties, often emerging market countries but also poverty-ridden LDCs.

8.3 Major public goods

8.3.1 Definition and principles

It is evident from the previous section that the lack of financial stability is a public bad. It entails very high costs, which fall mainly on the poor countries. The world has a very large interest in the smooth functioning of the financial system, so a stable financial system is a global public good. It permits the grasping of the benefits of an efficient allocation of goods and capital on the world level.

The devising of a regime that is capable of maintaining stability (in other words, capable of preventing the occurrence of crises) and coping with financial crises (that happen notwithstanding these preventive measures) is thus of utmost importance (Wyplosz, 1999). But this is more easily said than done. First, our understanding of crises is very imperfect. Crises may have different origins as is exemplified by a number of recent crises in the financial world. For example, the currency crisis of Mexico in 1994, the real estate crisis of Thailand in 1997, the private sector debt crisis in Korea in 1997 and the stock market crisis of the new economy in 2000. However, the current data do not enable us to define the exact causes of a crisis and hence it is difficult to predict a crisis and to set up effective mechanisms of prevention.

Second, the issue of principles is largely unsettled.[4] In matters of finance, the liberal ideology has not acquired dominant position. Indeed, the case for the free movement of capital is not as strong as in matters of trade; protection can have beneficial effects. So the design principles for the regime for finance need to take into account both situations of freedom of movement and of control. In matters of exchange rate stabilization the case is not as clear either (see Annex 8.1 to this chapter). So, the financial regime has to take into account a variety of different views as to the best arrangements. This leads to the conclusion that one need to develop principles for both the prevention and the cure of the disease. Although the specialist finance literature is largely silent on the issue, we propose (see also Chapter 12) the following principles, based on a comparison with other regimes:

- *Prevention*. In similar circumstances (environmental regime) the principle of precaution has been developed. This principle may be applicable here as well. Although we do not know exactly why, when and how crises occur, we know that the chance they occur decreases in case certain conditions are met. These concern, in particular, harmonization and standard setting of prudential regulation of the financial sector. So the precautionary principle would lead to the adoption of such measures even if their exact need has not yet been established.
- *Cure*. For this part the principle of solidarity should be applicable. It means that an international organization should draw on means provided by all members in order to combat a financial crisis emerging in one of its members. This organization can ask the beneficiary of the support to create the conditions for a rapid return to normal. This is the principle of conditionality. This principle does not have an overriding value, however. First, it conflicts with the principle of state sovereignty. Second, its application (therapy) is quite difficult in view of the uncertainty as to the type of problem (diagnosis). We come back to this point in a later section.

8.3.2 *The regime: national responsibilities*

At the level of *governance* the adoption of the principles cited means that mechanisms have to be put in place at two levels, national and international. On the national level the primary objective is prevention, in practice creating conditions so as to minimize the risk that a crisis actually develops. To reach that objective three types of action are needed, which can be specified as follows:

- *Adequate institutions and policies.* The design of the national institutions and policies can be adapted so as to create the macro conditions for an optimal functioning of the economic process in general and of the financial sector in particular. These involve first the basics, such as the effective enforcement of property rights, the legal obligation for shareholders to commit themselves, and bankruptcy laws making sure that the burden of failure of individual firms will be borne in an equitable way by all those who have taken risks. Moreover, they involve the creation of macro-economic conditions that are conducive to growth and stability, which implies sound public finances, an adequate exchange rate regime, a tax system that brings as little distortion as possible and a sustainable current account. Finally, they involve adequate institutional requirements in such diverse areas as labour and equity markets.
- *Regulation, innovation and supervision.* The quality of the financial system depends critically on the quality of the major actors, that is on the banking and insurance sectors. The individual consumer of the services of these financial institutions cannot judge whether they are trustworthy. He is unable to evaluate whether a bank will be able to pay back deposits, or whether an insurance company will be able to pay in a few decades from now the pension that it has promised to the subscriber of a life insurance. So public authorities have to provide that trust. They do that in two ways. First, by limiting the access to the trade to firms that meet the basic criteria for sound finances. Second, by prudential control of the financial intermediaries; that means by constantly preventing financial firms from taking risks that may endanger their long-term viability. So, adequate rules for such prudential control will avoid the occurrence of failures in the system. However, such regulation also has a negative side in that it may hinder innovation. Innovation is needed for increasing the performance of the system. The increase in sophistication of the products increases the complexity and decreases the transparency of the system. So, in order to deal effectively with the risks of modern financial markets ever more sophisticated forms of surveillance are necessary. The problem is thus to strike the right balance between rigorously applying the results of proven good practices and prudently experimenting with new forms.

- *Market functioning.* The proper functioning of markets implies that the various actors have as much information available as possible. In many cases the information actors provide is difficult to interpret, as firms use different terms for the same notion and vice versa. So the setting of standards for accounting and the setting of minimum rules for reporting (with respect to content and frequency), all mean that actors can react adequately and timely to market signals. The proper functioning of markets implies the free flow of international capital. This is rather uncontroversial for long-term capital flows that serve to improve the structure of the economy (see evidence in Section 3.2.5). However, the case for free short-term capital flows is less compelling, as they tend to create high volatility and thus increase the risk of a financial crisis. This leads many countries to operate systems for monitoring and controlling capital movements in order to limit the occurrence of financial crises and to reinforce the capacity of the country to cope with an emerging crisis. However, the effectiveness of controls of capital flows is limited, notably when the fundamentals are seriously wrong. Moreover, they come at a cost in terms of a loss of macro-economic efficiency. Temporary controls of capital inflows to prevent the overheating of the economy can be effective and have a positive welfare effect. These welfare gains may, however, disappear and even turn negative when controls are maintained (Reinhart and Smith, 2002). Again, the problem is to strike the right balance between liberalization and control.
- *Intervention.* All the previous measures may not be enough to prevent a bank getting into serious problems. In order to avoid its collapse and the ensuing contagion, central banks (CB) usually assume an active role. When the problem is only one of illiquidity, the CB may act as a lender of last resort and provide the bank in difficulty with the necessary finances to see to its obligations. When the problem is one of insolvency, the CB will try to put a safety net into place, followed by an orderly take over by another player from the private sector. In this way, moral hazard problems are avoided (see Section 8.4.1) and the consequences of the taking of undue risks will be with the shareowners of the bank.

We may conclude that it is notably sound fundamentals and strong institutions at the national level that limit the chances of a crisis occurring. The resilience of the system has been shown in such cases as the euro–dollar misalignment of the past decades and the 'new economy' hype of the turn of the century. Neither one has led to a financial crisis. However, the dangers of failure even in developed economies still exist. An example of a currency crisis is the pound sterling being forced by financial markets to leave the EMS at very high cost to the UK. An example of a banking crisis is the failure of the Credit Lyonnais to cope with the liabilities entailed by its (reckless) international expansion. In the latter case, a long-winded and extremely costly rescue operation by the French government has been necessary to re-establish confidence and get the situation back to normal.

8.3.3 The regime: international responsibilities

On the international level there is a double objective. First, to create the conditions that prevent a crisis from occurring. Second, if a crisis has occurred, to manage it nevertheless in such a way that it does as little harm as possible. We can specify the consequences of this for the design of an international regime as follows:

- *Adequate surveillance.* Countries are autonomous in their policies. However, as we have seen, if these policies are not adequate the probability of a crisis occurring increases. So there is a need for the setting of international norms and standards. In the past, much work has gone into the elaboration of such standards, applicable both to developed and developing countries (Schneider, 2002).[5] Next, there is a need for international monitoring of the way individual countries perform. If information on what goes on shows cases that do not comply with the norms, it should of course be followed by action. However, the possibilities of coercion are limited, so the system should at least provide the country concerned with the best practices available. The problem is, of course, that the norms are stricter the weaker the situation and the higher the risks. On the other hand, the capacity of the country to deal with the problems will be weaker the more risky the situation. So adequate measures for technical and financial help in the early stages in which such national problems develop are in order.
- *Adequate management.* Once a crisis has occurred it needs to be managed effectively in order to limit its negative consequences. There are various stages to this:

  1 *Diagnosis.* For adequate policy reaction one needs to know where the problem arises and how it develops (Dornbusch *et al.*, 2000). The adequate establishment of these facts is much more difficult than many think.[6] First, there is often very large uncertainty about the fundamentals. Moreover, instability is not always due to bad macro policies; actually there is an unlimited variation of self-fulfilling elements (see Box 8.1). Finally, notwithstanding our increased knowledge of the anatomy of a crisis (see Figure 8.1), it is generaly unclear whether a problem will develop into a crisis situation or not.

  2 *Immediate response.* In view of the wide variety of developments and of the considerable uncertainties involved, those responsible for managing the crisis will have to make sure that they have room for

flexibility as to the way in which they handle it and as to the means they wish to adopt. However, there are a few lessons to be learnt from earlier crises that seem to have general applicability. First, the country in question should give up the fixed exchange rate, so as to limit the cost of defence against speculation. Second, the international community should make large-scale intervention possible at an early stage, so as to prevent the too little, too late problem. This implies the availability of very considerable funds to help countries to get back on track. Third, there should be a credible programme to take away the source of crisis. Fourth, a consistent programme of restoring equilibrium should be provided, specifying the objectives and means.

3 *Containment of the problem.* The first task is to contain contagion by providing as much information as possible about the character of the crisis and the way it is going to be handled. Here, a concerted action of the international and national authorities is needed. A big issue here is the containment of moral hazard as a certain number of the concerted policy measures risk favouring economic actors that by irresponsible behaviour were at the origin of the crisis.

8.4 The organizations involved in the provision of the public good

8.4.1 Major players

In the previous sections we found that a number of actors are critical in the understanding of financial crises. Paramount among them are financial intermediaries (mostly banks and insurance companies and their specialized branches). So there is a need to clarify the rationale and the role of such intermediaries (Crockett, 1996). Financial intermediaries are institutions that help to solve a problem of market imperfection. This can be explained in the following way. Asymmetric information in financial markets gives rise to the following two problems:

- Adverse selection occurs because borrowers tend to have better information on the risk-return profile of investment projects than have savers. If the market price for loans were uniform, investors with the greatest risk will chose to borrow, while investors with a smaller risk, finding the market rate too high, will opt for self-financing. This adverse selection process tends to reinforce itself. Indeed, the presentation of a disproportioned number of bad projects for financing on the market, coupled with the self-financing of good projects, would push up the price of loans, inducing more good investors to opt for self-financing.
- Moral hazard occurs because once a contract has been concluded, the borrower has an interest to change his behaviour in such a way that it

adversely affects the interest of the lender. He will be tempted to accept a situation where risks are larger than initially foreseen.

In order to avoid these imperfections of the market, financial intermediaries have been created. They attract savings and pay them an average price. They use this pool of savings in their borrowing operations. They limit adverse selection by the evaluation of risks and by price discrimination between different types of borrowers. They limit moral hazard problems with their clients by monitoring their performance and behaviour over time. Financial intermediaries have used their position to broaden their services. One of them is adapting the products to the time preferences of their depositors and creditors, so as to increase liquidity in the market. As long as lenders and borrowers maintain their confidence in the capacity of the bank to meet its contractual obligations, it is unlikely that any problem will occur. However, as soon as doubts arise, a bank run may follow. The mechanisms are given in Box 8.2.

Box 8.2 **The bank run**

Banks are essential intermediaries to a good functioning capital market. They match supply and demand for capital and adjust where necessary the time horizon of assets and liabilities. This makes banks vulnerable. On the one hand, their liquid liabilities are repayable on demand at par. On the other hand, their illiquid assets can only be realized at short notice by accepting a discount on book value. In general this is not a problem. Indeed, a commercial banks' portfolio is stable when withdrawals by depositors take place randomly over time and assets are held to term.

However, if something happens that accelerates the rate of withdrawals, it becomes rational for all depositors to withdraw their deposits. This is because they all know that if withdrawals continue, the bank will be forced to sell illiquid assets, incurring losses and eroding its capital. Bank depositors, concerned about a possible run on their bank would gain collectively by agreeing to refrain from precipitate withdrawals. Since depositors are too numerous to be able to effectively collude, however, their individual interest lies in withdrawing their deposits first, while the bank is still able to pay.

The solution to this is massive public support which restores confidence. However, this support is only warranted in case the bank is, in principle, sound. Hence there is a need for a continuous surveillance of the solidity of commercial banks.

Source: Adapted from Crockett, 1996.

The major public players are central banks. In many countries they have been given the responsibility to regulate and supervise the banking system. In some countries separate regulatory bodies exist. In most countries the CB is given the task to intervene. There is considerable variety in the division of responsibilities over the central bank, government and other institutions (Brealy *et al.*, 2001). However, in almost all countries CBs assume the task of prudential banking supervision. This is true for both industrialized and developing countries. The smaller and less developed the country, the more extensive is the range of responsibilities of the central bank.

8.4.2 International organizations

In matters of the stability of the financial system a series of institutions play their role. Among the intergovernmental organizations, the IMF takes pride of place. (We will discuss the IMF in more detail in the following sections.) Organizations such as the G7/8 (Dobson *et al.*, 2001), the Bank for International Settlements (BIS, 1997) and the OECD also consider world financial stability as a matter of their concern. Since the major crises of the 1980s, two new forums have been created. The first is the Financial Stability Forum, created by the G7, which regroups the major economic powers. It has gone somewhat in the direction of regionalization by setting up regional working parties. However, as developing countries are completely absent from its top structure another group has been set up. The G20 (see Chapter 6) is an informal gathering at the highest level of national government representatives discussing proposals for change in the financial architecture.

None of these institutions assumes operational responsibility for coping with the problems of financial markets. The only one to do that is the IMF. There is not much formal coordination (let alone consensus building) between the various international organizations involved. Some coordination is done in practice (albeit in a fairly dispersed way) by the national government officials that attend the meetings of several of these institutions. On the regional level, only very few organizations have a strong position. A case in point is the EU, which has done away internally with currency crises by adopting a single currency. Initiatives in other regions are fairly timid (see Box 8.3).

Professional associations complement the work of the intergovernmental organizations. They work on the adoption of standards and good practices. The most relevant ones are the Basle committee on Banking Supervision, the International Organization of Securities Commission for stock trading and the International Accounting Standards Committee for accounting practices. The IMF refers to the standards adopted by these organizations.

On the regional level, there are few organizations that deal with the stability problem. We can cite the European Union with its independent European Central Bank almost as an exception to the rule. For each

---

Box 8.3 Is regionalism a solution? The case of Asia

Regional initiatives in Asia are not self-evident. East Asian countries have a history of enmity, competition and uneven distribution of power. Most countries in the region see their integration in the world economy as their first priority. So there was not really an impelling need to engage in regional arrangements. ASEAN has been created for trade integration, but the organization is far from having good geographical coverage, its institutional set up is rather weak and its achievements fall short of expectations.

Notwithstanding these inhibiting factors, East Asians have had two reasons for searching for a regional mechanism in matters of financial cooperation. The first is the major financial breakdown following the 1997 crisis that has seriously affected a number of countries in the region. The second is the slow progress on the global level in matters of providing an effective mechanism for preventing crises to occur and spreading out. The Chiang Mai Initiative regroups ten members of ASEAN and China, Japan and Korea. It involves a regional credit support mechanism for countries experiencing balance of payments problems. The advantage of such a scheme is that it considerably reduces the need for individual countries to keep large amounts of currency reserves. Pooling of reserves and making them available on certain conditions permits the creation of effective lines of defence against emerging problems. Its objective is to prevent an extreme crisis or systemic failure in a country and subsequent regional contagion. It creates time to work out other more structural solutions in cooperation with the IMF.

Source: Adapted from Park and Wang, 2000, Park, 2002.

---

continent there is a regional development banks, such as the Inter-American Development Bank. However, these banks have similar functions as the World Bank and do not assume functions on the regional level comparable to the ones of IMF on the global level (Bakker, 1996).

8.4.3 The objectives of the IMF

The objectives of the IMF are wide ranging. It aspires to:

- promote international monetary cooperation and exchange rate stability;
- assist in the establishment of multilateral system of payments;
- make its general resources temporarily available to those of its members experiencing balance of payments difficulties (under adequate safeguards);

- shorten the duration and lessen the degree of disequilibrium in the international balances of payments of its members.

In short, the IMF is paramount among the institutions responsible for the stability of the global macro-economic system.

Members have committed themselves to:

- inform each other about the exchange rate and the arrangements determining it;
- refrain from restricting the convertibility of their currency; and
- pursue economic, fiscal and monetary policies that will, in an orderly way, contribute to national and global wealth creation.

The IMF has no means of coercing member states to comply with their commitments other than the refusal to give more financial assistance. However, as alternatives are scarce, even the threat to use this instrument is very effective.

8.5 Governance

8.5.1 Information, surveillance and consultations

The first objective is to render the processes on international capital markets more transparent. This should help to avoid major market failures. The IMF does so by using the instrument of publishing regular and incidental reports on many aspects of the international capital flows, such as geographic patterns, maturity, etc.[7]

The second objective is the improvement of the consistency of national institutions and policies. The main instrument on this score is *surveillance* (IMF, 2001a). Financial stability is the result of a series of good policies. So the IMF evaluates the economic performance on a series of indicators for the entire membership. Traditionally, these involve aspects such as exchange rate policies, financial markets and external reserves. IMF surveillance has been extended in the past to include an increasing number of subjects. One very important element is the surveillance of banking soundness through financial sector assessment programmes. Other elements are good governance and the observance of international standards and codes of good practices. The IMF publishes reports on the observance of standards and codes. The assessment of the risks involved in member states (macro) policies is done more candidly. The IMF concentrates attention on countries where economic disturbances are likely to spill over to the international community. This bolstering of the surveillance task has been decided in the wake of a number of major crises that have shown the variety of origins and channels of contagion. The IMF has made special precautionary arrangements, including enhanced surveillance of countries that are in need of support for, and international confidence in, their policies.

The second instrument to improve consistency of national policies is *consultations* of IMF staff with representatives of the governments of each member country. These follow, in general, a standard procedure distinguishing several stages. In a first stage the staff members of IMF collect statistical data on a range of indicators such as trade, money in circulation, budget deficit, etc. Next, there are discussions with high-ranking government officials to establish the effectiveness of the policies of the previous year and the perspectives for the next year. Finally, a summary report on the country's performance is written and submitted to the IMF executive board and the government of the country in question. These reports often contain specific suggestions for the strengthening of weak points in the member state's policy.

8.5.2 Financial assistance

The third objective is to provide *sufficient official liquidity* to countries in crisis. The main instrument that the IMF uses are loans to member countries with payments problems. The origin of these funds is the quota each member has paid to the fund on its admission. A country with such payment difficulties can immediately draw the 25 per cent of its quota that it paid in gold or a convertible currency. If this is insufficient for its needs, a member may request more. It can borrow up to three times what it paid in as a quota subscription. However, when a country is faced with a sudden crisis, it may draw on the supplementary reserve facility, which provides short-term finance at somewhat higher rates.

The fourth objective is to come to *orderly debt work-outs* for countries that have got into severe long-term problems. The pursuit of this objective is important because it will enable countries to make a new start and to avoid a situation where permanently fragile countries become a threat to the system. The main instrument of the IMF has up till now been the co-ordination of groups of creditors; however, this has not been very effective.

Finally, the fifth objective is to provide sufficient capital to LDCs. Private capital flows are highly concentrated on a limited number of countries. The poorest countries are completely marginalized. So, official development assistance is of utmost importance for such countries. In this matter, the World Bank is the principal actor. However, over the past decades the functions of the IMF in providing loans have become closer to those of the World Bank. The latter started off by making long-term loans for investment projects, but moved into structural adjustment (that is non-project) loans. The former initially focussed on macro-economic adjustment but is increasingly involved in micro and policy adjustment by stressing conditionality.

8.5.3 A major debate: how far should the IMF go in the conditionality of its interventions?

Before the IMF releases its loan it may request the member country take a number of policy measures and sometimes even to embark upon in-depth reforms when the IMF considers that these measures are necessary to solve the fundamental problems that led to the occurrence of the financial problem. The reason for applying this principle is that the IMF wants to make sure that the member country in question will be able to pay back the money in a reasonable time period of three to five years.

The borrowing country that has run into difficulty will have to make sure that the conditions will be created for sound finances. These often depend on a series of reforms that will eradicate the source of the payments problem and prepare the ground for high quality economic growth. Along with its request for a loan, the potential borrower presents a plan for reform to the IMF. Such a plan often includes specific measures to reduce the budget deficit, tighten monetary policy, and deal with certain structural weaknesses. The latter can apply to measures of privatization of inefficient public enterprises, the breakdown of monopolies, etc. There is much controversy with respect to conditionality (see, for example, Killick, 1995; Goldstein, 2000). This is the more so because in recent years the conditions that the IMF has attached to loans have become more detailed and cover ever more areas of government activity.

The *proponents* of more conditionality argue that the IMF needs to go along this path of increased detail in order to:

- Make sure that the adjustment programmes of the member countries do not stop half way. The IMF considers that its long experience has shown that the basic condition for sustained growth is a consistent set of good policies and adequate institutions. It considers that countries are often not capable of implementing the necessary adaptations without IMF conditions due to opposition of the ruling elites.
- Prevent its bail-outs being used to facilitate bad economic policies and thus creating moral hazard problems at the expense of the tax payer (Jeanne and Zettelmeyer, 2001).

The *opponents* of conditionality (very often member countries that have to borrow from the IMF, in particular LDCs) complain about these conditions. Their arguments are that the IMF conditions:

- Put an unnecessary strain on their operations. In some cases the conditions of the IMF are indeed so severe that they have caused very serious social unrest, leading to the disruption of economic activity and of national institutions essential for growth (Ghai, 1991). In view of such restrictive conditions, countries may actually refrain from calling in IMF aid altogether.
- Interfere in an unjustified way with the sovereignty of the borrowing country. LDCs complain about the fact that the IMF demands very thorough structural reforms that it would never dare to ask from major developed countries, thus infringing on the principle of equal treatment.

Emerging economies reject the IMF recipes, as they want to develop their own institutional systems; such alternatives have proved to be conducive to growth (e.g. Crotty and Lee, 2002). Some go further in the sense that they claim that the IMF is based on a model of Western values and that the imposing of conditions is actually a form of ideological imperialism (see Chapter 5).

In recent times, voices have come from independent economists who challenge the involvement of the IMF on the basis of arguments that have to do with systemic features. They consider that the IMF should be careful in getting involved in deep structural reforms because of its:

- *Poor competence*. The IMF strays from its core competence of macro-economic and exchange rate policies into a host of other areas for which it is ill-equipped. This leads to poor crisis management and a loss of credibility of the IMF in this area that spills over into its core competence areas.
- *Poor operationality*. The criteria for getting the macro-economy right are fairly simple; on the contrary, criteria to measure the progress of structural reform are many (say over fifty) and performance is sometimes difficult to assess (e.g. on a total of 50, is a score of 25 good, 15 bad and 10 poor, a satisfactory performance?).

This controversy can best be arbitrated by evaluating the effects of the IMF measures in practice. In other words, can one establish whether the stepping up of conditionality has indeed been conducive to growth or not? Some empirical studies find that countries with higher compliance rates to IMF criteria have (after initial adaptation) also realized higher growth rates (e.g. Goldstein, 2000). This would thus justify the higher IMF involvement. Others are fairly critical with respect to effectiveness (e.g. Evrensel, 2002). In the absence of strong evidence, the IMF would be well advised to adopt a fairly strict interpretation of its mandate. It may then venture into other policy areas only when these have a significant macro-economic impact. Notably the highly sensitive areas of labour market and social policy are better left to others.

8.6 Evaluation of the past and options for the future

8.6.1 Major achievements

The macro-economic management is the specialization of the IMF. It has contributed to the notion that governments need to maintain a stable economic environment as this is conducive to growth. It has helped to create the conditions for saving and investment and it has helped to convey the right signals in terms of prices and policy measures. The support that the IMF has given to countries confronted with a sudden imbalance (shock) has helped these countries through difficult periods. Otherwise considerable problems would have cropped up, due to the macro-economic consequences of the exchange rate instability that such shocks in general entail. Although there is criticism as to the way this has been done in practice, the general record seems to be positive on this score (Killick, 1995). In the same way, one can evaluate the other aspects of the IMF tool box, such as the contribution to the setting of standards, etc. Unfortunately the latter are not always easy to implement by developing countries.

8.6.2 Inadequacies and challenges

In the past the IMF has been severely criticized both for its errors in setting the diagnosis and prescribing the therapy. There is abundant case material in the literature relating to the way in which the IMF has handled, for instance, the Asian crisis or recently the Argentina crisis. Very authoritative and insider criticism has recently been presented by Nobel Prize winner J.E. Stiglitz (2002). We give here the essence of his view:

* *Ideology and principles.* The actions of all international economic organizations are shaped by ideology (see Section 4.2: second layer influences third layer). The IMF has been created to help overcome the sort of problems that the crisis of the 1930s created. So, in its initial conception, the IMF was based on the recognition that markets did not work well. Recently, the dominant ideas in the Western and, notably, in the Anglo-Saxon world have shifted to 'market fundamentalism'. The IMF has aligned itself to this view in the so-called Washington consensus (US Treasury, IMF and IBRD). In this view, government involvement in the economy does not provide a solution to a problem of externalities or of market failure. On the contrary, government involvement is seen as causing the problem in permitting rent seeking, corruption and inefficiencies. More markets are seen as the solution to this problem.[8]
* *Instruments.* Founded on the belief of the efficiency of markets and the check on government, the IMF now provides funds only when countries engage in policies that are in conformity to this view. One of them is 'small government' politics involving small budgets (often meaning cutting expenditure and raising taxes) and privatization. The other is openness to the world, involving liberalization of exchange (often including capital markets). These types of policies may lead to adequate solutions for economic problems of highly developed Western nations with mature economies and sophisticated institutional systems. However, they tend to fail to produce good solutions in the case of many LDCs and transition countries, where economies are small and vulnerable and institutions are only effective if they relate to the

cultural environment of the country. The IMF has often pushed too quickly (and in hindsight often prematurely) capital market liberalization. It has put countries into crisis, forcing them to raise interest rates that lead to a contraction of the economy and to problems for indigenous business and hence to an increase in poverty.[9]

* *Interests*. The concerns of the Fund tend to be dominated by the treasury ministers of western countries and the major actors on the international capital markets. Part of the lending of the IMF seems to have been given more to bail out western capital providers instead of to help LDC economic activity to return to higher levels.

Other authors (e.g. Eichengreen, 2002) also point to this last anomaly. On the one hand, the Fund's operations allow international investors to escape without significant losses, which in turn encourages them to lend without regard to risk. On the other hand, the developing countries have ultimately to pay back, so the residents of the country that finds itself in crisis have to pay the bill. So, the operations of the IMF work out in an inequitable way and are at odds with the interests of the developing countries.

8.6.3 Proposals for improvement

There are a few sweeping proposals for a completely new set of organizations. These involve the set up of a world central bank or a world monetary authority. In view of the results of the theoretical discussion (in Chapter 5), one can see that such proposals have very little chance of being realized.

So, most authors writing about adaptation of the present global structures[10] part from the assumption that it is better to think about gradual reforms that have a chance of being implemented in the medium term. In practice that means that these suggestions apply to the national and the international aspects of the regime (Sections 8.3.2 and 8.3.3) and to the five categories of instruments of the IMF (Sections 8.5.1 and 8.5.2). The major suggestions for improvements are:

* Reduction of the *volatility of capital flows*. Proposals range from the prudent sequencing and segmentation[11] of capital liberalization for countries that still have controls, via the (temporary) reintroduction of controls in emergency situations (e.g. Griffith Jones *et al.*, 2001b), to the limitation of short-term borrowing in foreign currencies. Particularly hotly debated in this respect is the introduction of a tax on foreign capital movements (see Box 8.4).
* Improvement of the *supervision and regulation of capital flows*. This applies to the improvement of standards and the compliance with them. Practice shows that the global financial markets are very interested for efficiency reasons in common and clear standards and rules and the

Box 8.4 **Instruments for reducing volatility: the merits of the Tobin Tax**[12]

Introducing a tax on international capital movements would make such transactions more costly and hence would limit the number of transactions. In targeting more purely financial transactions, in particular, such a tax would limit speculative short-term movements that are the main contributors to the instability of the system. The tax has been named after one of its most well-known proponents Professor Tobin. The Tobin Tax would have several positive effects. It would:

- Raise tax revenue. This may amount to rather significant sums, of course dependent on the tax base, the rate and the negative effect on the number of transactions.
- Shift part of the tax burden from the immobile factor, labour, to the mobile factor, capital. This should alleviate unemployment problems (see Section 3.3).
- Stabilize exchange rates and make them better reflect the fundamentals of the economy (see also Annex 8.1).
- Enhance the efficiency of national macro-economic policy (see Section 3.4).

The opponents have actually two sets of arguments: the first set of arguments considers that it is undesirable for the following reasons:

- *Economic*. The efficiency of markets, which is a very important asset for economic growth, would be considerably decreased. Many question the validity of this argument. They say that markets have time and again shown that they are not efficient, while the negative aspects of volatility outweigh anyway the positive effects of efficient markets.
- *Logical*. Opponents claim that the real cause of the turbulence is not financial flows but macro-economic disequilibria. It is thus the latter that has to be addressed, not the former.
- *Political/ideological*. There are powerful groups in the major nations that consider any attempt to curtail the free financial market as an attack on the fundamentals of the Western economic system.

The second set of arguments plead that it is unfeasible. Difficulties would apply to:

- *Transactions*. All financial transactions in a foreign currency would be relevant. However, markets have grown to such sophistication that it always seems possible to define products in such a way as to avoid the tax.

- *Universality*. In order to be effective, the tax should be levied by all jurisdictions. This may be near impossible for countries that depend for their revenue on tax havens. Coercion by the international community, such as the exclusion of such countries from IMF membership or transactions in major financial centres, are very difficult to implement.
- *Revenue*. The tax has to be levied by national authorities. Those countries who raise much income may not be the most entitled to receive it. So, who should be the beneficiary of the tax? Proposals have been made to hand it over to the IMF so it can be used in pursuing its policy. However, the many distributional issues involved are politically very thorny.

The theoretical considerations that we discussed in Chapter 5 point to a low chance that under such conditions a regime change can be realized. To give but two illustrations, there is no consensus about the causes, neither is there a strong benefit with a small group that would justify collective action. So it is no surprise that the proposals have not even entered the stage of negotiations.

major private actors collaborate actively in their elaboration (Kuebler, 2002). Specific proposals concern, for instance, the introduction of bankruptcy codes so as to speed up restructuring. Institutional solutions such as a world financial regulatory authority seem to be far shots.
- Creation of an *international lender of last resort*. The advantage of a fully-fledged set-up would be that the support to countries in difficulties would overcome national recovery problems and prevent international contagion. However, it would create a moral hazard problem in the sense that its mere existence may lead to irresponsible behaviour of actors on the financial markets.
- Introduction of a *sovereign debt restructuring mechanism*. Such proposals intend to give countries in difficulties (risking insolvency) some breathing space to work out solutions with their creditors along the same lines as a private company would be able to do under national law (Raffer and Springer, 1996). Recently, the IMF has picked up the idea again (IMF website) and translated it into a proposal to give the IMF the authority to declare a standstill on payments, to organize restructuring negotiations and in cases where a qualified majority of creditors accepted the deal, it would also bind minority creditors. There is much opposition to this proposal, in particular because it would place the IMF in the double role of creditor and arbitrator. Some (Eichengreen, 2002) argue that a better option in this respect would be to include in loan agreements clauses for collective action and collective representation.

- *Provision of sufficient capital to LDCs.* Suggestions comprise mostly the improvement of the competitive position of the LDCs in general and the restructuring (and reduction) of the debt for the weakest countries in particular. Instrumental for reaching this objective may be the re-equilibration of the voting in the IMF so that they reflect more the legitimate interests of the developing countries. In practice it involves the limitation of the domination of the strong countries.

A last set of proposals explores the strengthening of the regional organizations. It is inspired by the positive track record of the European Union with the stabilization of exchange rates and the improvement of the surveillance of the financial sector. Initiatives for such financial arrangements have been taken in Asia and Latin America (Teunissen, 2002). Up till now these have failed to develop to the extent that they have a considerable impact on financial markets. However, increased trade integration and convergence of policies among participants may in future create the conditions for more elaborate and effective mechanisms.

8.7 Summary and conclusions

- Under influence of liberalization, the size and complexity of global capital flows has increased very considerably. This in turn has led to financial instability and recurrent financial crises.
- The cost of these crises are very high, in particular for the most vulnerable developing countries. So, prevention of crises is very important and financial stability is a global public good.
- The responsibility for the provision of this public good has been entrusted to the IMF. Each member country contributes part of the capital of the IMF in order to permit its functioning. Voting rights are associated with these shares. The Western countries dominate the IMF as they have the largest shares of the total.
- The IMF tries to prevent crises by creating the right conditions. Moreover, it tries to avoid the negative effects of crises by giving financial assistance to countries in difficulties. It attaches conditions to such aid; the inroads this makes on national sovereignty is a source of much controversy.
- The world financial system is confronted with two major challenges. First, adapting the governance rules so as to render them more apt to contribute to the capacity of LDCs to catch up and, second, to improve the macro-economic management of the world economy.

Annex 8.1 Exchange rate instability

A.1.1 The problem: exchange rate volatility

Countries pursue a number of policies to enhance their wealth. Paramount among these are:

1   Free capital movement, in order to improve the good allocation of resources;
2   Fixed exchange rates, in order to lower transaction cost for business and create long-term confidence, which stimulates investment and thus growth;
3   Independent monetary and fiscal policies in order to orient resources to the specific preferences of the country.

Now the problem is that these three elements are inconsistent. This can be easily shown.

- A country that wants to combine elements 1 and 2 must give up regime 3. If it sets its domestic interest rate to be lower than the interest rate of the country with which it has a fixed exchange rate, capital will start to flow out. If it sets a higher rate (for instance, in order to avoid the overheating of the economy), capital will start to flow in, leading to even further liquidity and the risk of inflation.
- A country that wants to opt for combining 1 and 3 must give up 2. An independent policy will lead to an interest rate differential that will entail very large capital flows. No country has the resources to go against the tide and effectively defend a fixed exchange rate that comes under serious attack.
- A country that wants to opt for 2 and 3 has to give up 1. Indeed, the differences in economic policy will lead to international interest differentials that can only be maintained when capital is constrained.

The choice that has been made almost world-wide now is to go for the advantages of the better allocation that capital movements bring. Moreover, as capital controls are difficult to make effective, most governments now have no other option. On the world level, there is no hope for coordinated, let alone unified, monetary and fiscal policies, so the only choice open has been to abandon the fixed exchange rates.

The enormous amounts traded now on world financial markets means that the exchange rates are subject to very strong pressures and consequently reveal very high variability. Unfortunately, international money markets do not always seem to be right. There are many imperfections that lead to misalignments. Some of them are based on imperfect foresight. But often they are straightforwardly speculative. The market sentiments that drive many exchange rate movements often seem unrelated to (or based on misperceptions of) the fundamentals.

A.1.2 Public good

A large volatility of exchange rates is a cause for concern, because it

- negatively affects macro-economic stability;
- distorts the allocation of real and financial resources;
- distorts fair competition, and hence;
- incites the emergence of trade conflicts and protectionism.

The markets can cope with some of the uncertainty (hedging) but many risks remain uncovered. These are a problem for all countries, but in particular for developing countries. So the stabilization of the exchange rates is a public good.

A.1.3 The organizations

In matters of exchange rate stabilization, the IMF now only plays a very modest role. The finance ministers (and sometimes the heads of state) of the G8, supported by central bank governors, play the role of a coordinating body in this matter. The implementation as to coordinated macropolicy-making has been put in the hands of the national governments, while the coordinated intervention in financial markets and the accompanying monetary policy has been entrusted to the central banks.

The advent of the euro has brought changes to this system. First, it has simplified the workings of the global system as it has effectively reduced many of the problems. Moreover, the multitier government, multi-institutional euro system has now been developed to such an extent that preliminary coordination of the members and post decision harmonized implementation of global measures can be made more efficiently than before.

A.1.4 Governance

The instruments available on the world level to reach stabilization of exchange rates are very weak and are of limited effectiveness. They concern:

- *Diagnosis.* What are the basic underlying trends? What is, in that light, an adequate exchange rate level? Can this be communicated to the market? Hence declarations are an important signal to the market.
- *Intervention.* How can one influence the markets so that they do not misalign? Here, early warnings by the authorities seem to have only limited effect. So a real intervention in markets is the only option. However, given the limitations of the institutional set-up and the uncertainty about the distribution of the cost and benefits, intervention is limited to times of a real or near real crisis.

How can the exchange rate be stabilized? There have been several proposals for exchange rate arrangements on the world level. One proposal that has received much attention is about target zones. Target zones are variation bands around a pivot exchange rate. The introduction of the system requires from the major actors that they agree on two things: first, on the ratio and bandwidth of the currencies and, second, on mechanisms to keep the rates within those margins. The EU has experimented extensively with such a system in the set-up of the EMS. It has experienced that the present size of the movements of capital make it very difficult to mobilize sufficient resources to keep currencies aligned.

A.1.5 Evaluation

The present regime has a number of weaknesses that imply as many constraints to the reaching of the targets in terms of the public good of exchange rate stability. As a matter of fact, the present system can at best be seen as crisis management. Indeed, only if certain very negative effects occur will authorities intervene. For the rest, the global system does not provide an adequate response to the quest for the public good that is stability of exchange rates.

9 Environment

9.1 Introduction

The world is confronted with a number of very serious environmental problems. Some of them have been with us for a long time (soil pollution), others have only recently cropped up (climate change). Coping with them is a matter of great complexity. The objective of this chapter is to show in what way global regimes have been developed to deal with a number of them. We have selected our examples on the basis of three criteria: (1) significance from a global point of view; (2) representative of the whole set of global environmental problems; and (3) illustrative of the dynamics of organizing effective global regimes.

We follow the set-up of the previous chapters, that is, definition of the problem, explication of the public good, description of the major organizations involved and instruments used. We will conclude the chapter with an evaluation that will show that, for the time being, we have only very tentative, limited and fragmented responses to the problems we are facing.

9.2 The problem

9.2.1 Categories of environmental problems

Economic activity implies the use of resources for production and consumption. Each of the links in this chain has a number of environmental consequences. Some of the most significant ones are:

- *Access to resource sites.* The organization of access to such resources is important for creating the conditions for a sustainable exploitation of the commons. Some resources are not yet appropriated, for example, the moon. For others the access is provisionally barred (seabed and South Pole).
- *Exploitation (extraction or production).* Here, several problems arise. One of them concerns the use of renewable resources, such as forest and fisheries. Unsustainable exploitation leads to depletion of the resource

and to several other problems such as loss of biodiversity, loss of capacity for regeneration (tropical forest), etc.

- *Processing*. The production of many goods implies the use of energy resources both for the transformation of raw material into finished goods and for the transport of these goods to the market. Most energy is still provided by fossil fuels. Burning these fuels produces gases that tend to fuse and lead to global warming.
- *Consumption*. Some consumption also involves energy use and the effect thereof adds to the effect of processing. However, most consumption results after some time in the disposal of the used good as waste. To this problem adds the disposal of waste that occurs at different stages of production. Together, this comes about as pollution both of the air, the water and the soil.

Many of the effects just described can be seen in economic terms as negative externalities (Siebert, 1998). It means that the cost they incur are not borne by the producer or the consumer but by a third party, often society at large. Such externalities constitute a failure of the allocation mechanism. Take the case of coal burning. The waste of coal burning is disposed of in the air that others need for breathing. Because the person responsible for burning the coal does not account for the cost of keeping the air clean there will be an overuse of the atmosphere as the waste bin of the energy users, while clean air for the whole population will be in short supply.

9.2.2 Major examples of global problems

A number of environmental problems have a fairly local character, such as waste disposal. These problems can be solved on a local or national level, as most of the time the externalities do not spread beyond national borders. Some other environmental problems, however, tend to transgress national borders, such as the pollution of river basins or the effects of acid rains. Many of these problems can be dealt with on a regional (supranational) level by cooperation between neighbouring countries. Finally, there are problems that span the whole globe. Global environmental problems come in two categories:

- Depletion of global resources, such as the loss of biodiversity (due to the extinction of species) or the depletion of water reserves.
- Pollution of the atmosphere, leading to ozone layer depletion and global warming. These problems have a global character for purely technical reasons: gases spread all over the globe and fuse in the atmosphere, so the whole world feels the negative consequences.

We will limit ourselves in this chapter to the second category.[1]

9.2.3 Stratospheric ozone depletion

Many processes lead to emissions of chlorofluorocarbons (CFCs), substances that tend to go into the outer atmosphere and lead to the depletion of the ozone layer. For a long time there was much uncertainty about the rate at which such depletion actually proceeded. At the end of the 1980s, however, the scientific evidence became very clear cut.

There are several problems associated with the depletion of the ozone layer. Most of them have to do with:

*   *Health.* They lead to an increase in the number of skin cancers and cataracts.
*   *Productivity.* They reduce production in agriculture and fishery.

So action is needed to avoid the emissions of CFCs or to repair the negative consequences of ozone layer depletion. For a long time it was difficult to measure the cost and benefit in terms of environmental damage and abatement. So little or no action was taken. At the end of the 1980s estimates have been made for the US that showed that the benefit–cost ratio of a set of measures was rather advantageous. On the basis of this information the US could even envisage implementing measures as an unilateral action. Other developed countries assumed similar positive relations. Action on the limitation of CFCs has been stimulated because, in the course of time, technological innovations (partly sparked off by environmental concerns) resulted in substitutes that were very cost-effective.

9.2.4 Climate change: global warming

A very substantial number of economic activities lead to the emission of so-called greenhouse gases. These tend to collect in the upper atmosphere, fuse there and change the constituency of the global atmosphere. This is believed to lead in turn to an increase in the average temperature all over the earth (see Figure 9.1), commonly called global 'warming'.

Problems associated with global warming are manifold. The main ones are:

*   *Ocean level rising.* This can lead to the inundation of coastal areas. As many of the urban areas have been developed along coasts, preventing inundation will lead to very high infrastructure cost.
*   *Large desertification.* Decline in precipitation in traditional agricultural areas leads to loss of capacity of food production.
*   *Increased unbalance.* In the rich countries (mostly in the north) the effects are limited and the capacity to deal with them is large. In the poor countries (mostly in the south) the effects are large, agricultural investment opportunities decline significantly and the resources of these countries to develop alternatives are limited.

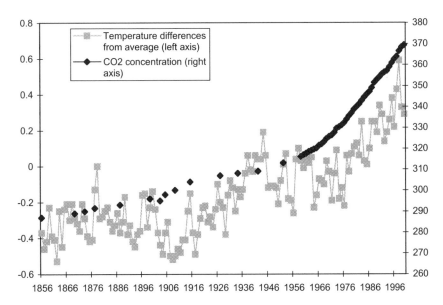

Figure 9.1 Temperatures rise as concentrations of greenhouse gases increase.

Source: Adapted from IBRD, 2000: 41.

- *Increased risk of contagious diseases (malaria etc.)*. This may lead to extra costs for health care.
- *Loss of non-human ecological diversity*. The habitats that are now characterized by a high diversity tend to be at risk, which already represents a loss. Moreover, the need for agricultural land to replace the land presently in use (that has become less suitable) will further limit ecological diversity on these lands.
- *Perverse effect on energy use*. The increased use of refrigeration and air conditioning will increase the use of energy, in turn accelerating the production of greenhouse gases.

The diversity of the problems and the wide spread of the sources of emissions make it very difficult to establish the cost of warming, the benefits of abatement (see, for an overview, Swanston and Johnston, 1999: 33–8) and the capacity for change. Estimates of the cost of warming range from small figures (some 1.5 per cent of GDP) for developed countries to very high percentages for low-lying islands that are faced with disappearing altogether. Estimates of the cost of abatement (that is of reduction of emissions) range between 1 and 4.5 per cent of GDP. The benefits of abatement are most difficult to measure. Moreover, any serious cost–benefit analysis is hampered by the problems posed by the long period that has to be taken into account and the uncertainties as to the development of the influencing factors. So reliable estimates are lacking for the moment.

9.3 The main public good

9.3.1 *Definition*

Climate change or global warming and the deterioration of the ozone layer are clearly global public 'bads'. They have a negative influence on everybody's wealth level. Hence the absence of such bads is to be considered as a global public good (e.g. Heal 1999). The two criteria of public goods, i.e. 'non-rivalry' and 'non-excludability', clearly apply. For instance, as soon as air pollution has been abated, nobody can be excluded from breathing the clean air (Perman *et al.*, 1999; Pearce and Turner, 1990). Moreover, it is non-rival: if somebody in Japan breathes clean air he does not preclude someone in South Africa from doing the same.[2] The main public good in matters of environment is often called 'sustainable development'. It is defined as the type of development that 'meets the needs of the present without compromising the ability of future generations to meet their own needs' (Brundtland report).

The values and basic attitudes that support the promotion of this global public good have converged to a large extent over the past decades.[3] This is also the case for the principles that determine the architecture of the regimes that need to be set up for the preservation of the global environment. A number of such principles are of particular importance. We deal here with them successively.

9.3.1.1 *The precautionary principle*

In matters of environment one is often confronted with uncertainty as to the seriousness of the problem, the cause–effect relation and the best instruments to deal with the problem. As we have seen in Chapter 4, such problems of uncertainty and incomplete information do have a bearing on the behaviour of actors. However, in environmental matters we are often confronted with irreversibility, that is if an ecological system has come below a certain stage it will not be able to recover and will result in a permanent loss. In order to cope with this problem the precautionary principle is adopted. In day-to-day terms it says, 'better safe than sorry'. In more elaborate words:

- When an activity raises threats to the environment precautionary measures should be taken even if some cause–effect relationships are not fully established scientifically.
- The proponent of the activity, not the public, should bear the burden of the proof.
- The process of applying the principle should be open, informed and democratic, including potentially affected parties. It must give an examination of the full range of alternatives, including no action.

9.3.1.2 The polluter pays principle

There is a tendency in market economies that polluters do not incur the cost of pollution prevention or of abatement themselves, but tend to let others deal with it and thus pay for it. A good example is the pollution of surface waters by a chemical industry. It permits consumers of the products of that industry to buy cheap goods. However, its implication is that water companies have to invest heavily in treatment to produce safe water, with the result that the consumer of water pays for the cost. The polluter pays principle is intended to achieve correct allocation in the economy. It obliges the chemical industry in this example to avoid the disposal of waste in the surface water. If to that end it has to make investment that increases the cost of its products, it means that these costs are internalized and borne by those who consume the relevant good. The consumer of water will have a lower price. In other words, the polluter pays principle obliges economic actors to avoid negative externalities, or to internalize the environmental cost of production, consumption and distribution. The principle is notably important in order to avoid situations with very high transaction cost.

9.3.1.3 Common but differentiated responsibilities principle

This principle has as its main elements the recognition by all states that they are collectively responsible for the solution to a problem, yet that they will contribute to that solution in a differentiated way. This differentiation applies notably to the developing countries that are permitted to do less than the developed countries. The difference in efforts is justified not so much on the basis of the limited capacity of the LDCs to contribute, but rather on their limited responsibility for the present problems. Many of these have indeed been caused by the developed nations. The principle does, of course, facilitate, first, cooperation to conclude multilateral environment agreements (MEAs) and, next, compliance with their obligations.

The principles discussed here have been adopted in a large number of instances, both on the national, regional (e.g. the EU, see Section 9.4.2) and international level (e.g. the UN framework convention on climate change, see Section 9.4.5).[4]

9.3.2 Collective action

A number of structural factors make collective action in environmental matters difficult. We mention here briefly the most relevant ones. They tend to be environmental illustrations of the general problem discussed in Chapter 5 (see also Perman *et al.*, 1999, Barett, 1990, 1999; Rao, 2002).

- *Pervasiveness of sources of pollution.* Environmental problems are created at each stage of the production–consumption chain. Decisions on production and consumption are taken in a decentralized way by millions of enterprises and by billions of consumers. Each of them is only a small contributor to a series of problems and a small beneficiary of the solutions to be found.

- *Entrenchment of problem in way of life.* A good example is motor transport. The widespread use of the motorcar has lead to the spatial separation of work, home, leisure and education. As people have adjusted to this spread it has become very difficult to limit the use of cars.
- *Uncertainty as to the cause/effect and the cost/benefit relations.* In environmental matters uncertainty exists as to the real causes and the type of damage done, the cost of prevention or of cleaning up, the seriousness of the impact, etc. This often leads in the first instance to denying the existence of the problem and next to endless debating about the adequacy and effectiveness of instruments. Even in the case of global warming the relation between emissions and effect is questioned.
- *Time preference.* In many cases the cost of environmental improvement will have to be borne immediately, whereas the benefits will tend to take years to materialize. So there is a strong tendency to postpone action.
- *Unequal distribution of cost and benefits.* For some of the measures the costs are borne by one group and the benefits by another. This would be justified if the polluter pays principle led to the charging of the cost on the major producers and users of the goods and services causing environmental damage. However, the implementation of this principle has been very difficult, both at the level of national states and at the level of groups within countries. Economic cost prevents even rich countries accepting abatement.
- *Weak institutional framework.* New forms have to be invented for coping with new problems.[5]

In view of all these problems, one may ask the question how is it that international cooperation does, in a number of cases, seem to work out. After all, we can observe that it has been possible to conclude a number of important environmental agreements committing large numbers of countries. Here, too, a number of general factors (see Chapters 4 and 5) are particularly relevant in environmental matters.

- *Collective action.* The stronger the public concern, the scientific consensus as to the cause and seriousness of problem, the economic substantiation of the cost–benefit relation, the actions of lobbies and pressure groups and the influence of the media, the better the chances for change. Collective action can be set in motion by the determined action of the first mover (see Box 9.1). It may be furthered by the concerns about damage to reputation of major players without agreement and by the use of credible threats towards nonsignatories.
- *Equity.* Agreements are made easier if the burden sharing is done in a way that is perceived as fair by all. In international matters this may

Box 9.1 **The bandwagon effect**

The process of environmental standard setting may be started by one country, with increasing numbers joining in time (bandwagon). An example of such a process, where the strong commitment of one country has induced others to join, is car exhaust gas standards. Car exhaust gases are an important component of greenhouse gases. The limitation of car exhaust emissions starts best with the introduction of new technology on car engines and petrol additives. The adoption of such new technology by car producers and oil refiners will be dependent on the passing of legal norms on car exhaust emissions. International negotiations on the setting of such norms were very long-winded due to the many implications for international trade in cars and the competitive positions of major producers.

In this situation, California broke the stalemate by unilaterally passing a regulation setting maximum standards on exhaust emissions from vehicles registered in the state. California decided to act unilaterally for two reasons: first, it was most affected by pollution from this source and, second, it was most sensitive to the problem given its high standard of living. After the passing of the regulation there was a pressure on all car manufacturers that wanted to maintain their sales in California and in the states that were inclined to follow.

The US example induced the German government to stimulate the use of unleaded gasoline, and the European Commission to start thinking on regulation for exhaust levels of new cars. Some European producers (notably those with either significant exports to or assembly in the US) moved quickly and adapted engine design. The public reacted favourably to the new technology and public authorities helped by setting fuel taxes in such a way as to favour the use of unleaded gasoline. The early movers among the car manufacturers were able to realize production cost cuts.

The demand for unleaded petrol by German tourists in Italy forced petrol stations there to supply the product alongside the traditional product range. This spill-over occurred in other countries too. The reduction in cost to consumers in follower countries (for both cars and petrol) facilitated the switch over in the whole EU to unleaded gasoline and to cars with engines in conformity with new EU norms. In the wake of that, the association of European car manufacturers made an agreement with the EU Commission in 1998, in which it committed itself to a reduction of new car emissions of 25 per cent over the following 10 years.

lead to the use of the instrument of side payments to countries that have a particular high cost of pollution abatement and little direct benefits (Carraro and Siniscalco, 1993, 1998; Petrakis and Xepapadeas, 1996).

- *Institutions*. Existence of previous MEA do set precedents and show the way to resolving a new problem. Moreover, in many cases one can use the combination of national execution with international monitoring.

9.3.3 National measures

9.3.3.1 Command and control: direct regulation

The method consists in instructing the subjects of the regulation on the norms they have to meet. This is the most used instrument in national matters because it has two advantages:

- *Transparency*. Rules specify clearly for everybody the limits to pollution and the punishment to offenders.
- *Certainty*. Resources committed to enforce the rules make compliance credible.

9.3.3.2 Market forms such as pollution rights: tradable quotas

The point of departure for this instrument is to limit (by regulation) the total quantity of pollution that will be permitted (effectiveness aspect). The next step is to design a system for distribution that is efficient in economic terms by dividing the total into a maximum number of permits to pollute.[6] The third step is to design a system of trade that determines who has access to market and that sets the rules for the trading.

With the instruments of tradable pollution rights, polluters choose themselves the modalities of abatement, which has three advantages:

- Permitting the optimal choice of investment. The cost-effectiveness of measures can be higher in a foreign country than in one's own. Those who face the highest cost of abatement will buy permits and those who face abatement costs that are lower than the price of a permit will sell them.
- Avoiding the problems of application of outdated and hence inefficient technologies because of time pressure. In this way, sectors that need to adapt their technology get sufficient time to do so.
- Putting a minimum demand on the institutional set-up and avoiding bureaucracy.

There are, however, some complications with this system (Bertram, 1992; Smith, 1992). These are in the following domains:

- Putting property rights on free goods is politically very difficult and the initial assignment of property has proved a very delicate matter to decide on.
- Establishing a market regime: it is difficult to design a minimum institutional set-up, to avoid high transaction costs in trading, to make sure that there will be no dominant player and finally that intertemporal trading is possible.

These problems can be overcome; indeed, tradable pollution rights systems have already been put in place in some countries and have proven to be operational (Tietenberg, 2003).

9.3.3.3 Taxation and excises

The basic idea here is to affect the price of polluting goods. On the national level, an effective instrument is to tax the polluter, so as to stimulate clean production and consumption, on the one hand, and to mobilize resources to compensate for the damage, on the other. Indeed, price changes due to differential taxation are theoretically more efficient than quantity controls (Pizer, 2002). Incidentally, much of the effectiveness of environmental policy actually starts with the removal of the opposite of taxes, as in many countries the use of polluting goods is actually subsidized. The effectiveness and distribution aspects of such measures are intertwined, in the sense that one has to determine the type of polluters that will be taxed and the level of taxation that is necessary to arrive at the desired reduced level of pollution. Governments have the difficulty to find a way to share the burden internally in a manner that is perceived as equitable (see Box 9.2).

9.3.3.4 Private litigation

The problem of implementation and compliance can be lowered by giving any person, firm or NGO the right to sue offenders of environmental law before any national court of their choice.

9.3.4 International measures

International environmental agreements cover, in general, the following three aspects:

- *Effectiveness*. Ascertain optimal aggregate resource use or alternatively determine levels of reduction of pollution.
- *Distribution*. Allocate the user rights or the obligations for action (abatement targets) over the various countries.
- *Implementation*. Create monitoring and enforcement mechanisms.

Box 9.2   The feasibility of greenhouse gas abatement by carbon taxes: the case of Mexico

Mexico is currently the fifteenth largest emitter in the world of greenhouse gases and by far the largest source of such emissions in Latin America. Thus, from a strategic standpoint, Mexico's decision to subscribe to carbon emission restrictions is a matter of significance. Mexico has found itself under intense pressure to join the world's industrialized economies and develop a plan for limiting its use of carbon-based energy sources in the future. Such a plan would, of course, entail economic cost and could significantly limit consumer welfare.

A large producer of air pollution is transport. Now, considerable emission reductions could be realized at relatively low cost by improving the technical quality of the engines of buses operating in the city. However, this is difficult to implement because the necessary measures would bring a cost to a public enterprise without the possibility of the government to get income back from higher transport fees. So a solution has been sought where the income side improvement would actually compensate the cost of investment. The carbon tax was the logical candidate.

A carbon tax (leading to an increase in fossil fuel prices) is, in general, an effective instrument in the sense that it does reduce the growth rate of carbon emissions. However, its introduction does also depend on political economy (distributional) considerations.

Consumers may be mobilized in favour of the introduction of the tax as it is found to have a progressive effect on welfare levels, meaning that it would harm less the groups with lower income levels. Under high rates of technological change it would even lead simultaneously to a reduction in the rate of growth of carbon emissions and an increase in welfare for all income groups.

Producers are likely to be against the introduction of carbon taxes as they have to make very costly adaptations. As the sectors that will be most affected are relatively concentrated, they are likely to be able to mobilize an effective lobby against the carbon tax.

Government has a preference for the present taxes on capital and labour. First, because the distributional effects of it are well known, whereas the distributional effects of carbon taxes are highly uncertain. Second, because there is some uneasiness about the stability of the revenue of the carbon tax once energy reduction is realized.

Given the power balance between the different groups and the fact that business is a concentrated and well-organized interest group, while consumers are ill-informed and poorly organized, it is unlikely that a proposal for a carbon tax will become enacted.

Source: Based on Boyd and Ibarraran (2002).

The problem with these categories is that during negotiations they tend to be discussed together and become blurred, which adds much to the complexity of these negotiations.

There are several instruments available to realize the production of a public environmental good. They are not all equally effective in an international setting. We will analyse the most relevant ones.

9.3.4.1 Direct regulation

Direct regulation has two disadvantages while applied in an international environment. First, the cost of designing rules are very high as they have to take into account a considerable diversity of situations, economies and legal systems. Second, the enforcement is difficult as there are often no means of coercion. In order to improve compliance sanctions could be considered, but these are difficult to agree on (asymmetry between the rich and mighty versus the poor and weak) and even more difficult to make effective (Bertram, 1992).

9.3.4.2 Market forms

The efficiency of the system of tradable permits can be much enhanced where the market can be organized on a global scale.[7] This international trading framework needs to bring order into the diversity of the various national (or regional: EU) systems and elaborate minimum standards as to aspects like the definition of the quantities, the interchangeability of the various pollutants, the price setting system, the guarantees against price manipulation, etc.

9.3.4.3 Taxation

In international matters the instrument of taxation is less easy to apply, as most governments do not accept an inroad into their sovereignty and are very reluctant to hand over considerable resources to an international institution. The former problem could be circumvented by a system whereby governments pay a contribution that is proportional to the pollution they produce. The second problem could be solved by agreeing on a system of redistribution for repairing the damage to the environment. However, both presuppose the existence of a strong institution, which is not available on the global level. A system of harmonized national taxes would be easier to implement, but is not effective in reaching the targets of lowering the public bad (Hoel, 1992).

9.3.4.4 Private litigation

Private litigation is an instrument that is not easy to transpose on the international level. It can only be done on the precondition that governments sign an international convention that specifies the standards to which all polluters would be obliged. This is very unlikely to happen, because it would encounter all the difficulties we cited under direct regulation. And even where an agreement could be reached, mighty polluters have the power to stall lengthy procedures while the sanctions that the courts might eventually impose are difficult to make effective (Bertram, 1992).

So, by studying the various options, it seems as if the combination of direct regulation and market forms are the best options for the instrumentation of international environmental agreements.

9.4 Organizations involved in the provision of the public good

9.4.1 The changed role of the major actors

The effective protection of the environment calls for an international regime. The elaboration of such international environmental regimes necessitates the cooperation of a number of major actors (national states, business and NGOs). All three have seen their role change over the past few decades.[8]

National states have become increasingly aware of the need to take environmental concerns into account. The increased capacity to deal with the relevant problems at home has contributed to accept practical solutions for problems that transcend the national ones. The most advanced states have, of course, felt the need to improve on the quality of the environment first. So, in line with the model described in Section 9.3.3, most actions have come through a coalition of advanced states, very often with the triad US/EU/Japan at their core. This group has been joined by countries that have given only lukewarm support, because for them the balance between perceived benefits and cost was only marginally positive. LDCs have, in general, taken the position that environmental problems have been caused mostly by the activities of the developed countries, so that the latter should also take the responsibility for finding solutions. LDCs have tended to ask for compensation of the cost when joining the rest of the countries in collective action.

Business logics have increasingly integrated environmental concern in firms' strategies. Many firms have done so because of the responsibility they have in societal matters. Others have been compelled to conform to this larger responsibility because they have been the 'victim' of specific targeting of NGOs that have threatened firms with a considerable commercial impact due to a loss of reputation. Finally, many firms have understood that 'green' products and production processes is just good economics. A technology lead (e.g. in car engines) gives a competitive edge. New production technology may lead to substantial cost savings.

Non-governmental organizations[9] include scientific associations such as the International Council of Scientific Unions and a wide range of organizations that advocate improved protection of the environment. The most well known among them are Greenpeace and the World Wildlife Fund. All these NGOs have improved their finance, their organization, their technical know-how and their capacity to get the media interested in their actions and points of view. This means that they are increasingly capable of influencing both public opinions and hence decision-makers. The increased means of low-cost communication via the Internet has also greatly enhanced their effectiveness.

9.4.2 International organizations

There are a large number of international organizations that take responsibility for at least part of the global environmental problems. The most relevant ones are:

- *UN*. When the UN was founded there was very little concern about environmental problems. So one need not be surprised that the UN Charter does not mention the issue explicitly. However, in the course of the 1970s a number of new scientific results and major disasters sparked off a great concern and UN action. Enhanced action resulted by the end of the 1980s in the Earth Summit of Rio de Janeiro, which engendered a whole series of initiatives and fixed a number of the principles that govern environmental policy. At this moment more than 170 international environmental treaties have been signed. Among them are very important ones such as the Montreal Protocol of 1987 and the Kyoto Protocol in 1997 (see later in this chapter). Paramount among the UN activities is the United Nations Environmental Programme (UNEP). Other relevant institutions are the UN Commission on Sustainable Development and the Global Environmental Facility (see also World Bank hereafter).
- *OECD*. The environmental policy committee of OECD was formed in 1970. The OECD exchanges information about best practices in national environmental policy-making and regulation. The quality of the policy process is enhanced by a system of peer reviews. The OECD also stimulates the negotiation and signing of international environmental commitments (OECD 1999a, 1999b, 2000). These include codes of conduct and directives for multinational firms. Past experience has shown that such codes are effective as stakeholders in many MNFs check the compliance of their company with the code.
- *G8*. Environmental matters have taken an increasing part in the attention of the G8 over the past decades. Sometimes this organization has been used to try to break stalemates in negotiation situations. However, its role in the total effort to come to international environmental agreements has been limited.
- *WTO*. There is a close connection between trade and environment. The WTO starts from the premise that trade measures apply to goods and

services, not to the way they have been produced. So, under the rule of non-discrimination, it is not permissible for countries to take action against products from countries that do not respect the importers' sustainable production standards. NGOs have consistently tried to change this situation and to 'green' the trade regime. Up till now this has not resulted in a change of the WTO stand. The WTO accepts, however, product bans where international environmental standards have been agreed upon. The WTO supports the setting of such standards by its competent sister organizations.

- *World Bank.* The bank has been rather slow to integrate environmental concerns in the selection of the projects it supports. In 1990 it started to finance operations in the framework of the global environmental facility, providing funds on favourable terms to projects that have a beneficial effect on the global environment (now, notably, climate change and biological diversity).
- *Regional schemes.* Many environmental problems that extend beyond national borders have a regional dimension. So a large number of agreements have been concluded to cope with such effects. Moreover, regional integration schemes are also dealing increasingly with environmental matters (see Box 9.3).

9.4.3 Objectives of major organizations

Many international environmental regimes are created by means of a framework convention. The choice of this form of organization can be explained on the basis of elements of the theories of collective action and of transaction cost.

The main characteristics of a framework convention are:

- Recognition by the signatories that there is global public good to be safeguarded;
- Creation of a set of soft obligations to foster the realization of that public good;
- Attribution of a high status to the agreement, but initial acceptance of a low content in order to maximize support;
- Acceptance of ambiguities in text and a differentiated interpretation of them;
- Agreement on the need to deal with detailed matters of content in separate protocols.

The chain of events that leads to the conclusion of a framework agreement and subsequent protocols consists of the following links:

- NGOs voice their concern and enjoy political support in one or more key states;

Box 9.3 Regional schemes for environmental protection

Most regional integration schemes deal only with matters of trade and investment. Some go further in matters of the environment (NAFTA, and in particular the EU). The EU has even gone beyond the interrelation of the internal market and the environment and quickly developed an environmental policy in its own right.

The *North American Free Trade Association* (NAFTA) integrates the markets of the US, Canada and Mexico. Right from the start of the negotiations on this scheme, environmental concerns were taken into account. The preamble to the NAFTA agreement calls on the contracting parties to pursue their programme of trade liberalization so as to promote sustainable development. This is given substance in a number of ways. First, NAFTA acknowledges that members are permitted to maintain environmental policies even when these impact on trade. In the event that disputes arise with both trade and environmental aspects, the agreement provides for procedures where environmental experts have their role alongside trade experts. Members are not allowed in such trade disputes to refer to WTO procedures. Moreover, the NAFTA negotiations have been paralleled by environmental cooperation negotiations. These have resulted in an environmental side agreement to NAFTA. This side agreement set up a development bank to support investments in environmental infrastructure on the US–Mexican border. It also set up a Commission for Environmental Cooperation that serves as a forum for cooperation on environmental issues and monitoring of compliance.

The *European Union* (EU)[10] started its activities in the 1950s at a time when environmental concerns were not yet on the agenda. Since 1972 the EU has integrated environment in its policies. In 1987 care for the environment got its constitutional foundation (Treaty Title XVI). The EU policy aims at a high level of protection. The treaty specifies that the policy shall be based 'on the precautionary principle and on the principle that preventive action should be taken, that environmental damage should as a priority be rectified at source and that the polluter should pay'. In practice, the policy is given direction and substance via action programmes. The EU has developed a range of instruments to bring its policy into effect. A whole series of 'directives' (EU law) have, in the meantime, been adopted on a whole series of subjects. The EU pursues a pro-active role on the global scene and cooperates with the competent organizations to promote measures at the international level that can improve the environment. It may enter into agreements between the EU as a whole and third parties. The EU has assumed in particular an active role in the field of climate change.

- A key state with a technology lead asks for a global regime;
- Negotiations lead after some time to a weak global regime that is gradually put in place;
- Disaster leads to an increase in global concern and in the recognition of a change in the cost–benefit relation;
- The regime is strengthened both in detail of commitment, instruments and coverage.

International environmental agreements are designed to deal with one specific problem and are composed of sets of explicit principles, norms, rules and decision-making procedures that are specific to this problem. As a consequence they tend to have idiosyncratic sets of institutional characteristics. We will consider two of them somewhat further: the Montreal Protocol on stratospheric ozone depletion and the Kyoto Protocol on global warming.

9.4.4 Case study 1: the Montreal Protocol (MP)

In 1977, UNEP convened an international conference on the ozone layer that concluded that there was a need to act. The Vienna Convention (agreed on in 1985) created a framework for future cooperative efforts. The acuity of the problem became apparent to an increasing number of states, and parties agreed on limitations of the emissions of CFCs in the Montreal Protocol of 1987. After coming into force, the protocol was amended twice to become more committed and to speed up the actions of signatories.

The amended version commited parties to a full phase out of all substances that cause ozone depletion before 1999. The MP established the principle of 'common, but differentiated responsibility'. This permits the separation of the abatement target from the cost burden involved.

In order to bring as many countries into the sphere of the agreement as possible, there have been a number of measures taken (compare the discussion in Chapter 4):

- *Incentives*. Industrial countries have agreed to make side payments in order to cover the incremental cost of compliance by the LDCs. Moreover, project support, for instance by the World Bank, can be made conditional on the joining of the protocol (see Box 9.4).
- *Free rider deterrence*. Signatory countries apply trade sanctions to nonparties that continue to trade substances that have been ruled out or goods that contain such substances. This may be a serious threat as it may lead to relocation of economic activities to countries that do comply.
- *Minimum commitment*. Setting of a minimum threshold for the number of signatories creates a strong incentive for hesitant countries to agree to sign, because the effort put in to reaching an agreement and the

> **Box 9.4 International aid to encourage LDC compliance with MEAs**
>
> Institutional and financial support is often needed to enable certain weak countries to meet their obligations. One of the outcomes of the 1992 UN Rio Conference on Environment and Development was the Global Environment Facility. It was set up as a joint undertaking of the UNEP, the UNDP and the World Bank (see Chapter 6). Its objective is to help developing countries finance the incremental cost of new environmental investments with global benefits in four areas: climate change, preservation of biodiversity, protection of the ozone layer and protection of international waters.

public good provided by the agreement would be lost if the threshold, in terms of the minimum number of countries, was not reached (Black *et al.*, 1993).

9.4.5 Case study 2: the framework convention on climate change

The basic text (framework convention) was agreed during the 1992 Earth Summit in Rio de Janeiro. In a follow-up conference that was held in 1992 in Kyoto, the so-called Kyoto Protocol (KP) was adopted. It will enter into force after having been ratified by 55 countries, accounting for at least 55 per cent of all 1990 emissions. Ratification became uncertain when the US decided to withdraw. However, the EU remained very committed and at a conference in Bonn in 2001, 170 countries finally came to an agreement about a detailed filling in of the KP targets and instruments. This was only obtained at the cost of a longer list of exceptions.

The Kyoto Protocol commits the signatories to limit the emission of greenhouse gases by 2012 to the level of 1990 or below. The objective of a reduction can also be formulated in terms of acceptable pollution levels. These can, again, be formulated in terms of pollution rights. The allocation of these rights over the countries participating in the programme calls for certain criteria. For the KP, the negotiating parties have come up with several proposals that have run into as many objections (see, for example, Cooper, 2000). The two most extremes are:

- *History*. Present pollution levels are representative of the present level of development and the choices in terms of energy use. To give an example, the US is responsible for 25 per cent of total emissions of carbon in the world; Western Europe for some 17 per cent; the Far East for another 25 per cent, while the whole of Africa accounts only for 4 per cent. For the newly industrializing countries this would mean that they have to confine their development in the limits of their present pollution. That would imply very costly devices both in production and consumption and would seriously hamper their growth. It is felt as utterly unfair and for that reason will not be accepted by LDCs.

- *Population.* The principle underlying this criterion is that every citizen of the world is entitled to an identical share of the worlds' resources. Whatever the moral appeal of this criterion, it is unacceptable for the incumbents. It would either limit very drastically the present production and consumption levels in the most developed countries, or in the case of tradable permits would lead to an immense transfer of resources from the latter to the LDCs.

In the end, the allocation of pollution rights has been an example of political horse-trading. Each country or region (e.g. the EU) has finally negotiated a level of pollution that it considered feasible in technical terms, acceptable in political terms and fair in comparison to the effort of other negotiating parties. So, the targets of reduction vary from country to country. The major developed countries would reduce by about 7 per cent.

An important aspect of the KP is the application of the principle of 'common but differentiated responsibility'. It implies that no targets have been set for LDCs. This is understandable from the point of view of their low contribution to the problem.[11] It can also be understood from the point of view of transaction cost (it would probably have held up the negotiations indefinitely). However, this exclusion poses a number of problems. First, the problem of effectiveness, as many of the larger LDCs have become substantial polluters. Moreover, the inclusion of the LDCs would tend to level the marginal cost of abatement over all polluters in the world, which makes the system tend towards the most advantageous overall cost level (Bosello and Roson, 1999). Finally, the increased cost effectiveness would generate means that could be used for transfers that could induce the LDCs to join the protocol.

These national targets can be translated to specific targets on the level of various actors by every country in the way it suits best its internal situation. Countries will then act on:

- The main polluting plants by setting emission limits and by structural measures (fuel switch); this implies investment in projects that reduce the emissions of such plants.
- The multitude of smaller emissions by product regulation, price incentives, civic behaviour, tax incentives.
- The capacity of the country to absorb emissions by so-called carbon sinks. As carbon is fixed by wood or by other vegetation, the more vegetation, the lower the need to use the two former instruments.

The KP still has insufficient ratification. It has been rejected by the US. The arguments put forward are two-fold. The first is largely political; it says that the KP leads to an unequal sharing of the burden. (Consider, however, that the US is the largest single contributor to the problem.) The second argument is of an economic nature: it says that the KP instruments are largely ineffective and lead to very high cost for those who have to implement them (see, for example, McKibbin and Wilcoxen, 2002).[12] However, the EU is determined to proceed; it is now elaborating the necessary legislation (see following section). Russia and Canada have said that they would also implement the KP. They recognize the shortcomings of the KP, but a better alternative that could be implemented relatively quickly has not yet been put forward.

9.5 Governance

9.5.1 The catalogue of KP instruments

The cost of pollution abatement can differ very much from one country to another. Countries that have already high standards and use modern technology will face high marginal cost for further abatement. Countries that use still older technology may realize considerable environmental improvements at relatively low cost. It is thus good economics to stimulate common efforts so that worldwide abatement is done in an efficient way. The way to do this is to accept that reductions need not be realized in one's own country, but may also be realized in other countries. The KP permits the signatory countries to use the following flexible mechanisms to come up to their targets for abatement:

- *Recognizing foreign efforts.* This comes in the KP in two forms. Joint implementation applies to countries that are both signatories of the KP. An example of such a project may be the investment of Shell in clean technology in Poland. The clean development mechanism applies when the host country is not a signatory of the KP. An example would be the investment of Shell in a clean technology project in Ghana.
- *Emission trading.* The mechanism of this trading has been given in Section 9.3.4.2. The KP obliges developed countries to achieve at least half of their reduction in their own country. The rationale for this limitation is two-fold. First, to prevent LDCs immediately selling their emission rights at a low price, with the risk of needing them later for costly projects. Second, to stimulate the highly developed countries to search for innovative ways to decrease the cost of abatement. However, withdrawing this restriction from the regime would lead to a substantial reduction of the cost (by half according to Manne and Richels, 2000; Buonanno *et al.*, 2000).

The mechanism of joint implementation is indeed subject to a number of problems. The major ones are that the system is subject to corruption and fraud and that measuring compliance is very costly. So, much attention is now given to putting emission trading into operation.

9.5.2 *Organizing the trading system*

Over the past decades a number of countries have been experimenting with the set-up of systems of emission rights trading. Consequently, a number of differences exist between these systems. It has not yet led to an international system. For that reason we consider, by way of example, the EU system (as it has been agreed on by the end of 2002). The main characteristics of this system are the following:

*   *Attribution of rights*. Each country can use its own rules as to the allocation of rights to companies for the coming few years. National plans have to be set up and submitted to the EU for approval. Up till 2008 this will be without cost to the firms concerned. After that date rights may be auctioned.
*   *Trade*. Companies can use their rights for their own purposes. In case they exceed their right they have to pay a fine of €40 per ton of CO_2; this amount will go up to €100 per ton after 2008. To avoid this, companies can buy the rights of those who do not exhaust their rights. The price has to be settled by the market. It is expected that initially this trade could amount to some €10 billion per year.
*   *Coverage*. In the first instance, the system is set up for the industries that are responsible for the largest part of the emission (40 per cent). It regards some 4,500 companies in the EU in the sectors of oil refineries, basic chemicals, fossil fuel fired power stations, steel, cement, pulp/paper and ceramics.

For the time being, the EU system has not yet been adopted as an international one. Such a system is being elaborated in conjunction with the other signatories of the Kyoto Protocol. At a later stage, other polluters and other pollutants will be included in the EU system as well.

9.5.3 *The problem of enforcement*

Multilateral environmental agreements (MEAs) provide for very few instruments to improve compliance. Nevertheless they are effective. The question is then, how strong will the KP be in this respect? How likely is it that the efforts that were agreed will actually lead to the actions needed and of course to the targeted effect? The following factors are important in this respect:

*   *Design of the agreements*. A good set-up takes away much of the need for compliance instruments. This applies notably to the limitation of the possibilities of countries to take a free ride. In this respect, the KP is very weak; many possibilities exist even for the major players to desist from making the effort.

- *Sanctions*. The use of this instrument is very controversial. Sanctions are very difficult to make effective internationally. The WTO is here an exception, but even for trade the instrument of retaliation is besieged with problems (see Box 12.4). Maintaining a high emission level is hardly a credible threat, as countries are unlikely to pursue self-damaging policies. Suggestions for financial measures, for instance fines on non-compliance, have not survived in the negotiation rounds that preceded the conclusion of the KP.
- *Dispute settlement system*. The KP does not provide for such an instrument. Yet it might have been helpful to use the experience of the WTO as an example of best practice in this respect (see Box 7.3).
- *Transparency of compliance by partners*. The effect of this factor is based on reputation. It does play an important role in the KP in the sense that monitoring mechanisms are foreseen. NGOs can hold governments accountable for their (non-)compliance, which may increase the political support for the measures needed.
- *Incentives*. Some of these are actually used in the KP. They come notably in the sense of other international organizations (e.g. the World Bank) to link aid with environmental issues (see Box 9.4).

The general conclusion of this analysis is that the KP is still in the infancy stage of an MEA. One has to wait for the problems to become more acute, the instruments to become more effective, the means of coercion on non-participants to become larger, in order to see the KP develop to the stage it will be able to produce the public good of a stable climate.

9.6 Evaluation of the past and options for the future

9.6.1 Achievements

Over the past decades global environmental concerns have attracted considerable public interest. This has incited national governments to cooperate on a range of issues. Such international policy-making has resulted in a rapid expansion of global environmental regimes. Most of them have been developed in the framework of the UNEP. The main legal form used was the multilateral environmental agreement (MEA). These are separate legal arrangements. They concern notably the preservation of biodiversity, the sound management and trade in hazardous chemicals and the promotion of lower emissions and cleaner production. Most MEAs have created conferences of parties that do most of the decision-making. The elaboration of major new regimes has gone hand in hand with the use of innovative instruments, such as tradable pollution rights, etc.

Over time, the interface between environment and development has been elaborated. A major principle now generally accepted in international environmental law is 'common objectives, but differentiated obligations'. A clear example of this is given in the Kyoto Protocol. It means that developed countries take on most of the burden of abatement and support (financially) developing countries in their efforts to meet international obligations.

9.6.2 Inadequacies and challenges

There is considerable and widespread concern about the inadequacy of the present regimes and organizations to deliver the global public good of environmental sustainability. This inadequacy is closely linked to the organizational weakness of the environmental regimes. Over the past decades a broad range of regimes has developed on a case-by-case basis, all concerning very specific issues. The UNEP has not provided a unifying framework for an encompassing environmental regime. Neither is there a standard format of obligations and instruments. This incoherence and lack of standardization mean that the transaction cost for participants in the process and the information cost of stakeholders are higher than needed. It means, moreover, that there are very few mechanisms to internalize externalities that underlie global environmental failure. These are notably related to aspects (dealt with in Chapters 4 and 5), such as free-riding, ambiguous property rights, time inconsistency and lack of possibilities for issue linkage.

Compliance is essentially based on non-judicial instruments (for instance, reputation). It applies not only to governments, but also to firms. The UNEP, for instance, promotes the global reporting initiative developed in partnership with leading multistakeholder organizations to encourage voluntary environmental reporting by companies around the world. Non-compliance often results in further diplomatic activity and negotiation. It often involves the search for means that can facilitate compliance of the defector, rather than punishment (Faure and Lefevre, 1999). Dispute settlement mechanisms are very rare and, when in place, have been used very rarely. The International Court of Justice has so far never dealt with a purely environmental conflict.

Finances are another point of concern. The finances of the UNEP consist of voluntary contributions. This makes the room for manoeuvre of the organization subject to significant uncertainties. Additional finance for enhancing the compliance with MEAs comes from the so-called global environmental facility. There is still widespread concern, notably among developing countries, about the lack of resources of this facility, the priorities it sets (allegedly favouring the interests of the developing world) and finally about its cumbersome procedures (unsuited given their limited administrative capacity).

9.6.3 Proposals for improvement

The proposals that have been made to remedy the organizational weakness of the world environmental government do mostly address the following three aspects:

- *Reducing the organizational diversity and improving consistency between regimes.* This starts with more and better coordination among the various MEAs, notably between those that cover similar areas (biodiversity, toxic waste, etc.). It continues with pleas for an umbrella organization that would oversee all MEAs now in place.
- *Stabilizing and enlarging the financial basis.* This applies in the short term particularly to the Global Environmental Facility. The financial basis needs to be considerably enlarged and it needs to be made more predictable (that is, commitments must be made for several years);
- *Improvement of compliance.* This would imply three elements. First, a surveillance mechanism, which would not necessarily have to be inter-governmental; one could also give accredited NGOs the right to lodge complaints. Second, the installation of an international body to analyse the case and give a judgment. Finally, it would imply a set of measures that the international community can apply to sanction violators. In this respect there is a strong pressure by environmentalist NGOs to use trade sanctions to countries that do not comply with MEAs. They point towards the fairly direct relation between policy measures concerning production, consumption and the environment. This view is opposed by trade specialists, who fear 'corruption' of the regime. It is also opposed by certain security specialists who claim that trade sanctions have generally proved to be ineffective in trying to force countries to comply with other values, such as race equality, human rights, etc.

To many these proposals do not go far enough and actually address the wrong problems. They favour the replacement of UNEP (and other global environmental organizations) by a newly created World Environment Organization (WEO). For the set up of such a WEO one can seek inspiration from the model of the WTO (Whalley and Zissimos, 2002; Tussie and Whalley, 2002). The basic elements of the proposals can be described as follows:

- *Objective.* The WEO would facilitate, encourage, administer and take actions aiming to advance cross-country negotiations on the environment, whose effect would be to raise environmental quality.
- *Form.* A northern country that is interested in the preservation of a rainforest can strike a deal with a country that has the custody of such forests. One can imagine that the latter commits itself to maintaining a prespecified fraction of its land area as unspoiled rainforest for the coming 30 years. In return, the former commits itself to pay a certain sum to the latter. In a sense, this is similar to the exchange of trade concessions in the WTO. However, in the WTO side payments are not allowed, whereas here they are an essential part of the system.
- *Guarantor.* A new organization needs to be set up to make sure that each partner in the deal will live up to his commitments as soon as the other has done so. In this respect, it may be necessary to work together with the IMF and the World Bank.

- *Compliance.* In principle the partners in the trading of environmental commitments have to verify themselves whether the commitment is put in practice. On the level of the WEO, one could however foresee something like an environmental policy review (similar to the trade policy review in the WTO).
- *Deal maker.* The WEO would manage all MEAs and would work on the harmonization of their objectives and structures. The most important aspect of this integration is, however, that comprehensive (cross-issue) deals are possible that make sure that every partner receives some benefit (compare the so-called tariffs rounds of GATT). The seeking of comprehensive deals limits the problem of free-riding.
- *Centralized dispute settlement mechanism.* The form in which disputes are likely to arise are different from the WTO. In the latter they tend to apply to the interpretation of general rules; in the WEO it will be more about the fulfilment of individual deals. However, the mechanisms to deal with the issues need not be much different. Sanctions are not evident; the retaliation as in trade does not work, so sanctions are likely to be of the financial type.

Up till now, support has been very limited for this proposal (the reasons for such lack of enthusiasm have been given in Chapter 5).

9.7 Summary and conclusions

- The world is confronted with a number of environmental problems that have a truly global character. Many consider global warming to be one of the major problems.
- To avoid such problems, global regimes have been elaborated. Environmental regimes are based on three principles: (1) precaution, (2) polluter pays and (3) common, but differentiated responsibilities.
- There is a plethora of international environmental agreements most of which have very weak organizational structures. The strongest among them is the United Nations Environmental Programme which has custody for important regimes, such as the one combating global warming (Kyoto Protocol).
- Governance aspects differ widely from one regime to another. One of the most salient features in this respect is the system of internationally tradable emission permits which is elaborated in the framework of the Kyoto Protocol.
- In future the 'system' is confronted with three challenges: to strengthen the organizational structure, to integrate the various regimes in one framework (comparable to the WTO for trade) and to improve the effectiveness of the instruments.

10 Transport and telecommunications

10.1 Introduction

Throughout modern history the growing integration of the world economy has increased the exchange of goods and services. Such exchange is physically made possible by transport and communication.[1] The increase in volumes transported and information communicated has gone hand in hand with considerable technological development. Existing modes of transport have seen their modes of production revolutionized. Sea transport, for instance, has seen the changeover from the sailing ship to steam-powered vessels and then to diesel powered ships. New modes of transport have been added (e.g. air transport). Overall, transport and communications have increased much faster then GDP.

The public sector has at one stage or another seen the need to regulate the international aspects of the use of the (new) technology. This has been the case for both ocean-going transport, for border-crossing railways, for air travel and for telecommunications. The form chosen was generally the intergovernmental agreement that set up a specialist international organization. These covered typically aspects such as technological standards (to guarantee safe switching between national systems); rules for cost and revenue sharing and so on. The aim of this chapter is to explain the wide diversity of forms that have been chosen for the different modes.[2] We will go subsequently into the cases of sea transport (mainly goods), air transport (mainly passengers) and telecommunications (mainly speech and data) and the Internet (mainly information and data). The set-up of each of the sections will follow the same pattern that we followed in the previous chapters. The sequence is description of the problems (mostly of two types: stability of markets and safety), definition of the public good, characterization of the organizations involved, assessment of the instruments in use and finally evaluation of the case.

As usual, the chapter will be rounded off with a summary of the findings.

10.2 Sea (ocean) transport

10.2.1 Introduction

In the course of history, ocean shipping has played a crucial role in the international economy. For most goods, shipping is a more efficient way of transport, notably compared with land transport. So the lion's share of the global exchange of goods is actually carried by ocean shipping. For quite some time no single state could exercise effective control over long distance shipping. Ships sailed the seas in a legal no-man's land. In the sixteenth century this situation was transformed into the principle of free access (*mare liberum*) and became international law.

Over time, the growth in the volume of trade has gone hand in hand with considerable technical improvements. Ships have increased in size, have become specialized (tankers, containers), and equipped with new devices for the efficient handling of cargo and safe voyage. As a consequence, the cost of ocean transport has gone down dramatically (see Figure 2.1).

The services offered can, for practical purposes, be grouped into two main categories. On the one hand, we have liner services, ships operating on a specific route (possibly with ships calling at a string of ports) according to a fixed schedule. As most non-bulk cargo is now containerized, most liner services now concern container ships. On the other hand, we have bulk cargo (such as oil and ore) that travels in specialized ships, mainly on a charter basis. Most sea transport services are delivered by private companies.

Efficient sea transport depends critically on efficient ports. In most countries the public sector has taken responsibility for the considerable investments needed to accommodate the ever larger and technologically more advanced ships. The justification of this involvement comes mainly from the fact that a considerable part of the benefits of the investment are not private, but come in terms of positive effects on the rest of the economy. So most ports are now directly or indirectly controlled by the public sector. On the other hand, it is the private sector that provides most port services, such as handling and storage. Some of these private companies have become multinationals and offer their services at several ports around the globe to serve international clients.

In recent years, there has been some tendency to integrate port and shipping services in one company, notably within the container business.

10.2.2 The problems

The ocean shipping industry is confronted with market disequilibria. In times of economic downturn, capacity cannot be reduced easily so considerable price fluctuations occur. In the past these have jeopardized the continuity of certain services. In order to shelter somewhat from such fluctuations and to be able to capture the advantages of economies of scale, liner conferences and alliances (Button, 1999) have been created (see Box 10.1). The liner conference system is from an economic point of view very controversial.

***Box 10.1* Liner conferences**

Definitions
*   agreement among shipping companies
*   for a specific trade route
*   to provide regularity and cut costs
*   by decreasing competition
*   sometimes with government recognition

Mode of operation
*   restrict membership
*   set rates and allocate business
*   regulate capacity
*   set schedules
*   pool revenues and cost

Loss of influence of liner conferences due to change in
*   technology: increase in containerization and bulk cargo
*   industry structure: vertical integration of shipping and terminal operating
*   market power: shippers tend to dominate the market and exert effective pressure to bypass conferences
*   policy: actions by competition authorities (such as the EU Commission).

*   Advantages of this system are the possibility to create regular services or to increase frequency of the service on a route. In the past this was considered to be an advantage in those cases where countries had a particular interest in a regular service for transport of overseas goods (relations with overseas territories).
*   Disadvantages of the system are that it is basically anticompetitive, so that it may set prices too high by barring access for other suppliers to markets.

Safety at sea is another matter of public concern. The sector of ocean shipping has always been subject to stiff competition. Under such conditions operators are inclined to cut costs, including costs that are needed to maintain safety. Inadequate equipment, insufficient competences of the crew and low maintenance levels can cause damage to third parties. These may be at sea (collision with other ships), but also ashore (e.g. the pollution of the shores due to the wrecking of oil tankers). Part of this damage is directly measurable in terms of cost of abatement and loss of economic activity (consider the loss of income from tourism). For other damages (e.g. deterioration of ecosystems) the cost are not easy to determine. In practice, it has been difficult to charge the polluter in this respect.

10.2.3 Public goods and regime

In order to cope with these problems governments of coastal states have, for centuries, taken a keen interest in ocean shipping. Many others have more recently become involved. They have considered that high quality ocean transport is a public good for one or more of the following reasons:

- security (available capacity in times of turbulence and war);
- colonial administration (part of infrastructure of governance);
- safety reasons (protect third parties against damage);
- environmental concern (prevent pollution);
- labour conditions (maintain certain standards and wage levels).

The first step taken by many governments to provide this public good has been to stimulate the building up of a national ocean shipping industry (by protecting it from foreign competition). This has been initially the case for the major trading nations (such as the UK, the US, France or Japan[3]). After decolonization a large number of new states have also followed this course and mobilized the support of UNCTAD. A second step has been the regulation of the industry according to national norms fostering the public good aspects listed above.

The international regime that has evolved under these conditions is based on two principles:

- open access to high seas (international oceans) and innocent passage through territorial seas;
- joint sovereignty: by nature the industry is dependent on two (home and destination) states to permit a shipping service.

Other essential features of the regime are:

- national policies: flag state jurisdiction over ships wherever they sail. Port state control over entry of ships and on market access;
- private: inter-enterprise agreements with respect to liners and industry standards with respect to safety (based on Lloyds insurance);
- international conventions: intergovernmental cooperation on mainly technical and some economic matters.

10.2.4 Organizations

In the course of the post-war period, a number of organizations have emerged under the auspices of (specialized agencies of) the UN that deal with one or other of the public goods that we have just defined. These are:

- *International Maritime Organization (IMO).* This organization was created in 1958. The IMO deals mostly with technical (or non-economic) matters, such as standards for construction in order to improve safety, traffic rules in order to avoid collisions, and environmental standards to avoid pollution.[4] At its creation it became the custodian of a series of existing conventions and has since worked on new regulations.
- *Geneva Convention on the high seas.* The first United Nations Conference on the Law of the Seas held in 1958 specified the competences of the coastal (or port) states (countries where the ship calls or passes) and the flag states (countries of registration of the ship) to implement international rules.
- *Code for liner conferences.* The instrument was adopted in 1974 by UNCTAD and entered into force in 1983. Its objective was to counteract the power of the major liner conferences that were all based in industrialized countries. The arrangement aimed at serving the interests of developing countries by reserving part of the market for their own shipping companies. To that end the '40–40–20' rule was introduced. This rule split up the total traffic into 40 per cent reserved for liners from the importing country, 40 per cent for liners from the exporting country and 20 per cent for liners coming from third countries.

Apart from these intergovernmental bodies there are also some private organizations. The first is the Comité Maritime International, an organization of international maritime lawyers founded in 1897. Its purpose is to formulate draft conventions on primarily private aspects of maritime law. Much of its work is given legal form through the IMO. Next to this are a number of industry associations that try to influence regime setting. Of particular importance is the International Chamber of Shipping in London, composed of national ship-owners associations. It focuses mainly on commercial issues.

10.2.5 Governance

The main instruments by which the national governments make sure that the regime in question is implemented are distributed over the home and destination country as follows:

10.2.5.1 The flag states

- Registration of the ship (after check on technical norms);
- All aspects of commercial and operational performance (including maintenance);
- Promotion of national interest for commercial and strategic reasons;
- Clarity about applicable legislation on board while on voyage.

10.2.5.2 The coastal states

- Full sovereignty over access and use of ports and coastal waters;
- Freedom of navigation, so no discretionary national norms about aspects of labour, environment and safety, etc. However, coastal states have the right and obligation to implement generally accepted international norms in these matters.

10.2.6 Evaluation and outlook

The regime has mainly two elements. The first is technical. Now the need for technical cooperation and regulation is obvious and we will not discuss its adequacy in this book on economics. The second part of the regime regulates markets. This part no longer seems to be adequate, as it maintains many aspects of protection. Such limitation of markets to specific nationalities is at odds with the general tendency towards liberalization. Moreover, the arguments that justified this protection in the past no longer hold. Indeed, the security and competition arguments are no more valid in the case of sea transport than in many other cases, such as food supplies or telecommunications. The development argument does not seem to carry much weight either, as witness the fact that the UNCTAD code has never been widely adopted, and has even declined in importance, as many countries have in the meantime phased it out.

So it seems that a separate regime is no longer needed and that sea shipping could very well become part of the WTO. This is notably the case now that the WTO has made arrangements about services in general and sectors such as telecommunications in particular.

10.3 Air transport

10.3.1 Introduction

The air transport industry has grown from very small beginnings at the start of the twentieth century into a large sector of economic activity. Although more and more freight (notably high value or urgent goods) travels by air, the main purpose of air transport is passenger transport. In international passenger traffic the airplane has almost completely displaced other modes, such as the ocean liner.

The growth of the industry has been stimulated by a considerable technological development. Airplanes have increased in size and the comfort offered; they travel much faster, while at the same time costs have decreased (see Figure 2.1). The total number of passengers has increased considerably over the past century. Moreover, the distribution has changed: the share of the US and EU has decreased relative to that of South Asia.

The services offered can, for all practical purposes, be divided into scheduled flights and charter flights. The latter are often operated by specialist companies. Recently, the distinction has become somewhat blurred as many links operated by charter have become so frequent that they resemble scheduled flights.

Air transport is dependent on the efficient operation of airports. Given the huge investments needed and the diversity and magnitude of the external effects of such investments, the public sector has mostly taken responsibility for this part of the infrastructure.

10.3.2 The problems

The problems that occur in the air transport industry are mainly of three types:

- Safety in the air depends on the technical quality of the aircraft, on the possibility to prevent accidents and to deal with political risks (terrorist attacks and hijacking);
- Pollution has become a major problem as air transport contributes to emission of greenhouse gases (see Chapter 9), while aircraft bring problems of noise and air pollution during take off and landing.
- Access to commerce has been a point of concern for many governments as the US dominance in air transport after the Second World War has been overwhelming.

10.3.3 Public goods and regime

A number of historical events have shaped the type of solution that governments have found to the problems of the emerging air industry. The air transport industry has been considered to be a public good for the same type of reasons as sea transport (although the specifics are different for the two modes):

- *Security*. In the First World War, aviation had shown how effective it could be in warfare. Countries established their exclusive sovereignty over the national air space, implying the authority to grant or deny permission to fly over their country and or to land at their airports and to pick up passengers.
- *Safety*. Consumers can judge neither the quality of the service nor that of the equipment. So governments have set norms that suppliers have to meet in order to limit the possibility of technical or human failure. These include standards that are designed to make technical specifications of aircraft and ground facilities match.
- *Environment*. In order to prevent pollution, national governments set limits to noise levels and exhaust gases.
- *Quality of links*. Every country considered it in its national interest to participate in international air communications. They stimulated national

aviation companies for economic and prestige reasons (flag carriers). The control of national air space was an important instrument in this respect.

The international regime that has evolved under these conditions bears some resemblance in its structure to sea transport. It is based on two basic principles:

- Open access to air space above the high seas (international oceans);
- Joint sovereignty: by nature the industry is dependent on two (home and destination) states to permit an air flight service. The destination state has the lead here as it controls access.

Other basic characteristics of the regime are:

- National policies: flag state jurisdiction over aircraft wherever they fly. State control over its air space and landings;
- Bilateral agreements between countries: these concern the number of flights (detailing the type of aircraft, etc.) awarded to the airline of each country. So the nationality of the airline determines market access;
- Private: inter-company agreements (code sharing, repair, other);
- International conventions (mainly technical harmonization and recognition of standards: only very limited economic agreements)
- Dependent on the policy of the country, one or more of the so-called freedoms may be awarded (see Box 10.2).

In other words, the regime (established by the Chicago Convention, see next section) 'recognises each contracting states' complete and exclusive sovereignty over the airspace above its territory, the requirement that aircraft should have a nationality by being registered in one particular state and the consequent need for aircraft registered in any state to obtain the permission of a state in order to operate air services to or from its territory' (Button and Stough, 2000: 63).

10.3.4 Organizations

The centerpiece of the international regime for civil aviation consists of bilateral agreements of national governments on allocation of the links between the two countries to airlines of their countries (agreements of the Bermuda Conference of 1946). This regime is not administered by a specialist organization. There are two international organizations that deal with international aviation matters, but from a different perspective:

- *ICAO.* The International Civil Aviation Organization resulted from the Chicago convention of 1947. It acts now as a specialist body of the UN.

> *Box 10.2* **The eight freedoms in civil aviation**
>
> Liberalization in the international air transport industry has been a slow process. It is entirely dependent on the degree to which national governments accept limits to their full control. The following steps are usually distinguished (also called first, second, etc. freedoms). They provide the right of an aircraft of one country to:
>
> 1 Innocent passage over the territory of another country
> 2 Stop in another country (while on route to a third country) for refuelling, technical assistance, etc.
> 3 Fly from home state (state of registry) to destination state
> 4 Fly from destination state to home state
> 5 Fly between two foreign states on a route beginning and ending in home state
> 6 Carry traffic between two foreign countries via its home state, i.e. a combination of freedoms 3 and 4
> 7 Operate stand alone services between two foreign states with no links to the home state
> 8 Operate a service between two points within the territory of a foreign state
>
> The international situation as to the degree to which these 'freedoms' have been attributed is very complex. The most far-reaching multilateral liberalization has occurred internally in the EU. The most far-reaching bilateral international agreements are the ones concluded between the US and other countries in the framework of so-called 'open skies' agreements.

Its main purpose was to set technical standards and procedures so as to enhance safety. It has over time also assumed some functions in terms of exchange of information on commercial matters.

• *IATA*. The International Air Transport Association was created in 1945. Members are air companies. As most of them were monopolists in their own country, the IATA quickly developed into a cartel of national monopolists that organized the market by making agreements covering fares, frequency of flights, type of aircraft, services on board and commercial practices. IATA activities were organized by regions (compare conferences in sea transport). There are two types of members, those who participate in the full range of coordination just mentioned and those who participate only in facilitation.

The difference between the intergovernmental set-up of the ICAO and the private organization IATA quickly became blurred. As governments were often the only or the major shareholder of the aviation company involved they tended to set the terms for the commercial negotiations conducted by the directors of the companies. Moreover, as deals that had been reached in the IATA had very important economic effects, governments required that these deals be submitted for their approval. The result was that governments had a very significant influence in the dealings of an organization that in principle was meant to be a private company.

10.3.5 Governance

The main instrument, with which governments control the present regime (Richards, 2001) are similar to the ones used in sea transport:

10.3.5.1 Flag states

- Registration of the aircraft and check on technical norms, etc.;
- Legal control over the aircraft while flying (safety, security, etc.);
- Stimulation of the commercial interest of the carrier by either ownership or at least strategic control.

10.3.5.2 Airport states

- Control of access to their country of foreign aircraft;
- Application of international norms to specific aspects having an effect on market positions such as environmental norms (noise and pollution);
- Control of other services, such as airports, ground services, connecting transport and rules for their use.

10.3.6 Evaluation and outlook

The regime for air transport[5] is at odds with the principles that govern trade of most other services branches. There has been increasing pressure over the last decades to also apply these general principles of trade to air transport. The main problem with the present situation is that the tangle of bilateral agreements precludes the realization of international mergers of airliners (Hanlon, 1999: 257–62). As in other industries these mergers are needed to rationalize operations, to cut costs and to improve service. However, under the present rules an international merger would oblige the respective 'tutor' governments to resolve a very complicated game, whereby one government has to leave its sovereignty to another government that has to renegotiate the whole list of bilateral agreements. Implied in this is the risk of losing a series of links.

A global open skies agreement would be in line with the regime aspired to for other services. The 50th anniversary conference of the ICAO in 1994 was devoted to this subject, but could not come up with an agreement. It was not feasible due to diverging positions:

- The US is in favour as it thinks that many of its companies can be the centrepiece of the new global companies.
- The EU countries are divided on the issue. The Commission wants to regionalize the issue as it thinks it would add to efficiency.
- Many countries in the developing world are opposed, as they fear being marginalized by the major powers.

A partial solution to this problem has been to conclude global alliances between airlines. All major companies are now members of such an alliance; the major advantage is that code sharing induces international passengers to stay with companies of the alliance for the whole trip. The problem this creates is one of competition; and in the absence of an international regime on competition (see Chapter 11) national authorities have in different ways been trying to come to grips with the intricacies of the operations of alliances (Oum *et al.*, 2000: 185–92).

So a new regime is needed implying a considerable liberalization of the international links and greater commercial freedom for airliners to organize their operations in line with demand. The set-up of this new regime could actually benefit from the experience with liberalization of national air traffic in many large countries (US) and in (groups of) national states (EU).

10.4 Telecommunications

10.4.1 Introduction

The sector of telecommunications has seen very important technical changes over the past centuries. In the middle of the nineteenth century the wired telegraph expanded very fast over the major countries of the world. By the end of the same century telephone communications over wired networks started to develop. In the twentieth century radio communications started, notably for specific purposes such as communications between ships. After the Second World War telephone communications took over as the dominant technology, irrespective of the mode of linkage. The development of telecommunications was boosted by the development of computers and the ensuing digitalization. It greatly enhanced the possibilities for transmission of speech, data and video. Capacity of transmission was greatly enhanced by the development of satellites, mobile phones and fibre-optic cables. As indicated in Chapter 2, these revolutionary developments dramatically reduced the cost of communication.

These profound technological changes did not bring a change in the market structure however. Supply of telecom services had been generally seen as a natural monopoly (on the basis of the need for a cable network). In order to prevent abuse, most countries had decided to operate the telecom services by a public (nationalized) company or government agency. The justification for this choice was corroborated by a number of other factors. First, the interest states took in the uninterrupted provision of a vital 'public' service. Second, to make possible cross-subsidization of peripheral users by users in dense areas.

The need for international communications led to the creation of international organizations (see Chapter 2), notably the International Telecommunications Union (ITU), which quickly developed into a cartel of national monopolies. These persisted for over a century, from the mid-nineteenth century up to the 1980s. They agreed on every important aspect of the regime: principles, ownership of joint facilities, prices, etc.

A major tendency towards liberalization has changed the picture profoundly. It has changed telecommunications from a public service into a regular market service. There are a number of factors that explain the emergence of this wave of liberalization:

- The technical reason for a natural monopoly has been eroded by innovations such as wireless mobile phones and satellites.
- The competition reason has been shown to be at best of limited value. Indeed, many natural monopolies soon turned out to be inefficient service providers. On the one hand, they permitted rent seeking by specific groups (trade unions for labour conditions, politicians for favouring certain types of access of positions). On the other hand, they permitted politics to interfere in both access to service and price of the service.
- Lack of competition also meant a lack of innovation in the type of services provided. This point became particularly important when it was realized that a cheap and diverse supply of telecommunication services was an essential prerequisite for participation in the information society, the area where the best chances were for employment growth.

The tendency towards liberalization that showed itself so powerful at the national level soon showed its effect on the international level. New service providers no longer accepted being governed by the old cartel. The corollary was that governments accepted creation of the same conditions at the international level they thought necessary on the national level. It meant a split in the functions of the international organizations: the ITU remained responsible for technical matters, but the market-oriented aspects were considered by an increasing number of nations as a classical service and hence were transferred to the WTO.

From a historical perspective it is interesting to study the former regime for telecommunications. However, for our purposes it seems more beneficial to leave this behind and to concentrate on the regime that is in the process of being elaborated. Consequently, we will focus on the present and future aspects in the following sections.

10.4.2 The problems

The problems that occur in the telecommunications industry are mostly of the following types:

- Technical and procedural barriers can lead to lack of possibility to connect the various national telecommunication systems and hence to loss of international services. Indeed, there is national ownership of the technical equipment on either side of the telecommunications network. So standardization is needed.
- Use of the global commons by one state does in some cases interfere with the use of others (damage control). Indeed, the available radio frequencies, the available orbits for satellites have a limited capacity.
- National states will want to control the activities that are executed within their territories. In some cases this has given rise to the jamming of what were considered propaganda messages from another state. This has become less easy in recent times as technical devices allow to circumvention of such controls in many instances.

10.4.3 Public goods and regime

The public goods of free flow of information and commerce (open communications) are furthered by the principles of:

- Open access to international spaces and equitable distribution of the global commons;
- Qualified open access to national spaces (similar to innocent passage);
- Free flow of information; no control of home state over content;
- Right of states to license activities to firms (both local and foreign).

In practice, the telecommunication regime consists essentially of three elements giving answers to the three most important problems, as cited in the previous section.

In the field of standardization, the regime has two dimensions:

- *System interconnection.* Systems in different states need to be able to work together in order to safeguard the free flow of content (free commerce). Governments and private providers have to conform to this basic rule in order to make sure that the international service can be established at all.
- *Equipment standardization.* This is mainly a question for the providers to make sure that the systems not only function, but that they function efficiently. Far-reaching standardization makes it possible to cut cost and to provide better services. This point has, however, been always very difficult to reach due to the big national industrial interests involved. They led many governments to protect their own equipment manufacturers by applying technical standards that the latter had developed. The progressive integration of computers and telecommunication has enhanced the need for an international standardization on many more points; that is not only for switching equipment between national systems, but also for domestic networks and terminals. Moreover, there is also a tendency to standardize central elements of the software.

In the field of damage control, there are also two major rules to observe:

- States register their use of specific frequencies with a special Board of the ITU and other states respect this 'prior use' right. This ensures that the use they make of them is not interfering with established rights.
- The necessary planning norm specifies that states have the obligation to coordinate (through ITU) their use of the spectrum with other states. Recently, technical innovations have meant that capacity has greatly increased, so that a much higher load in communications can actually be accommodated.

In the field of content control, the restricted intentional interference norm stipulates that states should refrain from jamming. Exceptions are allowed in case of the threat of peace, order and security of the state.

In the past the various governments have also cooperated in order to establish market shares, rate setting and dividing revenues. These have now, for the most part, been abolished or have become part of commercial transactions between the companies concerned.

10.4.4 Organizations

In the field of telecommunications, technology has determined to a large extent the emergence of international organizations. The major ones are:

10.4.4.1 ITU

The International Telecommunications Union was established in 1932. It merged the activities of other much older bodies that had regulated specific technologies, the most important example of them being the International Telegraph Union, created in 1865 (others covering telephone and radio). In 1947, the ITU became a specialized agency of the UN. The main task of the ITU is the setting of technical standards about equipment and use. However, because telecommunication firms were until recently almost universally public monopolies, aspects of a commercial nature also came to be dealt with by specialist committees.

10.4.4.2 WTO

The liberalized telecommunications industry has become the subject of specialist trade negotiations. In 1998 the agreement on basic telecommunication services came into effect (voice, fax and data). This means that the two basic rules of the WTO now apply to the telecom sector. Under the most favoured nation discipline, concessions given to telecom suppliers in one WTO member country must be offered to suppliers from all WTO countries. Under national treatment, foreign telecom service suppliers established in a country must be treated identically to a supplier from the home country. Moreover, an agreement has been reached on regulatory principles, covering subjects such as competition safeguards, interconnection guarantees, transparent licensing processes and the independence of regulators. The latter elements are introduced to ensure that market access is not nullified by an incumbent's (former monopolist) anticompetitive behaviour.

10.4.4.3 Private

Given the close relationship between national governments and national telecommunication companies, there was until recently no need for an IATA type of organization (see previous section) of private telecom business.

10.4.5 Governance

The instruments used to make the present international regime effective are very much dependent on the actions of national governments. The most important instrument in this respect is licensing. Given the importance of the quality of the service, the government may open up the market only to providers that respect certain technical (interconnectivity) and other rules (privacy). As there is, in general, only a limited capacity, governments will often auction the licences among the firms that qualify.

10.4.6 Evaluation and outlook

In the recent past a drastic change has occurred from a cartel of national monopolies to a free market for diversified services with many players. This change has had a profound impact on the international regime and international organizations.

Problems of technical standard setting on infrastructure will stay with the ITU. This is an important public good as interconnectivity is very important for all players and notably for the consumer. The more so because there is competition from some private firms that set their own business standards (from computers) and try to impose that on the market.

Market-oriented development of the international telecommunication regime will be undertaken through the WTO (GATS), which is responsible for telecommunications in the same way as it is for any other service.

10.5 Internet

10.5.1 Introduction

Technological change constantly brings possibilities for new products and services. The latest major event in this respect is the development of electronic data processing coupled with telecommunications. Soon after the emergence of the computer the need was felt for an exchange of data and information between computers. To that end, networks were created. It is no surprise that the first application was used in military matters. Linking the various networks (Internet) largely facilitated the exchange of strategic and operational information and saved cost of computer time. The advantages of a network soon became apparent to the research community. Later, other organizations (such as multinational firms) saw the strategic interests of intracompany linking of national computers.

With the spread of the personal computer, the network became more and more used for private purposes. Next, the business sector started to recognize its potential for intercompany information exchange and for commercial purposes. Now, the Internet is used not only for information and communication, but also for trading (so-called B2B (business to business)), shopping (so called B2C (business to consumer)), banking, studying, voting, etc.

A distinction should be made between carriage and content. The first relate to the communication infrastructure, it includes cables, computers, satellites, etc. Content comes technically in the form of text, pictures, sound, etc., and economically in the form of services such as advice, instruction, games, etc.

10.5.2 The problems

The very quick spread of the Internet has entailed a multifaceted set of problems (e.g. Graham, 2001). We have selected the following six for further scrutiny.

10.5.2.1 Dominance over content

The characteristics of the Internet mean that there is an increasing risk of commercial or special interest groups taking over control of certain parts of the net. This may lead to a *de facto* limitation of information. Limits to information may come from two other sources. The first is the Internet service provider. Most consumers are unlikely to subscribe to more than one. Some of these gateways are run as a largely integrated subweb with a wide range of services. Under such conditions consumers are unlikely to access other supply of services. The second is the browser. This determines what is found and what not. If the cost of switching is high, consumers can get locked into one system.

10.5.2.2 Dominance of market

There are very many companies active on the net and this would suggest that there is little chance of dominance. Yet cases such as Microsoft show that the danger is real. The problem becomes particularly acute when market power is connected to power over content. The negative effects are the ones usually related to lack of competition; consumers pay too much and innovation is retarded.

10.5.2.3 Provision of illegal goods and services

This is particularly important in case the service provider breaches fairly important and rather universal values and rules. Cases in point are paedophillia.

10.5.2.4 Cyber crime on commercial activities

Many people and firms now rely on the Internet to do business or to operate transactions. The net is the market place, but the transaction that is made there has to be followed by some physical delivery and the compensating financial transaction. Each element of this chain may be subject of fraud and crime; the quality of the good is not what has been promised; credit card numbers are used for other purposes (crime); money transferred is diverted, etc.

10.5.2.5 Breach of privacy of individuals

The exchange of information that is done for medical purposes brings with it the danger of these data coming into the hands of third parties. Other problems arise with the use of the data on patterns of personal preferences (including shopping, information search, etc.).

10.5.2.6 Tax evasion

The delivery of a service is subject in most countries to a sales or value added tax. Many of the transactions that are made on the net are of an international character. They may escape taxation in both the origin and destination country. This distorts competition (due to the higher market price that service providers who stay within the national area have to demand) and leads to the erosion of the tax base of national states.

10.5.3 Public goods and regime

The public good character of the Internet (looked at as a system) is a matter of debate. There are many arguments in favour and others against (Spar, 1999).

10.5.3.1 The arguments in favour are:

- *Non-excludability*. The system is there and everybody can use it, provided a minimum of technical means (PC, telephone, software) and willingness to pay for access facilities.
- *Non-rivalry*. The use by one does not preclude the use by others.

10.5.3.2   The arguments against are:

- *Excludability.* The net is increasingly commercialized. This implies that an increased number of services ask for pre-payment.
- *Rivalry.* Simultaneous use of the web by many customers produces congestion. This can be avoided by paying for enhanced services.

However, the previous section has made clear that many aspects of the functioning of the Internet have a public 'bad' character. So avoiding them provides as many public goods. We can list them in line with the six public bads from the previous section as follows:

- *Diversity of sources of information.* The Internet provides an unprecedented means of instant information gathering at very low cost. It opens possibilities such as tele-education. The right of access of citizens to such diverse sources of information is certainly a public good.
- *Good functioning of the market.* Fundamental to the market economy is fair competition. The new forms under which competition presents itself in the Internet world needs further analysis and, based on the result thereof, new regulation needs to be elaborated.
- *Absence of illegal services.* Countries wanting to protect their citizens from attacks on certain values will want to block the transmission of offensive material such as publicity for drugs or information about terrorist methods. They will want to prevent children being confronted with hard pornography. Although a number of such cases are clear universal public goods, many others are subject to considerable controversy. Indeed, values differ and what seems part of the basic rights in one civilization may constitute an offence to public morale in another (drinking alcohol). The universal character of the Internet here poses a clear challenge to policy-makers.
- *Smooth functioning of e-commerce.* The Internet opens a whole set of possibilities for new types of business. It brings down cost of transaction to many users (efficiency criterion). Moreover, it presents opportunities for improved distribution: firms that are located in distant places will now be connected in a similar way to potential partners as those in central locations. This also holds for developing countries that have better chances for catching up as the Internet puts very low demands on cost of infrastructure.
- *Safeguarding of the privacy of individuals and firms.* The public good character of privacy is clear from the very strict laws that some countries have passed on the subject. However, there is controversy about this point as some countries consider that the 'excessive' protection of the individual constitutes an undue limit to normal commercial practices, on the one hand, and on the capacity of the state to safeguard security, on the other.

- *Capacity to tax*. Governments need to fulfil certain tasks. To that end they need income. Their most important source of income is taxes. Lack of tax income means loss of public goods provision. The equitable distribution of taxes is certainly also considered a public good as it determines the solidarity of citizens.

If there are so many public good aspects involved, the question then is 'Should one intervene or not?' In the first instance, intervention would imply public regulation.[6]

Arguments for intervention are that regulation:

- Prevents public bads, such as paedophillia and loss of privacy. Prevention cannot be effectively done with other means;
- Stimulates the type of technical progress (filtering of information) and legal progress (effective regulation) that is necessary for bringing things forward (compare the provision of environmental public goods (Chapter 7)).

Arguments against intervention are that regulation is:

- *Bad economics*. Bridling market forces, while unleashing them would produce growth of new services and hence overall growth. Moreover, it risks fossilizing structures that may only have a temporary value[7] given the great uncertainty as to the direction of development of the system.
- *Unconstitutional*. People have the right of free speech and gathering of information; public surveillance of information access can give rise to larger problems than leaving it free.
- *Ineffective*. Even if one would like to regulate it, it would not work as people can always circumvent regulations.
- *Unneeded*. Self-regulation has (for the time being) worked out rather well.
- *Unfeasible*. Bringing all states together would be a too lengthy process and the chances of it leading to any good solution are limited.

Given the debates described, it is clear that reaching an international consensus will be faced with many problems. For the moment, the design principles for any regime are not yet very clear. However, the actual situation would imply that the most important principles are:

- Free flow of information: no bridling even where important negative aspects prevail;
- Self-regulation instead of state jurisdiction.

10.5.4 Organizations

The Internet has until now been largely aloof of public regulation. The present regime was developed rather bottom up. Its rules are the result of consensus building among its users. This has been made possible as the initial users and designers of the Internet were notably engineers and computer scientists who had their strong professional codes and shared understandings.

- *IETF*. The process of policy formulation is largely carried out by the Internet Engineering Task Force and by the World Wide Web Consortium. These bodies function as online communities of interested parties and are in charge of the development of technical standards, such as communication protocols.
- *ICANN*. The problem of names is dealt with by the Internet Corporation of Assigned Names and Numbers (ICANN). It is a hybrid form of an online community (such as IETF) and a traditional government structure. It comprises accredited organizations such as the World Intellectual Property Organization.

So far this original decision-making structure has proven remarkably robust, notwithstanding some inherent flaws. The question is however, whether this self-regulation can survive in view of the importance of the public good elements involved.

Two types of solutions have been tried out to cope with this problem:

- *National governments* try to regulate access to parts of the Internet. However, national regulation can in the end not be the solution; on the contrary, the diversity of the sort of regulation may actually constitute a new problem.
- *Private initiative*. Companies provide software for multinational firms that is capable of checking compliance with the rules of the countries where they are working. However, this increases the cost to business without removing the problem.

So the conclusion must be that it is increasingly necessary to come to harmonization of the national regulations and to rethink governance of the Internet, including international regulatory institutions and codes of conduct. For the time being, these have not, however, been crystallizing. The organizational set-up is not clear but given the capacity of the ITU to adapt to new technologies in the past, one could think of adapting the structures of the ITU to accommodate this new technology too.

10.5.5 Governance

The tools that governments have in making sure that the provision of the six basic public goods identified in the previous section are safeguarded come in a number of categories. They take as their point of departure either the possibilities of technology (including software) or legal measures. Most basic in this respect is, however, the physical infrastructure; if this is lacking or not sufficiently developed, the safeguarding of all the public goods can only be realized by the (public) provision of the necessary infrastructure.

- *Dominance over content.* A first instrument to be used in this respect is regulation. Governments may oblige providers to realize a minimum of interconnectivity, so that consumers are not trapped in a subsystem. Moreover, they may step in with public production in case the private market shows important failures. Comparable cases are public broadcasting.
- *Dominance of market.* The instruments that government have on this score form part of the regular competition policy. They are not typical for the Internet. The specific features of the Internet make their application far from easy however (Graham, 2001; Cave and Mason, 2001). That is why the international harmonization of national competition regimes has a very high relevance in the case of the Internet (see Section 11.4 on competition).
- *Provision of illegal goods, services and information.* Here, the main instrument is of a technical nature. It consists of the filtering of information that can be accessed by the users of Internet. Some governments have tried to do such filtering themselves, such as the Chinese. Others (like the French) have tried to implement policy with this instrument by obliging the providers to comply with national law and make sure they do the filtering.
- *Safeguarding e-commerce.* A part of the instrument is of legal character; that is, the recognition of such elements as the electronic signature. Most of the instrument is again of a technological nature. Firms wanting to make sure that the partners they deal with are sound have to accept identification rules and verification rules that pass through specific devices on their computers. Governments may oblige Internet firms to apply standardized devices.
- *Safeguarding privacy of individuals.* Here, technical devices (including software) is essential. Governments should make sure that providers of access to the Internet do apply such software. A first start in this sense has already been made for the EU.[8] The USA is against such measures but the EU and the USA have agreed to disagree on the subject.
- *Avoidance of tax evasion.* The only way to make sure that trade over the net is taxed in the same way as trade in traditional form is by countries coming to agreement. Recently, the OECD has made a code on the subject and it is likely that more will follow.

10.5.6 Evaluation and outlook

The Internet is still in the early stages of its development. The world has not yet come to grips with the dilemma it presents to society. It permits instant global switching of information and in that sense does away with

geography. Many feel that in this sense it has done away also with territori-
ally based laws. In the absence of international regulation many global
public goods are not provided.

However, we may expect that as the latter become more precisely defined
and the effects of instruments better assessed, a regime that goes beyond
the present one of merely user-driven codes is likely to emerge. Given the
lessons learnt in the previous chapters and sections, this regime will
probably first take the form of a set of agreements among the most concerned states, followed by a light form of international organization.

10.6 Summary and conclusions

- There are considerable differences between the various regimes for
  transport and telecommunications. The regime for sea transport came
  on top of a basically market-oriented activity. The one for air transport
  was set up under heavy government control right from the start. The
  one for telecommunications evolved under the logic of cooperation of
  national public monopolies. The Internet regime has been developed
  outside the control of government.
- The regimes integrate technical and economic aspects. The economic
  rationale for having specific regimes has practically vanished; in fact
  they all concern trade in services. For that reason they can best be
  brought under the auspices of the WTO.
- The Internet is a very special case of regime building. One may expect
  that over time the obvious public good aspects of the web will lead to a
  stronger influence of intergovernmental international organizations on
  its functioning.

Part IV

Evaluation

11 Complementing the system

11.1 Introduction

In the previous chapters we have described how the global system gradually evolved. In the distant past, the dominant feature of this system was a combination of national regimes complemented with some international additions. These additions have increased in importance as increasing globalization called for an increase in global regime building. We have described in detail the evolution of the global regimes that are directly impacting on the economy: trade in goods and services, finance, environment and finally transport and telecommunications.

Many observers have pointed to the deficiencies of the system and have suggested the filling in of some missing elements.[1] We consider that the present architecture is insufficient on two main scores.

The first concerns the missing elements of global markets of production factors; in practice, capital and labour. We will go into these aspects in the first two sections of this chapter; for capital we concentrate on investment, for labour we concentrate on the freedom to move (in other words, migration).

The second element that needs to be covered better is the conditions under which markets function. The most pressing need for some form of global regime building is in matters of competition. The second is in matters of labour standards and social policy. We will deal with these issues in the last two sections.

As before, this chapter will be rounded of in a short section that gives the major conclusions and an outlook into the future.

11.2 Production factors: investment[2]

11.2.1 Why investment?

As evidenced in Chapter 2, FDI (foreign direct investment) has grown very rapidly over the past decades. This is the consequence of the progressive liberalization of FDI flows, as many countries have unilaterally done away with restrictions on incoming FDI. The rationale of these policies can be found in the better allocation of resources that this provides, benefiting both the industrialized countries that are the major source of FDI and the developing countries that are increasingly important as a host for FDI.

The importance of FDI for the present world economy is evidenced in the annual World Investment Report published by UNCTAD. Table 11.1 gives an idea of the present importance of FDI in the global economy.

One sees that the size of FDI has grown much faster than GDP and that it has engendered similar growth of the total international production. For the developing countries, FDI is of particular relevance as over the past decade it accounted for the lion's share of total capital flows to these countries.

11.2.2   The anatomy of the problem: the changing character of international investment

The liberalization policies of individual countries and of regional group-ings (such as the EU and NAFTA) have created a situation in which much of the global FDI flows are now practically free. This is definitely the case for the developed countries and also, to some extent, for many developing countries. However, liberalization is not a panacea. Presently, FDI is mainly confronted by two types of problems:

*   *Barriers.* There are still many obstacles to FDI. Many of these come in the form of so-called performance requirements, obliging the MNF, for instance, to minimum levels of local procurement or to transfer of certain technologies. Even where FDI is liberalized by national policy, a problem of credibility remains. Indeed, as long as this policy is not locked into a multilateral commitment, it can unilaterally be suspended.
*   *Distortions.* The main problem is the behind-border government influence on investment. As FDI is of critical importance for develop-ment and as FDI tends to locate in countries with particularly favourable conditions, many governments of areas that show less favour-able conditions have set up incentive schemes to attract investors. Governments tend to compete for FDI with incentive schemes (sub-sidies and other advantages, e.g. tax relief or R&D subsidies). Such

Table 11.1 FDI and foreign production (billions of $)

Year	1982	1990	2001
FDI inflows	59	203	735
Total assets of foreign affiliates	1959	5759	24,952
Exports of foreign affiliates	670	1169	2600
Gross domestic product	10,805	21,672	31,900

Source: UNCTAD, 2002.

schemes are justified by developed countries on the basis of regional restructuring policy and by developing countries on the basis of growth stimulation. A problem may also be that they are combined with relaxation of standards of labour and environment.

The way in which different governments have responded is often inconsistent, which increases cost and uncertainty for international investors.

11.2.3 The need for a regime

The relevance of a comprehensive regime for international investments has been identified on several occasions.[3] However, in the first instance, most attention went into the direction of the most pressing problem, which is some form of international insurance against actions of host governments that could jeopardize the value of the FDI (mostly expropriation). The combination of liberalization to do away with barriers and the setting of common standards to limit distortions can be seen as an important public good.

Some doubt the need for an international regime. They consider, on the one hand, that countries that want to attract investment have no interest in preferring one origin to another. They consider, on the other hand, that MNF have anyway to come to grips with the intricacies of the legal and regulatory system of the country they invest in, so that the transaction cost argument should not be exaggerated. They say that MNFs can, in many cases, negotiate a regime that is as favourable as the best one available worldwide. Moreover, a number of countries have unilaterally set a regime of protection *ergo omnes* that does away with the transaction cost of individual negotiations. These arguments seem to apply to countries that can provide a good institutional environment. However, it does not do away with the credibility gap that countries with a poor record face if they want to pass towards international norms for good governance. Finally, national codes and even more discretion open possibilities for corruption; a problem that has been found to inhibit seriously economic growth of LDCs.

Assuming that the national option is not sufficient, we see that multi-lateral action is needed. The locking in of national reforms by a credible external commitment to a multilateral framework will enhance the confidence that investors have in the continuity of the regime. It can also help to achieve other goals, such as reduction of corruption, money laundering and tax evasion.

Of course, these advantages in regime building come at a cost; that is, a reduction of sovereignty, in other words with the capacity of national and local governments to choose the combinations of policy measures. The cost–benefit relation may be more advantageous in a regional (e.g. EU) setting than in a global setting.

A FDI regime will typically be designed on the basis of the following principles:

- *Freedom of entry.* Giving foreign firms the right to invest in the host country.
- *National treatment.* Foreign firms will be treated in the same way as local firms.
- *Most favoured nation treatment.* The host country will not discriminate between investors coming from different nations.

However, this is not all that is needed to set up a regime for international investment. Host governments and home governments of MNFs are often very much concerned about the possibilities of these MNFs to elude national regulation on taxes due to transfer pricing systems that favour tax havens. They thus tend to set specific rules for MNFs to avoid such behaviour. Together, these give rise to a tangle of different rules on the global level, increasing transaction costs for MNFs. A multilateral regime that provides international rules on accounting, corporate governance, tax, and repatriation of funds can bring down such transaction costs and is therefore an important public good.

11.2.4 Organizations

The most important rules at this moment with respect to foreign direct investment come from the following international organizations.

11.2.4.1 ICC

The International Chamber of Commerce is an organization of private enterprise that has over the post-war period worked on the issue. In 1972, this resulted in guidelines for international investors, giving recommendations for both investors and host governments.

11.2.4.2 IBRD

In order to provide insurance against political risks for investments the World Bank set up the Multilateral Investment Guarantee Agency in 1988, which has been joined by over 100 countries since then. The notion of political risk covers a number of categories: currency restrictions, repudiation of contracts, expropriation and armed conflict.

11.2.4.3 OECD

The OECD has a long history in this respect. This begins with the 1961 codes on the liberalization of current investment transactions and on the liberalization of capital movements. In 1976 there followed the national treatment instrument. The OECD guidelines for multinational enterprises are a set of recommendations (which means they have no binding character and form no legal obligation) by the governments of the OECD countries to MNFs operating in their countries. They ask firms to behave not only in accordance with rules and laws of the host countries, but also to respect certain standards concerning such diverse issues as environment, competition, industrial relations, etc. The OECD has gone beyond this by setting up the Multilateral Agreement on Investment (MAI) (Witherell, 1995). However, the draft of this agreement fell victim to anti-globalist forces (see Box 11.1).[4]

11.2.4.4 WTO

The WTO has concluded the Trade-Related Investment Measures (TRIM) as part of the Uruguay round package. The agreement obliges countries to provide market access and limits the range of performance requirements. It mostly addresses trade-distorting policies; not so much investment issues. The TRIM has left many ambiguities and therefore the implementation is far from perfect. Mostly developing countries have difficulties with the obligations.

Box 11.1 The MAI: an aborted FDI regime

The background to the agreement

In 1991, the OECD ministerial conference asked two working groups to study the feasibility of a multilateral framework for investment. In 1995, official negotiations started for a Multilateral Agreement on Investment (MAI). The idea was to establish a treaty that would set high standards of protection and rights for foreign investors. To that end, the group of negotiating partners was limited to OECD members (accounting for some 90 per cent of outgoing foreign direct investment around the world). Other partners would be invited to join the agreement later if they so wished. In 1997, negotiations resulted in a draft text.

The characteristics of the MAI

This draft for the MAI had the following characteristics:

- *Free standing*. The MAI would not be part of any of the present international organizations. It would rather take the form of an agreement among signatories, more or less like the GATT (see Chapters 6 and 7).

- *Comprehensive*. Covering all types of investment (both cross-border establishment of enterprises; portfolio investment and intangible assets); all sectors of activity, all phases of investment (before and after establishment, privatisation, etc.) and applying obligations to all levels of government (federal, national and local).
- *Principles*. Signatories have to observe both 'national treatment' and 'most favoured nation treatment'. In order to safeguard the application of these principles, rules of transparency have been set.
- *Protection*. It would provide the highest standards of treatment of investors against expropriation and disturbances, such as armed conflict. Free transfer should be given to all payments related to the operation.
- *Evolutionary*. Liberalization was to be progressive; the protection of important national interest would be safeguarded.
- *Balanced*. MNFs have to recognize societal concerns, such as environmental protection and labour standards. They have to conform, moreover, to the standards of the host country in terms of responsible corporate citizenship.
- *Performance requirements*. Prohibition of setting conditions concerning the transfer of technology: R&D, location of headquarters, employment of locals, domestic content, local purchases, exports, etc.[5]
- *Dispute settlement mechanism*. Disputes between states were to be settled by an arbitral panel. Disputes between states and MNFs were to be settled by arbitration in accordance with international commercial regimes (such as the one of the International Chamber of Commerce).
- *Safeguards, exceptions, etc.* Possibility to maintain certain regimes that are not in conformity with MAI. Possibility of dispensation of capital movements in the event of serious balance of payments difficulties.

The causes for the lack of success

During the negotiations, cooperation was restricted to governments that had a collective interest in an orderly regime. A number of other stakeholders had been kept informed but had stayed on the sidelines. On the basis of the progress made, one might have thought that the MAI negotiations would have been concluded successfully. However, things took a quite different course as the result of the development of the positions of both supporters and opponents.

Traditional support for multilateral liberalization of investment came from the business community. Such support was given to the negotiators during the process, notably through the business and industry advisory committee of the OECD. However, in the wake of the increased criticism, this coalition of industries broke down and support for the MAI vanished. A possible reason for this was that much of the interests of MNFs had already been realized with the GATT/WTO trade liberalization. Further efforts to have the MAI recognized were thought to bring only limited returns. A consideration in this respect may have been that the large MNFs are able to exert strong pressure on individual governments for obtaining the tailor-made advantages they wish for investing in a particular location. Here, the immediate private interest of firms seemed to have been more important than the longer-term collective interest of a good regime.

The opposition to the draft text came essentially from two groups:

- *Developing countries*. LDCs were confronted with an awkward dilemma. Accepting the MAI in the form presented would remove the possibility of using certain instruments they think of as essential to reaching policy goals. Staying outside would make them lose attractiveness for incoming FDI and the ensuing possibilities for growth.
- *NGOs*. A rainbow coalition of pressure groups considered that the consequences of the MAI would be disastrous, as it would guarantee to MNFs the possibility of realizing its investments, without governments and civil society having the possibility to check the environmental, labour and societal consequences of such investments.

The opponents launched a very heavy attack on the texts. They used the MAI as a focal point for their criticism of the insufficiencies of the whole multilateral economic system and on the way decisions were made about that system. They were able to mobilize much political support in the negotiating countries. In view of this internal opposition, some governments withdrew their support. These defectors to the plan notably comprised those who had reservations with respect to parts of the text and those who considered that many of the advantages could also be grasped by bilateral and other deals anyway.

In the face of this strong opposition, neither the business community nor the governments saw a sufficient need for committing themselves to a binding multilateral agreement. The whole process petered out and the draft text of the MAI has not been submitted for ratification. It has only served the purpose of clarifying the issues and helping negotiators of other bilateral and regional arrangements to come to conclusions.

11.2.4.5 UN

The strenuous relations between host governments and MNFs induced the UN to work out a code of conduct on transnational corporations. The code gives recommendations with respect to issues such as: ownership, taxation, industrial relations, technology transfer, etc.

11.2.4.6 Regional

Many regional arrangements (in particular, the EU and NAFTA) contain rules for FDI (see, for example, Brewer and Young, 1996)

11.2.5 What should a new regime look like?

Given the shortcomings of the present system, a global comprehensive regime for investment is a desirable goal. However, the failure of the MAI will make it extremely difficult to reiterate the same type of set-up as long as conditions do not change significantly. We have seen that a number of the questions could be attacked from a different angle. The most important ones are:

- *Sectoral.* The WTO has already integrated some of issues related to FDI for a limited number of sectors. The suggestion that the WTO might be the framework for a series of other investment agreements and thereby would develop gradually into a more comprehensive trade and investment organization is a realistic option. The WTO Doha conference has recognized the case for a multilateral framework to secure transparent, stable and predictable conditions for long-term cross-border investment. It should reflect in a balanced manner the interests of host and home countries. Negotiations will begin shortly.
- *Regional.* Regional arrangements (e.g. EU, NAFTA) are a second-best solution. They provide geographical subsets of investors the type of protection that they were seeking through the MAI. This protection may include investor state dispute settlement systems.

Does the regional solution imply many foregone benefits if compared with the global one? Some observers think that the risk of regional agreements creating a harmful discrimination to third parties is probably less important than in the case of trade.

11.3 Production factors: migration

11.3.1 Why migration?

In economics the major markets are those of goods and services, on the one hand, and those of production factors, on the other. In the latter we distinguish capital and labour. In matters of global regime we see that the WTO covers most of the international trade in goods and services, while the IMF covers international flows of capital only in a very limited way. We saw in the previous section that attempts to come to a regime for FDI have not yet materialized. For labour, the situation is even less developed. On the point of international movement of persons (labour), there is at this moment at best only an embryonic regime.

The question, 'How to deal with international migration?' gets quite different answers depending on the ideological basis from which it is approached (compare the social embeddedness in Chapter 5). To individualists, the freedom to migrate is seen as an unalienable right. To those who put the interest of the community first, the migration decision resembles that of becoming a member of a club; the individual applies and the club can put conditions on individuals before accepting them.[6]

To the economist, there is a clear advantage of openness, that is international migration will, according to textbooks, improve the allocation of labour and thereby increase overall welfare. This would lead to the adoption of the principle of free movement of persons. However, this macro view does not take into account two major aspects. One is the distribution of benefits and cost. For those whose source of income is threatened by immigration, there is a cost and they will oppose immigration. Moreover, there are important externalities to migration that bring additional cost and benefits, and challenge the assumptions of the macro neoclassical theory (e.g. brain drain for developing countries and the further concentration of wealth in a limited number of areas). The results from empirical economic studies into the effects of immigration are not conclusive,[7] and thus leave considerable room for political arguments to shape the policy. So the conclusion is that migration is only beneficial for all concerned under specific conditions.

In the following sections we will go somewhat further into the dynamics of international labour movements, into the public good aspects of a regime for labour and into the reasons why up till now international institutional development has not got off the ground. Finally, we will give some idea about the possible set-up of a new international regime.[8]

11.3.2 The anatomy of the problem: the changing character of international migration

Over the past decades international migration has increasingly been felt as problematic for a whole series of reasons. The most important are:

- Mere size. Massive inflows have been registered for the major host countries, such as the US and the EU, but also for some developing countries. Emigration movements are driven by problems of security (war), famine (climatic or environmental disasters), politics (repression of human rights) and economic factors.

- Unpredictable character. The huge variability in influx makes it extremely difficult for a host country to react adequately.
- Large number of origin countries. The increased diversity of immigrants increases the difficulties of integration for each host country. Migration movements stretch over the whole globe and are not confined to the same region. This is due to the increase in the possibilities of communication (mobile phones, television) and the decrease in transport cost.
- Illegal situation of many (some estimate at one-fifth) of the immigrants. Their mere presence poses a challenge to the basic principles of the rule of law in host countries. Moreover, they are thought to use public services while not contributing to their financing.
- Sense of insecurity by the present population of host countries, induced by evidence that some sending countries tend to stimulate the emigration of criminal or terrorist elements.

To many, the problems caused by the present migration flows are only a foreshadow of what is to come. They point to the considerable potential for international migration that is building up. The three factors that determine migration (push, pull and friction) are all likely to lead to larger migration flows. The main push/pull factor is the very large difference in wealth levels between the most developed countries and the poorest ones. On the push side, we find the problems mentioned in the first bullet point of the previous paragraph. On the side of friction, we observe that the cost of communication and transport have significantly decreased, while the friction costs are lowered further due to the development of international traffickers who bring people by all sorts of means into the destination countries. On the pull side, there is in the developed countries a constant demand for immigrant labour coming from the black economy and from the group of activities that are threatened by international competition. Policies to stem migration by doing something on the causal factors tend to be rather ineffective; this goes both for development aid, sanctions on non-registered employment, etc.

11.3.3 The need for a regime

The conclusion of the previous section is that in the future the world will have to come to grip with a migration problem of considerable size and complexity. The present 'non'-regime is largely constituted by unilateral rules for immigration. The reason for this is that migration touches the heart of the national state. Indeed, each national state wants to keep the right to determine who will belong to its community and who will not. So, up till now, countries have preferred to do without a multilateral regime for migration.

This non-system is coming under increasing pressure, as it is apparently incapable of coping with the problems. The main failure is in the incapacity to control effectively migration flows. 'Once national governments close the front door of legal immigration more or less strictly, most of the entries take place through the side (asylum seekers, refugees, family reunification) or back door (illegals)' (Straubhaar, 2000). This is increasingly a problem in the sense that the nation state as a club can no longer provide the sort of good to the members of the club that these members expect from it. Illegal users challenge this exclusivity criterion, which leads to a rise in congestion cost for existing members without a corresponding decrease in the membership fee.

So, some sort of multilateral solution needs to be worked out. To see in which way this would be possible, it is necessary to look for the common interest of the participants. In the past, transaction cost could be minimized in a national setting, which is actually an institutional solution based on territorial exclusivity and legal rules for citizenship. Transaction cost theory (see Chapter 4) predicts that it will be easier to come to grips with the problems of openness that challenge this national state in a regional setting than within a multinational setting. This does not seem to lead to concrete actions though. The EU, for one, still struggles with the setting up of a common external regime, although it has passed some agreements with neighbouring countries to protect it from a too heavy pressure, notably of illegal immigrants. In America the same concern has led to some coordination between the US and Central American states.

However, as we have seen in one of the previous sections, these arrangements tend to be at best only partial solutions, as the migration problem is now really a worldwide phenomenon. So, multilateral solutions need to be worked out.

What would be the *objectives* of a new multilateral system? It would have to make sure that the flows of migration are indeed beneficial instead of disturbing. So the global public good in matters of migration is the prevention of negative economic effects. As these are not the same for all participants, the set-up of such a regime is not self-evident. There is a parallel here with capital movements: they are, in principle, welfare enhancing but under certain circumstances they lead to disturbances that can cause such damage that the principle of free movement cannot be accepted. That means that there is no similarity with the approach for trade; so there is no need for anything like the most favoured nation treatment. However, in most countries there will be a rule for 'national treatment' of foreign labour that has legally been accepted into the country (see Chapter 7).

Thus a regime should be created that prevents and manages crises. We recall that the international organizations responsible for the implementation of the regime in finance (Chapter 8) consisted of an intervention force (an improved and enlarged role for the UN refugee organization?) and that interventions were based on the principle of conditionality (equivalent to improving the conditions in the source country).

11.3.4 Organizations

The present situation with respect to regime building for international migration is very fragmented. The UN and its specialized agencies have realized various conventions. The objective of these conventions is to safeguard the rights of migrant workers and to establish standards for the way these persons and their families need be treated.[9] But there is no real regime in the sense that there is neither a clear-cut principle (such as the most favoured nation in the WTO), nor the organization to implement rules based on such a principle.

The regime for migration is provided by three organizations:

- *Labour*. Both the ILO (International Labour Organization) and the IOM (International Organization for Migration) are weak institutions in matters of migration. Neither of them has set any norms. Neither of them has much regulatory power.
- *Refugees*. The UNHCR (United Nations High Commissioner for Refugees) is a fairly strong organization that has emerged because of the need of governments (particularly those of the least developed ones) to deal with sudden upsurges in migration or with the persistent presence of masses of migrants. The principle is that asylum is given when there is a 'well-founded fear of persecution'.
- *Services*. The WTO (World Trade Organization) has included in its GATS (General Agreement on Trade in Services) some stipulations that relate to those who need to cross borders to deliver a service.

It is clear that this set-up is not capable of dealing with the type of problems we listed in the second section of this chapter. So, novel approaches need to be worked out.

11.3.5 What should a new regime look like?

The basic long-term premise of the new regime would be that openness is positive. Under stable conditions it would imply that people can freely choose where to live and work. This situation is a basic principle within most countries, and also in a supranational or regional setting such as the EU. Such a situation exists in practice for professions and for expert employees of MNFs. However, it is unlikely that this principle could also be applied on the global level in the near future to all migrants. So the demands on the regime will be rather to *improve the conditions for orderly movements of people and crisis management*. This contains three components.

First, the regime would need to provide effective measures for preventing the occurrence of sudden mass movements. In this respect the following elements need be looked at:

- National policies that promote growth and development in potential source countries. These include efficient markets, good governance and democratic government.
- National measures with respect to human rights, minorities, etc.
- International measures with respect to market access, development aid, stability of the financial system, etc.; in other words, make sure that the other international regimes work out well for economic growth in potential emigrant countries.

Second, there is the need for facilitating orderly movements of a regular character. In this category would fall such elements as:

- International principles for labour rights, taxation, social security, pension for migrants and their dependants abroad. There is a clear case for the extension of the ILO conventions in this area.
- Rules for entry, exit and re-entrance to which source and host countries agree.

Third, there are the rules that intend to balance the benefits and cost for both (potential) sending and host countries. These include matters such as:

- Migration tax to compensate sending countries for their loss in investment in human capital or to compensate the host country for the investment in club goods to which the newcomers have not contributed. This tax, already proposed a quarter of a century ago by Bhagwati (1976),[10] has a number of side-effects that make it difficult to implement in practice, while substantiating at the same time the basic principle of freedom of movement as much as possible.[11]
- Standard agreements between countries on waiving the migration tax when there is a sufficient bilateral compensation in terms of other aspects of the migration regime (for instance, development aid).[12]

The analysis up till now has been highly inspired by economic considerations. However, there are more aspects to regime building for such a sensitive subject as migration than economics. These refer to criteria such as comprehensiveness, transparency, accountability, etc.[13]

11.4 Market order: competition

11.4.1 Why competition?

The conclusion of the trade rounds in the framework of the GATT/WTO has made clear that a great number of problems that inhibit international trade have now been removed. That puts the accent on other aspects that can impinge on fair trade. At the end of Chapter 7, we listed a few of them; they constituted the so-called 'trade and' agenda. One of the major topics in this respect is the issue of competition (see Hope and Maeleng, 1998; Waverman, 1997). The definitions of competition policy vary considerably in scope between different countries. A fairly restricted definition limits competition policy to antitrust policy (in other words, to the control of cartels) and to the prevention of abuse of dominant positions. A wider definition would also encompass questions of dumping and state aid. This wider definition of competition policy is not very adequate here, as the latter aspects are already dealt with under the present WTO trade regulations and dispute settlement mechanisms.[14]

We will consider the global competition policy problems in the standard sequence in which we have addressed the other issues in this chapter: problems, public goods, actions by institutions, and suggestions for improvement.

11.4.2 The anatomy of the problem: no level playing field

Many MNFs now stretch their actions worldwide. With increasingly global markets it is clear that many mergers and acquisitions and business practices that restrict competition will affect the situation in several countries. On the other hand, the regulation of these activities is still a national affair. This coexistence of global markets with national jurisdictions poses two sets of problems with respect to competition.

11.4.2.1 Behind borders

The removal of many obstacles to trade has opened national markets to foreign competition. This is supposed to have positive welfare effects. These effects can, however, only be reaped in case the markets are really contestable, that is to say that the exporters can effectively access such markets under normal competitive conditions. However, anticompetitive behaviour of local producers may impinge upon such access. Competition law should put sanctions on this behaviour. If national competition authorities apply different rules to foreign companies than to domestic ones, the principle of non-discrimination is violated, which could have strong effects on trade.

11.4.2.2 Beyond borders

Competition authorities will have to judge cases that have implications far beyond their borders. For instance, if EU authorities block a merger of two MNFs with a global activity for domestic reasons, this may lead to a loss in efficiency in other countries where there was no threat to competition. So, international conflicts are to arise as a result. This implies that global markets require a global view on the objectives and principles competition policy.

The same is true for reasons that have to do with the effectiveness of competition policy implementation. MNFs may have their headquarters and hold their assets in a country outside the one where the offence takes place. This means that the competent authorities may be handicapped in two ways. First, in judging the case because they have no access to the relevant documents. Second, in making firms comply, as they have no means of coercion.

11.4.3 The need for a regime

Anticompetitive business practices can have a serious negative effect on the economy. Mainstream economics is fairly outspoken about the objectives and instruments of competition policy (see, for instance, Neumann, 2001). On this score it would not be difficult to define the public good of a fair competition regime. However, these views are not translated into public preferences. Indeed, the problem is that many countries have very different views about the need of a textbook-inspired competition policy. This absence of universally accepted criteria makes collective action for a regime providing this global public good a difficult exercise.

There is not even sufficient agreement as to the principles on which a multinational competition regime should be based (Katzenbach *et al.*, 1993; Lloyd, 1998); there is, in particular, much difference in opinion between Asian and Atlantic countries in this respect. Transition countries have only recently set up competition laws. Although there is quite some convergence between the EU and the USA in matters of competition regimes, one should not forget that even in the EU some countries have only recently started to adhere to the principles of the EU treaty that abides by three rules: no cartels, no abuse of a dominant position and no state aids. The middle one is particularly important as competition authorities can actually forbid mergers and acquisitions that may lead to such a dominant position. In cases where MNFs are involved, this gives rise to disputes about the extra-territorial application of national competition rules.

The arguments for intervention (e.g. Meiklejohn, 1999) on a global scale are:

- Avoiding discrimination; this improves allocational efficiency.
- Recovering the effectiveness in competition policy disciplining MNF; this enhances growth.

The arguments against come from different strands:

- Unneeded, because the present trade-related measures cope with most of the problems.
- Unfeasible because of difficulties in international cooperation.
- Unfair as Western MNFs will in this way get extra power to wipe local companies off the national markets of LDCs.
- Unjust as it impinges on national sovereignty.

11.4.4 Organizations

There is, at this stage, no international body that is responsible for competition matters. The arguments of the proponents of such a global competition authority have not led to international regime building (yet). The international organizations that have dealt in one way or another with the issue are the following:

- *OECD*. Work on competition by the OECD goes back quite some time. Since 1967 it has analysed options and adopted several recommendations on multinational enterprises that contain codes on anticompetitive practices (see e.g. OECD, 1987, 1995).[15]
- *UN (UNCTAD)*. In 1980 a set of multilaterally agreed equitable principles and rules for the control of restrictive business practices was adopted. However, these are recommendations and are not binding on member states.
- *WTO*. In the Havana Charter of 1947 it was envisaged that the International Trade Organization should have powers to investigate business practices that restrict competition and to recommend counter measures. However, none of these powers has been bestowed upon the GATT, nor upon its successor WTO. Some of the agreements arrived at in the framework of WTO contain elements of competition. These relate notably to trade in services (see Chapter 7). On the initiative of the EU, the WTO ministerial conference of 1996 agreed to set up a (study) working group on competition policy. However, during the 2001 Dohar conference the proposals to include competition in the agenda of the new trade round have not been accepted and the issue has been put off till after 2004.

In view of the present stalemate on the multilateral front, a number of other solutions are now being tried out:

- *Unilateral*. This option implies the extension of the powers of a national competition authority to outside its borders. The extraterritorial application of national competition policy is fraught with legal difficulties and often runs into severe problems of foreign policy. So it is an option that is only effective for very powerful countries, in practice only the USA and the EU.
- *Bilateral*. The most important in this respect is the US/EU relation. Indeed, here the potential conflicts are as yet the most important and the need to come to some sort of solution is the most pressing. The 1991 EC–US (transatlantic) agreement has been under severe strain on several occasions when either EU or US authorities judged cases in a way that was considered to harm the interest of the partner countries' firms. Both countries now cooperate better in matters of fact finding, principle setting, etc.

- *Regional*. The EU and NAFTA have set competition rules for their areas. The former regime is very strong and effective with many powers of the Commission to investigate competitive behaviour and to fine infringements. NAFTA has as yet a much weaker regime.

11.4.5 What should a new regime look like?

Although there are many factors that inhibit, for the time being, the setting up of a multilateral competition regime, the problems that are caused by the absence of a regime are real and have at some stage to be addressed and solved. One could start work on a fairly simple regime, setting a frame-work for cooperation between national competition authorities. This could cover:

- The exchange of general information and (mutual) technical assistance;
- Consultation on the application of law in specific cases;
- Support in investigating and judging cases;
- Mechanisms of settling disputes.

The proponents of a more fully-fledged regime discard such intermediate harmonization options (usually only based on international codes and recommendations) because they consider them to be ineffective. Indeed, the stakes of individual businesses and the nations that identify with these stakes are so high that only very binding regimes will do the job. On the other hand, we have seen on many other occasions that regimes tend to develop gradually and that the proposals set out before could very well create a start from which it is easier to move to the next stage.

The proposals that are under discussion tend to follow one of the two following lines:

- *WTO*. The attractiveness of the WTO for taking on board competition matters is based on a series of features. First, WTO already exists and extending the realm of an existing organization seems easier than creating a new one. Second, it is the only international organization that has both the competence (strong powers) and the experience in using them (including dispute settlement) that are a *conditio sine qua non* for an effective competition regime. Finally, there are strong link-ages between competition and trade, the prime task of the WTO. In some proposals the WTO should address all competition problems, in others (such as Mattoo and Subramanian, 1997) the WTO should only safeguard the enforcement of national competition law so as to safe-guard equal access to markets of foreign competitors.
- *A new institution*. Some consider that the case of competition is so important and so specific that it should not be mixed up with trade. Proposals have been made by competition policy experts from academia

(such as Scherer, 1994; and Graham and Richardson, 1997) to set up a stand-alone international competition policy office. The proposed organization should have both investigative and enforcement powers. Proposals differ as to the degree to which such powers should make use of existing national and multilateral organizations and instruments.

- *Intermediate.* The EU has consistently tried to introduce competition on the agenda of the WTO. However, a group of European experts has proposed a new institution as an add-on to the WTO (IATCWG, 1993). This organization should have very strong powers. Cases that transgress the capacity of a unilateral, bilateral or regional solution would have to be brought before this international antitrust authority.

11.5 Labour standards

11.5.1 Why labour standards?

Markets tend to function well only under certain institutional conditions. This is particularly true in labour markets where economic and social arguments interfere in a complex way. As a consequence, most countries have passed detailed regulation on labour markets. Labour standards are an important instrument in this respect. Labour standards are norms and rules that govern specific aspects of the labour market; that is, prices (minimum wages), quantities (maximum working time) and all sorts of conditions (such as health and safety) and the behaviour of actors (industrial relations).

On the national level, labour standards represent important choices as to the way in which society wants its labour market to function, taking into account the social values that pertain in that county and its level of development. The choices that many countries (developed and developing alike) have made in the past now come under heavy criticism. Critics claim that the density and level of labour standards distort the efficient allocation. They point to the waste of resources through rent seeking, to a lack of competition and hence innovation, and to constraints on investment and hence on economic growth. They claim that in many cases the benefits of regulation have been annihilated by the cost. So national regulation needs to be reviewed and has to justify itself in terms of effectiveness and efficiency criteria.

11.5.2 The anatomy of the problem: the changing character of social policy

The global economy has entailed increased competition from abroad. This in turn has given rise to a debate on the conditions under which such a further freedom of exchange can actually be accepted. Labour standards have a central place in this debate.

The arguments of those in favour of setting international standards come principally from workers that benefit from high labour standards in their own country and employers who are bound by them. They raise their voices against the perceived unequal conditions under which this stiffened competition is taking place. They accuse countries that do not observe high labour standards of unfair competition and social dumping. The argument runs as follows. Countries that have no or have low labour standards can produce at low cost. Countries that want to enter the market for certain goods are then obliged to match this low cost level, which will only be possible by accepting the same low standards. Hence the openness of markets leads to a race to the bottom in terms of labour standards. This loss of labour standards is a public bad for two reasons:

- *Economic*. Standards oblige firms to internalize the external effects of its functioning, including firing and hiring. Labour standards avoid the loss of social and human capital that accompanies sudden and profound economic restructuring. Moreover, standards are an asset to any country as they present a stabilization of the social fabric. It results in higher productivity due to increased motivation, higher investment in specific skills of the manpower and a decrease in conflicts.
- *Social*. Labour markets are highly influenced by power relations both on the demand and on the supply side. In some cases social groups are at a disadvantage due to such factors. Standards prevent the inequality between social groups widening. International standards notably protect the categories of labour that are most vulnerable to international shocks. They prevent a race to the bottom.

The arguments of those against are mainly economic. Two strands of thought can be distinguished:

- *Unneeded*. A straightforward relation between labour standards and (lack of) trade performance and or growth does not exist. The most important determinants for growth are technology and labour qualification. Labour standards have only small weight in the total balance. For instance, there is no relation between workers' rights of association/ collective bargaining and trade (OECD, 1996). So countries will choose their optimum labour standards in function of their competitiveness.
- *Damaging*. Markets need to function well in order to improve the chances for growth. If standards are set too high, this will actually diminish total welfare. This can be very detrimental to countries that are in the course of catching up. They need to be as efficient as possible. International standards cannot take the diversity of national situations into account. National governments are the closest to the problem, so their choices in matters of specifying labour standards tend to reflect best the optimal positions in aggregate welfare. In other

words, competition of regulatory systems does not lead to a race to the bottom, but to optimality in regulation.

In practice, the arguments for and against have been simplified and oppose the trade unions of developed countries that are in favour, to the governments of developing countries, who are against.

11.5.3 The need for a regime[16]

The need for regulation on a national scale is justified by the considerable improvements in social public good provision. Supporters of international labour standards tend to draw a parallel with the international level. Establishing a set of standards that would be applicable over the whole world would take away the risk of unfair competition based on social dumping. However, the transposition of the argument from the national to the global level is fraught with difficulties. On the national level there is, in general, full freedom of movement of goods services and production factors capital and labour. Often there is a way of compensating the regions that suffer from the imposition of such standards by means of regional development policies.

So a different set of arguments needs to be established. There are essentially three arguments here in favour of international labour standards:

- *Moral*. Certain labour standards are part of the essential universal human rights. This set of standards needs to be respected and should not be part of any discussion.
- *Economic*. Setting labour standards enhances total welfare under the condition that it is done in a gradual way and that it permits flexibility in forms and pace and is done in line with the productivity growth of individual countries.
- *Social*. The race to the bottom needs to be prevented. So all countries need to respect the same minimum standards on a wide array of relevant points.

On the international level, there is some agreement as to the standards that are to be considered universal. First among these are human rights; they tend to transcend all political, economic and cultural situations. So labour standards that embody basic human rights are universal ones. They also constitute the basic principles of a regime. As such, the following are considered (OECD, 1996):

- Freedom of association and collective bargaining, that is the right of workers to form organizations of their own choice and to negotiate freely their working conditions with their employers;
- Elimination of exploitative forms of child labour, such as bonded labour and forms of child labour that put the health and safety of children at serious risk;

- Prohibition of forced labour in the form of slavery and compulsory labour;
- Non-discrimination in employment, that is the right to equal respect and treatment for all workers.

There is no agreement whatsoever on the set of international standards that would respect these principles and would fulfil the social and economic criteria. The social argument loses much of its weight internationally since rich high standard countries restrict both trade and migration and are not always generous to compensate in terms of development aid. So this means that it is likely that the moral and economic arguments determine the evolution of the international regime in matters of labour standards. Indeed, recent history shows that this results in a constant search for political agreement on a wide geographical basis and on a wide spectrum of issues.

11.5.4 Organizations[17]

The most important international labour standards have been set by organizations such as the ILO and OECD, whereas other UN organizations have some involvement as well.

11.5.4.1 ILO

The conventions of the ILO constitute the most comprehensive set of international labour standards. They are binding on all countries that have ratified them. They can be grouped into the following categories (OECD, 1996):

- Fundamental human rights. In this category come freedom of association and collective bargaining, elimination of exploitation of children, prohibition of forced labour, and non-discrimination;
- Employment: minimum level of employment security, standard contracts, etc.;
- Social policy: minimum level of living standards, access to education, training;
- Labour administration: the setting up of a well-functioning labour market;
- Industrial relations: the setting up of consultation in tripartite organizations;
- Conditions of work: such as minimum wage, maximum hours of work, etc.;
- Social security: sickness, maternity and unemployment benefits, pensions;
- Employment conditions for vulnerable groups: such as for women, children, old and young people;
- Migrant workers.

11.5.4.2 UN

The UN has addressed core labour standards in several acts as well. These provisions are similar to, but less detailed than, the ones contained in the corresponding ILO conventions. They are important in the sense that they have to be observed by all UN members, so have almost universal application, whereas the ILO conventions are only applicable in the subset of countries that have ratified them.

11.5.4.3 Others

There have been numerous attempts to introduce labour standards in trade agreements. A first case to be mentioned is the charter of the aborted International Trade Organization. Other cases targeted the WTO. They have all fallen victim to the fierce opposition of mostly the less developed countries that see them as disguised forms of protection.

11.5.5 What should a new regime look like?

The world would probably gain if a number of social policy measures were more widely applied. Such an increase in standards should, however, be done without doing harm to the growth prospects of developing countries. There does not seem to be any need for a new institution or for new legal measures. Most of the needs with respect to labour standards can be taken into account through an extension of the present ILO system. This would then imply:

- Better coverage of the present conventions (more countries ratifying);
- Further extension of subjects (compare, for instance, the development of EU social policy);
- Search for equality of standards in countries with similar levels of development;
- Better compliance with the present conventions.

There are several ways in which such an improvement can be achieved, but all have certain disadvantages:

- Enhancing development aid. In so far as non-observance is due to poverty, the reduction of poverty is essential; the effectiveness of classical development aid is, however, questioned by many.
- Improving the monitoring system of the ILO. This would mean an agreement on detailed definitions of labour standards and enhanced international inspection powers. Some countries would consider this an unacceptable inroad into national sovereignty.
- Using the WTO trade sanctions to enforce better observance. This is a very controversial issue as the WTO has not been designed for the

purpose and many countries do not want to mix trade issues with labour issues. Moreover, the effectiveness of the trade sanctions instrument is open to doubt. Finally, the welfare effects of sanctions in both the targeted country and in the imposing country are so intricate as to make a well-measured use of this instrument very problematic.[18]

- Conditioning multilateral financial loans (IMF) to labour standards. Many difficulties arise here. It would target only countries that apply for such loans. The means may be counter-effective in the sense that denying access to such loans may block development and thus lock countries in a poverty trap. It would add to the conditionality problem (see Chapter 8).
- Conditioning regional or national programmes in respect of standards. We may cite in this respect the generalized system of preferences (trade) of the US or the EU and or the development assistance of these countries. The effectiveness of this instrument may be very good as bilateral aid is often given in the framework of a more intimate donor–recipient relation, which could cope with the intricacies of such a conditioned set-up.[19]
- Private sector standards. Firms are becoming increasingly aware of the negative reaction of consumers towards products that have been produced under conditions that lack respect for core labour standards. They will want to be known as socially responsible corporate citizens and make sure that their subsidiaries comply with standards. There will, however, always be discussion about the level of social protection that would qualify for such social labelling. Moreover, empirical research has shown that such codes are only effective under specific conditions.[20]

Overlooking the set of problems that comes with each of the avenues of improvement one can only conclude that the improvement of the present regime will be done in a piecemeal way and will take much time. Economic necessity points indeed towards flexibility. Given the controversy between workers and employers and between (groups of) countries, progress as to particular issues will depend on the particular configuration of the political forces for each of these cases.

11.6 Summary and conclusions

- The global 'system' of regimes as described in the previous chapters is not complete; there are important 'missing links' that call for action.
- Direct investment is a first case where action is needed. After the aborted attempt of the multilateral agreement on investment, a new regime should be elaborated. It should take more regard to the interest of the non-Western countries and should best be grafted on the existing framework of the WTO.

- The situation for migration is in stark contrast to the one for goods; the regime is entirely based on national controls. Migration movements do not need a WTO type regime. What is needed here is a regime that is capable of preventing (and if needed to deal with) sudden mass movements (crisis prevention and management).
- Diverging national competition rules risk distorting increasingly international economic exchange. Given the close link with trade and the need for a sort of dispute settlement, the WTO framework may be a good locus for global regime development on this issue.
- Labour standards have an important function: to safeguard social values and economic growth. A further strengthening of the ILO-centred global regime would be desirable for a wide array of detailed subjects.

12 Evaluation and outlook

12.1 Introduction

The preceding chapters have described how the growing interdependence between the various economies in the world has led to the development of international institutions. These chapters have shown that this global international institutional system is far from ideal. In the words of Nobel prize winner J.E. Stiglitz (2002: 21):

> We have a system that can be called global governance without global government, one in which a few institutions . . . and a few players . . . dominate the scene, but in which many of those affected by their decisions are left about voiceless.

> It's time to change some of the rules governing the international economic order, to think once again about how decisions get made at the international level – and in whose interest – and to place less emphasis on ideology and to look more at what works. Globalization can be reshaped, [to] . . . create a new global economy in which growth is not only more sustainable and less volatile but the fruits of this growth are more equitably shared.

This quotation[1] contains two elements: an evaluation of past development and a suggestion for future change. These are also the basic elements of this chapter.

In the first part of this chapter we will make an evaluation of the past. We will thereby follow the same systematic set-up that we used in the previous chapters. In a first section we give an overview of the basic features of the regimes analysed. In the subsequent sections we will detail for each of these features the most important findings. In this way we will deal with the basic rationale for regime formation, the major public goods provided, the principles on which the regimes are based and the modalities for implementation (governance). We will finalize this first part with a short overview of the major results and shortcomings of the present institutional set-up.

In the second part we will discuss proposals for the future. In so doing, we change the approach. Whereas the previous parts of the book were all based on theoretical and empirical studies, we now enter into the domain of prospective analysis, which has a good deal of speculative elements in it. However, while projecting lines into the future we will use as much as possible the lessons from the past development on the global level, and from developments on the regional level. In particular we will refer to the lessons from the most successful regional economic integration, viz. the EU.

As usual, we will round off the presentation with a short summary of the main features discussed in this chapter.

12.2 Evaluation

12.2.1 An overview of the main features of the regimes

Table 12.1 gives an overview of the main features (in the rows) of each of the major regimes (columns) that we have analysed in the previous chapters. The subjects in the columns reflect the choices that we have made for the set-up of the whole book in chapters, while the subjects of the rows reflect the set-up of the individual chapters in sections. In the top rows we refer to such basic notions as the definition of the common interest that countries have in order to get together; in other words, the motive for their collective action. This is made more concrete in terms of specific public goods that need to be provided to the international community.[2] In the middle rows we indicate the organizations that deal with the problems of public good provision,[3] followed by the basic principles that govern each regime.[4] Next, we detail some governance aspects, in particular the most important instruments that are used to get to results.[5] The bottom part of the table finally describes the results obtained so far in the provision of the major public goods and the open issues that still remain.

12.2.2 Rationale

Globalization has rapidly spread, largely under the impetus of multinational firms. It has eroded the capacity of national governments to deal independently with problems and thereby increased the need for international cooperation in the framework of international organizations. The efforts of these institutions need to be oriented towards a set of basic goals. Among them economic growth takes pride of place, in particular in those countries that have a considerable poverty problem. But other societal concerns also call for action. Among them are traditional ones, such as the safeguarding of open communications and the respect of human values. Also important in this respect is equitable development to be fostered by good regimes in trade and redistribution (development aid). Finally, we mention among the more recent concerns a sustainable environment.

Table 12.1 Basic features of the global order

	Trade	Finance	Environment	Sea–Air	Telecom	Labour
Basic rationale	Enhancing economic growth	Enhancing economic growth	Safeguarding sustainable development	Open communications	Open communication	Labour rights are universal human rights
Public good provision	Enhancing free trade in goods and services	Stable financial relations Avoiding crisis and contagion	Stabilization of climate Prevention of ozone layer depletion Maintaining biodiversity	Avoid market disequilibria Maintain safety Protect environment	Safeguard communications Control potential damage	Improve labour conditions Prevent race to bottom
Basic principle	Most favoured nation Non-discrimination	Precaution Solidarity Conditionality	Precaution Polluter pays Common but differentiated responsibilities	Open access to space Joint sovereignty	Open access National sovereignty (license) Equitable distribution of commons	Freedom of association Elimination of exploitation Non-discrimination
Main organization	WTO	IMF	UNEP	ICAO IMO	ITU	ILO
Instruments for realization and compliance	Dispute settlement Sanctions Retaliation	Standards Surveillance Financial assistance Incentives/aid	Standards Pollution rights Tradable permits Bans on products Reputation	Standards Registration of ships and aircraft (home country) Control (destination country)	Standards License by national state (home)	Standards Reputation Aid Tripartite negotiation (labour unions, employers, government) Complaint ICJ
Results	Considerable progress (lower barriers in more areas)	Reasonable in prevention Limited in management	Slow progress	Technical: OK Market: disputable	Very good	Slow progress Low impact
Open issues	Maintaining other values Conflict of principles	Inherent instability Choice of instruments	Further deterioration of situation No uniform framework	Market regime obsolete	Internet Privatization of infrastructure	Tension between 'social dumping' and gradual improvement

The definition of the common interest has not changed profoundly over time, notwithstanding very rapid and profound changes in the structure of the economy. We need but cite the change from manufacturing to inform-ation, the increased sophistication of products and services, the growing internationalization of business (trade and direct investment) and the increase in the mobility of capital. They all have influence (compare, for instance, the Internet) but most of this is on the lower level of analysis, some in terms of definition of public goods, but most in terms of governance.

The fundamental design criteria that characterize the socioeconomic institutional set-up of Western countries are very much based on a division and *hierarchization of functions*. In general, one distinguishes three elements. The allocation function has the objective to optimize the working of markets. The stability function has the objective of creating the conditions for the good functioning of markets. The social function (redistribution) function has to make sure that the results come up to social preferences. This notion has also shaped major Western regional integration schemes (see, for instance, the case of the EU in Box 12.1).

Each of these functions can be closely associated with a rationale in Table 12.1.

- The first function is mainly represented in the column of trade. How-ever, in the past a few tasks about market functioning have been entrusted to specific organizations (notably in transport). We have found that this historical relict is inadequate at present and that the market aspects of these regimes should be integrated with the trade regime. Such a move has in the meantime been made for telecom-munication.
- The second function is to enable the good functioning of the global economy. It is covered mainly by the public good of stable financial relations, as depicted in the second column.[6] This is very inadequate. First, the effectiveness and efficiency of the present regime are insufficient (see the recurrent financial crises and their effect on equity). Second, important elements for this function lack at the global level; a regime for competition has, for instance, not yet got off the ground.
- The third function is represented here notably with the public goods of sustainable environment and respect for the human factor (third and sixth column). Not represented in the table is the redistribution function (development aid).

On the national and EU level this fundamental set-up seems to be adequate. However, many feel that on the global level it shows a very serious imbalance. The allocation (market) regime is well developed with strong organization. The regimes for the other functions are ill-developed and are dependent on weak organizations (see next sections).

Box 12.1 Design principles: the case of the EU

The construction of the EU is based on three layers.

The foundation is formed by the internal market. The basic principle in this area is the free internal movement of goods, services, labour and capital. In this way the allocation function is enhanced, which is conducive to growth.

The middle layer consists of enabling policies. In order to create the conditions for a good allocation (and hence for growth) a number of common policies are pursued, such as competition, macro-economic stability, monetary, etc.

Now the outcome of these processes may not be always in line with social preferences. As such, we may think of the equality of income distribution over social groups and geographical areas, the access to jobs for men and women, etc. To improve the situation in these domains a third layer of policies is needed. This layer is composed of several elements. We cite here notably regional (cohesion) policy, to which the EU devotes a considerable part of its budget. Another component we cite is environmental policy, upon which the EU has spent a considerable part of its legislative effort over the past decades. All these third layer policies tend to respect the autonomy of first layer policies. For instance, in redistribution policies it is not allowed to introduce protectionist trade measures to support industrial development in backward areas. In environmental matters the efficient allocation is safeguarded by applying the polluter pays principle.

This basic set-up is not unchallenged. Time and again, pleas are made to introduce social considerations already at the level of the definition of market policies by setting constraints that are supposed to foster such social objectives. In some cases such actions have come to regime changes, but these do not affect the fundamentals just described.

12.2.3 Public goods

The next interesting point we have to turn to is the selection of public goods provided and to the sequence in which the need for these goods arises. Given constraints on collective action, regimes only come about when there are very good reasons (Section 5.3.4). Factors such as 'awareness' and 'knowledge' are important, but the factor that carries most weight is actually 'interest'. Now the aspect of economic interest can best be seen in the trade field. So the early creation and subsequent development of GATT/WTO is in line with these predictions and also in line with the results of studies in regional integration (see Box 12.2).

***Box 12.2* The stages of integration and the development path of the EU**

The theory of regional integration distinguishes several stages. In each stage a specific public good is added to the previous ones. There are sound economic as well as political reasons to start integration with goods markets (free trade area and customs union) and to continue with the markets for production factors (common market). The EU has indeed started with these subjects much like most other regional integration areas in the world. It took, however, half a century to arrive at near completion of these stages.

During the progressive development of the EU it became clear that other public goods could no longer effectively be provided on the national level. So the EU set out on a development path towards the stage of the economic union. It included from the start a fair amount of competition policy and an embryonic social and macro-economic policy. Later it integrated environmental policies and a series of others, notably cohesion policies, with the objective of coming to a more equitable income distribution. In the course of time these policies were intensified, in other words they covered more aspects of the general public good. With increased integration monetary instability became more and more of a problem and after some experimentation with intermediate forms of monetary integration, the EU moved towards a full monetary union at the turn of the century. Recently, the EU has also integrated aspects of foreign/security policy and justice and home affairs, thereby entering the stage of a political union.

Source: Based on Molle, 2001: 467.

The second early development has been in finance. The problems of the interwar period were still very vivid after the war and increased the awareness of the problem and the need to do something about it. The main public good has, however, gradually shifted from stability on foreign exchange markets towards the stability of the international financial system. This seems to be a logical step in the sequence of regime building. Indeed, the 'interest' argument applies here in full as actions for the improvement of exchanges in matters of trade (and investment) can only bear their full fruits in case stable financial conditions prevail. However, this sequence on the world level is only partly in step with the development on the regional level. Here, financial integration has not come to the fore at an early stage, presumably because there was no real need as the matter was already settled on the global level.

It is a well-known fact that the concern for environmental problems is taken seriously only after basic needs have been settled. The emergence of global environmental action and its subsequent development in the 1970s would then fit in the total picture of 'interest'.

Lack of clear interest would also explain the absence of progress on other scores (described in Chapter 11) such as competition, labour, etc. The case of the social aspects, notably of labour standards, is a particular one. Their development would have been stimulated by the almost universal interest in the subject. However, as Chapter 11 has shown, there are also formidable obstacles that explain why progress has been slow on this score.

12.2.4 Organizations

Reviewing past development we see that the main international organiz-ations that are responsible for governing the world economy were founded in the aftermath of the Second World War. This applies notably to the GATT/WTO responsible for trade and to the Bretton Woods institutions responsible for finance. Some of the UN organizations are even older, such as the ILO, dealing with social and labour issues. Others have come to the fore under the pressure of new needs, such as the UNEP, dealing with the environment. Organizational solutions to emerging problems have mainly been found within the present frameworks (e.g. the switch from GATT to WTO); only in rare cases were new organizations created (e.g. UNCTAD).

The total set up of organizations seems to suffer from two major problems. First, responsibilities of the various organizations tend to overlap each other (e.g. WTO, UNCTAD, IMO), giving rise to high cost and uncertainty. Second, there are gaps in the responsibilities leaving room for defaults of the system (e.g. investments, competition). Such a situation is neither uncommon, nor impossible to remedy as the case of Western Europe may illustrate (see Box 12.3). Of course this is subject to specific conditions that may not be fulfilled on the global level.

The question is, then, what lesson can be learnt from this European experience for the development of the patchwork of organizations on the global level. First, that it may take a long time before change becomes visible. Even on the relatively small scale of Europe, the development took half a century. So, on the global level much more time may be needed as interests are more diverse and solutions more difficult to reach. The WTO seems to qualify most as the nucleus for institutional integration, as the WTO is at this moment the strongest in terms of economic interest and governance. However, for the time being, the conditions on the global level seem to be so different from those at the EU level, that the application of the EU model to global organizational development seems somewhat far-fetched.

12.2.5 The role of values and ideology

The main regimes we analysed have all been conceived in function of the basic norms and traditions (ideologies) of the Western countries (see

---

Box 12.3 Dynamics of organizations: the European case

In Europe, the need for integration on a number of scores resulted in the creation of a whole series of organizations. In matters of trade, the first (in 1952) was the European Coal and Steel Community (ECSC), followed in 1958 by the European Economic Community (EEC) and the competing European Free Trade Association (EFTA). In matters of finance, we cite the European Payments Union. For security, the Western European Union (WEU) was created, while the Council of Europe took responsibility for cultural affairs and human rights.[7] The Organisation for European Economic Cooperation deals with all types of matters of economic policy such as budget, industry, productivity, tourism, etc.

In the fourth quarter of the twentieth century, the EEC emerged as the dominant organization. While the EEC developed into the European Union it took over the tasks of quite a few other organizations that have subsequently been phased out (ECSC, EFTA and WEU).[8] The determinant element in this evolution may have been the strong interest (economic growth), on the one hand, and strong governance structure of the EEC (qualified majority voting, unified legal instruments), on the other.

Section 5.2.2). They have different blends of liberalism and public intervention. As long as there were credible alternatives this situation precluded universalism for these major regimes. However, after the demise of the centrally planned economies and the transition of these countries to a market economy most major countries have now accepted the idea of a market economy along the lines of the West. A similar remark can be made with respect to the group of developing countries. After decolonization a large number of new independent states emerged that have tried to come to grips with the challenges they were confronted with in a way that suited them; their more interventionist attitudes have led to the creation of UNCTAD. Both transition countries (including Russia and China) and less developed countries have now become members of the global economic organizations described in previous chapters.

The dominant role of ideology can be illustrated for all three functions discussed in the previous section.

12.2.5.1 Optimizing allocation

This fundamental economic function has been attributed on the global level to the WTO. It is based on a liberal ideology (free access to markets for goods and services). For the movement of production factors the situation is less clear-cut. The aborted attempt for a direct investment regime (MAI) also parted from a liberal ideology and the regime was to create the conditions for optimizing the free flow. For other capital movements the practice has, even without a formal regime, become a widespread liberalization. For labour movements no regime has yet even passed the stage of proposal, but liberal ideology does not find a very fertile soil to grow here.

12.2.5.2 Creating conditions

The major institution in charge of this function is the IMF. It creates the conditions for growth with respect to macro-economic stability. The ideological basis for its activity is, in practice, shaped to a large extent by the dominant market economies, notably the USA.[9] Other institutions, such as those for competition, have not yet passed the stage of proposals, so the role of ideology is not very obvious.

12.2.5.3 Respecting social preferences

There is no clear overriding ideology at the foundation of the regimes dealing with social objectives. The world is very diverse in these matters. On the one hand, the US has a tendency to impose individualism. On the other hand, the Asian countries want their quite different values to be respected. The search for clarity and unity is still going on.[10]

12.2.6 The role of principles

The elaboration of the basic principles has been done in very idiosyncratic ways for the different regimes. Table 12.1 shows, indeed, that there is no 'meta' principle that could serve a unifying role. The emergence of a leading principle is often dependent on the contributions of different parties to the negotiation table. For reasons of transaction–cost minimization it is efficient not to talk about details but to see in how far one can agree on principles. In emerging regimes we can observe this aspect very clearly. Cases in point are the three principles in environment. The 'non-regime' of the Internet is interesting in this respect; it is based on the principle of free access to information. This is clearly inspired by a liberal ideology. However, as this conflicts with societal preferences, adaptations are proposed, which up till now have not been able to impose themselves.

In a number of cases the emergence of dominant principles has been facilitated by the unanimity in scientific circles about the basic working of the system. With respect to the contribution of the economics profession we see a diversified pattern. The case for the freedom of markets for goods and services is very strong. The case for free FDI is strong as well. However, the advantages of the freedom of other capital flows are still not sufficiently convincing to favour the setting of general principles there. In environmental matters the principle of the polluter pays is based on the conviction that it limits possible distortions. For global labour movements the net advantages of a free regime are actually very questionable in economic terms. So no principle has been worked out yet. For stabilization at the global level the situation is not as clear as in other cases either. Although here, too, the principles of precaution and solidarity seem to apply in much the same way as in some other regimes.

12.2.7 Instruments (governance)

International regimes are, in general, defined in terms of obligations of members. It means that the instruments used need to be made effective at two levels: application by national governments and the control of national governments by international organizations.

National states possess the governance structures that international organizations lack. So the former are major actors in the implementation stage of the latter. They may use the instruments that seem most adequate nationally to realize objectives agreed internationally (e.g. for the limitation of pollution, some may use taxation, others tradable permits). In line with the scheme of Section 5.2, we see that the higher layers of institutions do influence the lower ones. The governance of nations is indeed pushed into a certain direction that is consistent with the choices made at the higher level. To give an example, structural adjustment programmes that were based on the notions of a good functioning of markets and sound public finances were considered the only valid approach for coping with national economic problems.[11]

International organizations are, in general, weak in matters of compliance. They rely very much on elements, such as the setting of standards and principles. To make such situations work, countries must observe the rule of transparency. Only under that condition is a system of monitoring and surveillance possible at relatively low cost. The monitoring does not need to be done by the international organization in question. Some regimes rely on monitoring by interested parties (trade); others depend partly on NGOs (environment). Whatever the situation, the regime always has an interest in using instruments that optimize the situation with respect to transparency. The WTO has, for instance, consistently been pushing in this direction by the abolition of opaque measures, such as non-tariff barriers, and their replacement by transparent measures, such as tariffs. Once a good monitoring system is in place, reputation should then do most of the work in making countries comply with regimes.

Some regimes are stronger on measures for compliance than others. We may list the compliance mechanisms as follows:

- *Reputation.* All partners know that the quality of the deals they get in future will depend on their reputation. So this will not be easily foregone. NGOs target both companies and countries on the aspect of reputation to enhance compliance.

- *Coercion*. In order to create the conditions for financial stability, the IMF gives conditional loans. If the country in question does not agree to this the IMF can withdraw support for national plans and, as alternatives will be hard to find, a country will in general comply.
- *Sanctions*. The WTO admits retaliation in case a country does not live up to the result of a dispute settlement procedure.
- *Incentives*. The World Bank can give debt relief to countries complying with environmental programmes.
- *Indirect rewards*. Compliance to standards, for instance, signals to the international community that you are part of a respectable set, which leads to lower cost of capital or higher inward investment.

Although all these instruments have their merits, many of the ones in use are actually sub-optimal. Better instruments are available but are not used because they are difficult to implement on the global level (see Box 12.4).

12.2.8 Results

The global institutional system was devised in broad outlines half a century ago. Since then it has gradually developed. On many scores one can say that the system has been able to show progress; this is most visible in matters of trade and environment. On other scores, progress has been rather limited (labour) or even absent (investment).

The (lack of) progress has been dependent on a set of factors (see Section 5.3.5) of which we briefly highlight the most significant ones.

- *Effectiveness*. The delivery of a public good of free trade has had beneficial effects and hence the organization dealing with it has shown further progress. Something of the same sort has happened for environmental concerns (e.g. Montreal and Kyoto Protocols).
- *Power*. In the post-war period the dominance of the US was instrumental in creating a number of regimes. However, the power of the US is now often perceived as a negative point as it is thought to be used in favour of its own interest (e.g. climate) or its own ideology (e.g. finance).
- *Equity or fairness*. This point has bedevilled many discussions about regime change. It has even led to the creation of a new organization next to GATT: the UNCTAD. At this moment, many countries think they do not get a fair deal in the present international organizations and for that reason do not want to continue to develop them further. In other cases the equity point has been dealt with by excluding a group from bearing part of the burden (e.g. LDCs and climate change).

Box 12.4 Sub-optimality of instruments: the WTO and EU compared in matters of subsidies

State aid (subsidies) can have important negative effects. So both the WTO and the EU have policies that regulate the use of state aid. There are, however, important differences between the two on many scores.

The objective of the WTO regime is to prevent subsidies from nullifying the abolishment of protectionist measures, such as tariffs. For the EU the objective is the protection of fair competition on the internal market.

The procedure of the WTO is the lodging of a complaint, and the setting up of a panel (much along the line described in Box 7.4) that checks whether there has been injury to the complaining partner. The EU gets a complaint and that leads to the Commission investigating the case; findings of the Commission can be challenged before the European Court of Justice.

Compliance in the WTO has to be done by negotiation first and retaliation next. In the EU the Commission can oblige the member state to stop the aid and oblige the beneficiary of a non-permissible subsidy to pay it back.

The EU system is more economically sound as it takes away the origin of the problem, whereas the WTO system permits retaliation, which creates another distortion. Moreover, the institutions of the EU are more likely to come to economically sound conclusions. The EU does indeed rely on permanent staff in the specialist Directorate General of the Commission, whereas the WTO relies on trade diplomats that take alternate roles in the subsidy committee.

Source: Based on Messerlin, 1999: 167–74.

Progress should not only be measured in terms of setting up new regimes or in extending existing ones. There should also be progress in getting rid of the regimes that have been set up under specific historical circumstances and shown to be inadequate and ineffective. The transport sector regimes are cases in point. However, experience shows that these regimes are particularly resistant to change; the interest of those who want to change is rarely sufficiently important to lead to collective action that exerts sufficient power to overcome the defences of the combined vested interests of sector representatives and international bureaucrats.

12.2.9 *Open issues: a list of detailed problems and a general problem of lack of coherent government*

Taking an overview, one sees that there is a patchwork rather than a system. The patchwork consists of a large variety of international regimes and organizations, each of which has been created to cope with a specific (set of) global problem(s).

This 'system' is under heavy criticism as many consider it to be inadequate to cope with the problems of global public good provision, in other words with good global government. They deplore the lack of responsiveness to the needs of civil society and the lack of democratic control (very vociferously expressed by many political currents).

The different entries in Table 12.1 show that there are many open issues, and also that they are specific for each regime (bottom row in table). However, there is one issue that is more of general relevance, and that is the lack of consistency between the various regimes. In the present set-up, consistency is indeed difficult to organize. The considerable numbers of organizations in which international agreements are negotiated have different rules, different audiences and different objectives. Their dispersed actions are geared to effectiveness in a segment of the global 'system', not to bringing about improvement in the total system.

For some time, there has been some effort to come to better coordination. In matters of trade and finance, efforts have been made to come to a greater consistency between the main multilateral agencies dealing with trade, development and finance. Notably, trade-related assistance and market access for developing countries is a case in point. Cooperating organizations comprise the WTO, IBRD, IMF, UNDP, UNCTAD and ITU. More specifically, there has been a link (observer status on the level of the board members and cooperation on the level of staff members) between the IMF and WTO. Although these increased efforts for coordination help, they neither produce conformity in governance nor consistency in results.

The patchy character of the architecture poses three problems:

- *Transaction cost*. Regulatory forms are very different for the different regimes (compare, for instance, multilateral environmental agreements, conventions on telecom, WTO resolutions); all are very idiosyncratic. This diversity creates a high cost to economic actors, as they have to come to grips with a multitude of aspects of international governance.
- *Games and collective action*. As there is no integrated organizational framework, there is little incentive to agree package deals that comprise more than one regime of the type 'if you agree on making progress in the ILO; I will agree on progress in WTO'. So it is less likely that the most effective deals come about.
- *Special interests*. Regimes that are specialist tend to become influenced or even controlled by specific interest groups that tend to overlook broader societal interests. A very clear example here is the agricultural regime of the EU (see Box 12.5). Another case is the IMF, which is very much dominated by treasury ministries that tend to be sympathetic to interests in financial markets (Stiglitz, 2002: 19, 209). The present solution of compensating for this by allowing greater participation of non-governmental organizations may not be the most adequate one.

***Box 12.5 An unfortunate case of regime building: the EU
        agricultural policy***

The fathers of the European Union, while drafting the Treaty of
Rome, gave a special constitutional status to agricultural policy.
Budget outlays for agriculture fall in the so-called compulsory
category to which special decision-making rules apply. Such decisions
have been entrusted to the Council of Ministers on which sit the
national ministers of agriculture who have proven to be strong
defendants of their sectors' interest. They have elaborated a common
agricultural policy (CAP) that sets minimum prices for products. After
a while these were set well above the equilibrium prices, giving rise to
huge surpluses.

The CAP has a very poor record. Although it has realized part of
its objectives, it has done so at very high cost.

- *European Union*. Consumers in the EU have paid more for the
  products than necessary, while EU taxpayers have paid to get rid
  of products nobody wanted (surpluses). These costs can be
  estimated at some €400 per head of population per year.
- *Third world countries*. Notably developing countries have suffered
  in two ways: first, from poorer prospects for exporting to the EU
  and, second, from lower revenues of sales to world markets due to
  EU dumping. Thus the detrimental effects of the CAP have to a
  large extent annihilated the beneficial effects of the EU development policy.

Moreover, the CAP has put a constraint on growth by the mis-
allocation of production factors and resources that it has entailed.
This point is exacerbated as the policy has been found to be
susceptible to fraud.

The CAP has shown a particular resistance to change, notwithstanding this poor record. One reason for this state of affairs is that
specific political economy factors have been cast in constitutional
iron. Another reason is the ineffectiveness of the comprehensive
character of the EU that usually would have mobilized pressure for
adaptation. But agricultural interests are very heavily concentrated in
one country (France) and this country has been able to trade its
cooperation on new initiatives (such as enlargement) against continuation of the CAP. Anyway, the CAP is an example of regime building
that teaches very clear lessons about how to avoid the mistakes of self-
regulation.

Source: Molle, 2001: 324–35.

12.3 Proposals for improvement

12.3.1 Future risk: higher demands on an already inadequate system

The future of globalization is unclear. On the one hand, technology and business will continue to press for more interaction and openness. On the other, the forces that are opposed to openness tend to become stronger. There are a few reasons for this. First, the concerns about the possible negative consequences become politically more powerful and the capacity of the national state to provide shelter for the disadvantaged tends to decrease. Second, the process now moves out of the relatively straightforward matters, such as trade liberalization into the much more intricate issues such as competition, trade and environment, where cooperative solutions tend to be hard to find. Finally, the developing countries that find that they have got no fair deal in the past will be more critical on any initiative that may harm their interest.[12] All in all, we expect that the trend towards globalization may weaken in the coming decades, but is not likely to be stopped.

The present institutional set-up is inadequate to deal effectively with the problems. In future it is likely that even more demands will be put on the system. Anyway, there is already now broad dissatisfaction with the incapacity of the present system to deal with a set of societal concerns, such as poverty reduction and labour protection, and about the lack of voice that many countries have in the present system.[13] So there is a big need for adaptation. Bringing the system up to the needs of the global community of the twenty-first century is a big challenge.

Realizing such change is not an easy matter. There is a built-in resistance to change in existing organizations. The past shows that history matters a great deal. Initial set-ups of institutions represent the interests of the dominant states at the moment of their founding. This may very well no longer be in the present interest (for instance, aviation) of the same state, let alone those of other states. However, once regimes exist and show a certain level of effectiveness, it is difficult to adapt them, let alone to supplant them by others. However, change is possible provided one fulfils the right set of conditions (Kapur, 2002).

Moreover, there is a difficulty of organizing the power that should lead to change. Indeed, the theory of collective action shows us how difficult it is to reach cooperation between many parties. This is notably the case for subjects where the collective benefits from cooperation are real, but where the interests of each of the parties taken individually is small and tend to diverge in their specification. Finally, there is a strong inclination for countries to opt for free-riding on the efforts that other parties make.

12.3.2 Four options for improvement

All these considerations lead to the conclusion that action is needed.[14] We will define what precisely is needed first and show how it can be put into place next. In our proposals for change we distinguish four options. Change demands collective action. In Chapters 4 and 5, we have seen that collective action is more likely to succeed when one either limits the subject (function) or the number of participants (clubs). So we organize our options, on the one hand, on a functional axis according to the distinction: 'comprehensive/specific' (options 1 and 2) and, on the other hand, on a club axis according to the distinction 'globalism/regionalism' (options 3 and 4). On both axes the most far-reaching options (1 and 3) involve more radical change while the less ambitious options (2 and 4) involve rather incremental improvement.

1   The first option is the boldest one and involves a new grand design for comprehensive world government in which the presently existing regimes and organizations are integrated.

2   The second one is a much more timid one and consists essentially of incremental improvements to individual regimes, which are the basic constituting elements of the present 'system'. This second option is based on the detailed analyses made in the various chapters on individual regimes.[15]

3   The third option is a three-layer structure, in which many of the tasks of government are not shifted from the national to the global level, but to an intermediate layer of regional organizations. This option takes into account the increased need for voice of specific groups (e.g. LDCs), the fact that clubs can more easily be formed than large groups and the adaptation to the global level of the principle of subsidiarity.

4   Finally, the fourth option takes only the incremental change of the present global and regional institutions into account.

So, the more we move from option 1 to option 4, the more we take constraints into account in designing a new architecture of world government.

12.3.3 Option 1: striving towards an integrated world government system

The main characteristics of this option, which one could qualify as a 'grand design' for the reform of world government, are quite straightforward. It starts from the idea that all global public goods need to be provided via one united framework. It would apply the '*trias politica*' rules to the world system, defining a government, a parliament and a court of justice. It would detail these three functions in organizational and governance terms. For instance, 'government' should be further defined in terms of departments each responsible for a public good and governance in terms of power and instruments used to implement the regimes.

Now, for setting this system up we do not need to start from scratch. We can try to fit the presently available (sometimes embryonic) individual regimes into that new system. With respect to the function of government, the specialized agencies of the UN and various separate organizations could be seen as the ministries of trade (WTO), finance (IMF), environment (UNEP), etc. The General Assembly of the UN could act as a parliament. The International Court of Justice could be seen as the court.

The advantages of such a system would be considerable. First, one would have an effective world government that could take a consistent view on all the major problems. Next, one would save substantially on transaction cost by adopting a common set of legal instruments and rules of governance (within which some diversity could be accepted to accommodate the details of the various regimes).[16] Further wins could be achieved where a common world currency were adopted, as it would do way with uncertainty for international business and would also take away some of the causes of instability in the financial system. In order to evaluate the feasibility of this grand design, we can draw a parallel with the creation and growth of the EU (Box 12.6).

What are the chances for the realization of this option? Notwithstanding the intellectual attractiveness of this option, it does not seem that its chances of being put into effect are very good. Indeed, it is not the attractiveness of an institutional design that leads to action. It is the willingness (stimulated by interest) and the capacity of national governments to work together on a common project that determines change. Now, the latter points seem to be missing. There are a number of reasons for this:

- *Sense of crisis*. Regime building is a complicated matter. The previous chapters have made abundantly clear that only very specific circum-

---

Box 12.6 The grand design approach in practice: the case of the EU

The EU has been created with a double objective: first, to avoid security problems by increasing economic interdependence; second, to gain economic advantages by the liberalization of markets. To these ends, an original set of institutions was created. First, a system of main institutional actors, Commission, Council, Parliament, Court, European Central Bank, etc., that deal with all issues falling under the competences of the EU. Second, a set of decision-making rules; its system of qualified majority voting (that is weighted votes per country) has shown that one can effectively deal with the problem of the differences in size of member countries. Third, a system of governance, with legal and financial instruments for implementing its policies.

The system has been capable of integrating over time more functions and more countries; accepting, where needed, some variable geometry.[17] It has, for instance, developed an embryonic monetary unit and later adopted a single currency.

stances (such as those pertaining after the Second World War) force systemic changes. The present situation does not reveal such characteristics.

- *Distribution of power*. The present elements of organization do not fit easily into the new design. A particular problematic point in this respect is voting power. Whereas the US and, to a lesser extent, the EU dominate the organizations such as the IMF and World Bank, the LDCs dominate the UN by their one country–one vote system. The former need to be convinced that they have to distribute part of the power, the latter that a further concentration should be accepted, based for instance on weighted voting on the basis of population figures. It is difficult to see what factors would induce the various parties to leave their strongholds.
- *Ineffective bureaucracy*. Many governments consider that most international organizations are not very good at delivering the products and services they promise (lack of effectiveness) and what is worse, they are considered as very inefficient. Objective ways of performance measurement of international organizations are lacking. But public choice theory shows that bureaucrats, in general, tend to pursue their own objectives different from those of the organization and that bureaucrats of international organizations have particularly strong incentives to do so. Those concerned about such problems tend to consider a situation without international organizations as better than one with organizations that are 'hijacked' by specific interests. Their argument is that as the public good is not delivered there is no benefit, so the cost of the bureaucracy can be considered a waste.
- *Ideology and principles*. Many of the protests of the past can be interpreted as opposition to the further development of the liberal market and of its hallmark organizations, the WTO and the IMF, without due attention being given to societal concerns. The chances of a UN-dominated 'new system' to overcome this problem look bleak.

12.3.4 Option 2: partial repairing, incremental improvement, and better coordination of present global regimes

The main characteristic of this option is the separate improvement of each individual regime both in terms of the width of the coverage of public goods and the quality of governance. It accepts the inconvenience of the absence of a clear and consistent world system and works on the improvement of the present patchwork 'system'. There is a panoply of ideas for partial change of the architecture that we have reviewed in terms of practicability in the final sections of Chapters 7 to 10. One can distinguish in this maelstrom of thinking two main currents.

The first strives at the improvement of the capacity of each of the main organizations to deal effectively with their specific responsibility for societal concerns. This approach suggests the IMF to deal better with volatility, the UNEP with environment and the ILO with the enhancement of labour standards. This strategy is clearly advocated on the global level by organizations, such as the WTO that considers, for example, that all international labour issues need to be dealt with by the ILO and not by the WTO. A fairly far-reaching proposal in this respect is the creation of the World Environmental Organization (WEO) that should oversee all regimes in the environmental field (see Chapter 9). In a similar vein, can one find proposals for a world monetary authority (see Chapter 8). Somewhat more difficult to place is the proposal for a world social organisation (Hertz, 2001b) that encompasses both labour, environmental, welfare and human rights codes. It is actually halfway between our first and second options. Included in all such proposals[18] is the need for a better distribution of wealth over rich and poor countries and for a better distribution of power over the various categories of members.

The second tries to bring constraints on the basic rules of the major economic organizations. They advocate the use of instruments to influence the actions of present organizations in such a way as to foster side objectives (e.g. environment in trade matters). A case in point has been the past acceptance of the WTO of generalized systems of preferences for LDCs. A future case could be the use of WTO trade protection measures (including retaliation) to countries that do not fulfil labour standards agreed internationally. However, this comes at the risk that the new regimes become captives of the vested interests of the sector.

The advantages of this option are more limited than those of the previous option. However, a clear gain would be improved coherence and competence of the government of a specialist sector.

Now what are the chances of success? Many sceptics will point to the fact that in the past the progress on these scores has been slow to non-existent and that it is likely that this will continue into the future as the same conditions will prevail. They point, first, to the weakness of the factors that push for global regime development, second, to absence of consensus on the desirability or the feasibility (ideology and science) and, third, to the difficulty of collective action and the lack of leadership. More optimistic observers think that the gradual adaptation and marginal improvement of present institutions may very well be the only feasible option for the future and point towards the limited problems of collective action. The path that the development will take cannot be foreseen, however. It depends very much on the specific configurations of the future factors that push towards regime formation.

12.3.5 *Option 3: towards a world system based on three layers?*

The main characteristic of this option is the introduction of a minimal structure for a coherent global government (covering all important regimes), coupled with the use of reinforced regional integration schemes. This option is based on the observation that action by small groups forming clubs is much easier than large groups. This is, for instance, the case where the diversity of interests between regions as to governance precludes action on the global level, but where tailoring of a regime to the cost and benefits of the countries directly involved does permit action on the regional level. Recently, the EU has sketched a proposal to push regional cooperation in the interest of better world government. The proposal implies a three-layer hierarchical structure (global, regional, national), in which the middle part deals with regional matters for the nations and represents the national part on the global level.

The advantages of the option are three-fold. First, by limiting the demands on the provision of global public goods by providing more on the regional level. Second, by limiting the cost of collective action and trans-action by simplifying coordination and decision-making. Third, by improving the voice of (groups of) LDCs and thereby limiting the distributional issue.

What are the chances of putting this idea into practice? The ideological environment used to be negative. Under the influence of the dominant power (the USA) international organizations (WTO, IBRD, IMF) have for a long time been opposed to regional integration ventures. They were joined by many academics that considered that regionalism would push the global system on the wrong path. Several countries also do not want to divert attention from the improvement of the global government system, because they find that their interests are better served by enhanced integration in the world economy than in a cumbersome regional integration (e.g. Langhammer, 1992). After the switch in the position of the USA they have gradually accepted regional integration as a convenient middle station on the road to worldwide integration. The EU has always been convinced of the merits of this form of integration, also outside Europe (Memedovic *et al.*, 1999). It has supported the creation of regional trade arrangements in several parts of the world by giving technical advice on the way they should be set up and by giving financial support to the ensuing restruc-turing of the economy.

However, a sympathetic attitude towards regionalism is not enough. The tasks of combining the slimmed down version of the grand design of option 1 with a substructure of regionalization is formidable. It would be at two levels:

- *Global organizations.* The creation of a global organization, such as the proposed WEO (World Environmental Organization, slimmed down to do uniquely obvious global tasks such as climate change) comple-mented with the creation of a consistent set of regional organizations with the competences in a wide spectrum of fields is a formidable task.
- *Regional organizations.* On this level, too, the difficulties are immense. First, agreement would have to be reached on the mandate of the

regions in the global institutions and on the governance of the new set-up (including weighted votes). Second, the regions would have to be determined (where is Russia, where the Arab countries, etc.). Next, the value added of an additional layer would have to be proved and the risk of another level of bureaucracy put aside. Finally, a sort of unifying structure for the various regional and global regimes would have to be worked out.

So, the conclusion must be that it is very unlikely that this will be the way forward for the global system.

12.3.6 *Option 4: incremental globalism combined with incremental regionalism*

The main characteristic of option 4 is its linkage between some global regimes and their corresponding regional regimes. In a way, it consists of a slimmed version of option 2 complemented with enhanced regionalism. The idea to improve the existing global institutions and regimes in an incremental way could be easier to implement where regional organizations could be developed that would take away part of the burden from the global ones.

The advantages of the set-up are notably in the enhanced speed of realization and in the improved coherence on different levels with respect to individual regimes. A flaw of the set-up presented as option 4 is that the problem of governance without government is not solved. The need for general coordination and broad policy guidance could be filled in by an adapted version of the G8, whereby the membership would be based on the rule of one member from each of the regions.

How good are the chances to have this idea put into practice? The information in Box 12.7 clearly shows what hurdles have to be taken before the idea can be put into practice and made operational. The tendency to develop specialist regimes on the global level is not fully matched on the regional level. One tends to see organizations that first develop some strength in matters of trade. Some of them develop into more encompassing ones in terms of public goods, that is not only trade, but also labour, finance, environment, etc. (EU, to a lesser degree NAFTA). But going along that path is not easy as the example of Mercosur shows (Baer *et al.*, 2002). The conditions that the EU venture could fulfil and that made the EU a success are not easy to replicate in other regions of the world. They concern, for instance, unity of purpose, limited diversity and strong institutions (Molle, 2001). Indeed, one need but look at the situation of the diversity of interests and cultural backgrounds in a region such as Asia with two countries with a population of over a billion to take the measure of this problem. Moreover, the model of the EU is neither desirable nor feasible in most developing countries (Winters, 1997). So, the assumption behind the idea that the voice

---

Box 12.7 **The match between global and regional regimes**

The match between the global and regional regimes could look as follows:

- *Trade.* The WTO is the farthest developed international organization with clear objectives and a relatively strong institutional set-up. Notably, its dispute settlement procedure stands out in this respect. On the regional level, most ventures that have been set up deal with trade and related matters. Realizing the fourth option would imply a filling in of the missing elements in the puzzle in geographical terms and providing all regional integration organizations with the power to deal with WTO matters.
- *Finance.* The IMF as a global organization uses a direct line in its contact with nations. There is no equivalent structure dealing with monetary and macroeconomic matters on the regional level. The economic commissions of the UN are far from assuming a role as relay between the global and national level. The EU is the only regional organization having competence in these fields. Moreover, most authors have doubts about the capacity of regional organizations, such as ASEAN, to reform themselves quickly enough so as to be able to cope effectively with financial crises (e.g. Park and Wang, 2000).
- *Aid.* The WB deals directly with all countries involved. Next to it exist a number of regional development banks. The setting up of a confederate structure of these institutions would imply that regional banks would be the main operational arms, while the World Bank would limit itself to a role in worldwide redistribution and the exchange of information. The coordination problem between donors would be lessened, the more so when regional banks also assume this role for bilateral donors.
- *Environment.* The UNEP deals in a somewhat disparate manner with a list of global environmental problems, which has resulted in a series of individual international agreements. Kyoto on climate change is a case in point. Next to it are a host of regional agreements. These are all specific legal constructs and regimes, showing a great diversity as to geographic coverage, forms, instruments, etc. The EU is also the exception here, in the sense that as a regional organization it has extensive powers in matters of the environment. The value added of newly created regional institutions for the environment that assume responsibility for harmonizing regional matters consistent with global regimes is far from self-evident.

of the LDCs would be heard better and that their interests would be better represented in global regimes is probably easily realized.

That would mean that a further improvement of all existing regional organizations including the specialist ones has to be put on the agenda; hence the relevance of initiatives such as Chang Mai (see Chapter 8).

12.4 Summary and conclusions

- The global 'order' consists of a set of idiosyncratic regimes. They show very wide diversity on all relevant features, such as rationale, principles and governance.
- Notwithstanding this lack of consistency, the present (non) system has been able to provide the most important global public goods and adapt itself to cope with some new needs. However, for each regime there is a list of points for which improvements are due, many of them related to governance aspects. Moreover, there is a general problem of lack of government and consistency that needs to be dealt with.
- The factors that determine the dynamics of institutional development on the global level are quite distinct from those that have shaped the European institutions. Although some useful lessons can be learned from the EU experience, the EU is not a role model for the world.

The choice of options is dependent on their feasibility:

- The improvement of the situation cannot be realized by making a new grand design. Indeed, none of the conditions identified by the theory for such regime development will be fulfilled in the near future. The same, although to a lesser extent, applies to the model based on three layers of government in which the regional layer would assume a preponderant role. These options are probably unrealistic, in view of the enormous demand they make on the capacity of governments to come to agreements. However, they should not be forgotten. Just as in the European case they should be kept as a long-range perspective that can guide the actions on more immediate objectives.
- Options that improve the present regimes in an incremental way are feasible. They do demand considerable extra effort, but the lines into the future are better traced and can be made more concrete in terms of benefits and costs for different partners.

A double strategy is needed consisting:

- On the global level, in regime improvement, for instance of the type of the creation of the proposed world environmental organization or a new organisation for global macroeconomic management.
- On the regional level, in an increase in comprehensiveness of existing integration schemes.

Notes

1 Introduction

1 We will base ourselves thereby on a number of analyses and proposals that have been made by both academics and by civil society and put these in a rigorous theoretical framework.

2 However, in each chapter we will devote a section to the issue so as to make clear where the points of contact are between our interest in global matters and the regional issue.

3 I realize that my position is coloured by past experience and the European context of much of my work. Moreover, I am aware of the fact that there is an overwhelming supply of Anglo-Saxon literature notably by persons working for US-based organizations or institutions. This is reflected in my list of references. This limelight is likely to leave many other contributions from smaller language groups and from institutions that have less access to international publishers in the shade (such as universities in LDCs). I invite the reader to send me any relevant publications that can help me to provide a more balanced view.

2 The dynamics of globalization

1 We refer here notably to Kenwood and Lougheed (1999) to whom the text of the present chapter owes very much. See also Foreman Peck (1995, 1998), Bairoch (1993) and Pollard (1997).

2 See for a definition of institutions, Chapter 4, and for a description of the international organizations, Chapter 6.

3 The paradigm has been developed by Dunning (1993a,b) the text of this box is taken from the presentation of the OLI paradigm in UNCTAD (2000: 141).

4 See in this respect Hufbauer (1991), van Bergeyk and Mensink (1997) and the annual reports of international organizations, such as UNCTAD, on investment and of the IMF on capital movements.

5 Globalization has started in the West. Hence this chapter shows a strong accent on Western Europe first and the North Atlantic area next. This is not due to a lack of interest for developments in the rest of the world but a reflection of the way in which the West has for a long time dominated global economic relations (see, for instance, Table 3.1).

6 See for this period in particular O'Rourke and Williamson (1999).

7 The tendency described here did not proceed uniformly over the whole period; in the 1920s the growth of trade and output were about at the same pace, but in the 1930s trade volumes lagged considerably behind output.

8 The high level of the figures for the EU has been reached in the period before 1970; integration had actually already started in the 1950s.

9 For the definition of the organizations corresponding to the acronyms in the Table, see Section 6.7.

10 Under the influence of this liberalization, the FDI has increased 20-fold between 1973 and 2000, both in terms of flows and in terms of stocks. The share of world FDI in world GDP increased between 1980 and 2000 from 0.5 per cent to almost 3 per cent (UNCTAD 2001). Under the influence of the global crisis it decreased very considerably in 2001 to almost half the previous year (UNCTAD, 2002).

11 This crisis has many explanations. To some it marked the end of a major upturn in the very long Kondratieff cycle (about 50 years). To others the sudden rise of the power of the oil exporting countries sparked off a loss of competitiveness in the developed countries. This problem was aggravated because the illness has been cured with the wrong medicine (Keynesian stimulation programmes).

12 With the implementation of the euro, the situation has shifted once again and is now more in the left-hand bottom corner of the table. Up to now, the experience with target zones is not very encouraging. However, the situation of the dollar–euro relation may evolve in that direction.

3 Coping with the effects of globalization

1 There is ample evidence that the number of armed conflicts between countries that have strong economic links is less than between countries that have only a restricted economic interchange (Polacheck, 1980; Hirsch, 1981 for trade; Gartzke *et al.*, 2001 for economic interdependence including monetary and other interrelations). Moreover, the lack of international procedures to come to arbitrage in international trade conflicts is supposed to have significantly contributed to military conflicts in the nineteenth and twentieth centuries (WTO, 1998).

2 This applies both to general (globalization) and preferential trade liberalization (regionalism). Some claim that regionalism stands in the way of globalization. However, recent developments show that both are mutually reinforcing (Ethier, 1998).

3 LDCs claim that the distribution of benefits over the various groups of countries needs to be made more equitable. They want to redesign institutions and instruments so that they favour more the LDCs. The suggestions range from the traditional protectionist trade policy and control on the activities of multinational firms via an increase in the level of development aid to a recast of the world institutional system (WTO, World Bank etc.). In the next sections we analyse here somewhat further the trade policy and FDI aspects, as they as they have the most direct bearing on regime choices to be discussed in the later chapters of this book.

4 Prior to the industrial revolution the difference between somewhat differently defined groups has been estimated to be 2 to 1 (Bairoch, 1993).

5 Convergence has occurred in what is now the OECD club (Williamson, 1996). This is partly due to openness. Indeed, the long-term data show an increase in convergence during the periods when openness increased and the decrease in convergence when openness decreased.

6 Rich countries: OECD plus 'tigers'. Globalizers: top one-third of 72 developing countries for which trade/GDP ratios increased. Non-globalizers: other countries. The results are not significantly affected in case other categorisations are chosen.

7 The World Investment Report (WIR) from which this text is cited (UNCTAD, 1999: 156) describes for each of these points the way in which MNF and FDI can actually support the development of the LDCs. These points have been further elaborated in the 2002 WIR (UNCTAD, 2002).

8 Much of this section is based on earlier work of the author in this field published in Molle (2002).

9 This is the quantity aspect of the labour market.

10 See, for instance, for the EU Jungnickel (1996) and for the US Burtless *et al.* (1998).

11 This view is corroborated by the results of recent studies for the EU (Sapir, 1999) and for the US and Japan (Ghose, 2000). The latter author puts his conclusions rather bluntly as: 'Thus it is patently absurd to attribute the economy-wide unemployment in industrialiszed countries to trade in manufactures with developing countries' (p. 34).

12 See, for instance, for France, Arthuis (1993).

13 This is the price indicator of the labour market.

14 However, here too the situation is far from straightforward. No negative effect has been found by Lawrence (1996: Chapter 3, Wage inequality). The study by Ghose (2000) for the US and Japan leads him to conclude: 'Trade with developing countries cannot be held responsible for the growing wage inequality in industrialized countries either' (p. 34). However, Dasgupta and Osang (2002) find that about 50 per cent of the premium of non-production over production workers can be attributed to globalization.

15 See for a review for the EU case Molle (2001: Chapter 7).

16 A plea for the setting up of such a regime and ideas for the rules it should apply and its organization are given in the various contributions to the book edited by Ghosh (2000).

17 As an example we may take the theoretical and empirical uncertainty as to the effects of the minimum wage on unemployment; see in this respect, e.g., Dolado *et al.* (1996); Cahuc *et al.* (2001); Broadway and Cuff (2001).

18 See for a review of the literature Cluitmans *et al.* (1999), and for recent evidence about the negative influence of labour-related taxes, Daveri and Tabellini (2000). This result is corroborated by findings outside the European area, for instance for Canada, Stanford (1998).

19 See in this respect among many others Atkinson (1999); Franzini and Pizzuti (2001).

20 A special case that should be mentioned is for countries that are dependent on international sources for loans to finance their operations. International credit bureaux give ratings to countries based on their economic policies. Unfavourable combinations of policies lead to high cost of borrowing. This adds to the conditionality of IMF lending which forces countries very often to policies that are different from the ones they would have chosen independently.

21 We will discuss the aspects of labour market standards further in Chapter 11. The influence of integration on environmental standards is given in Levinson (1996).

22 We will not go further into this point, but suggest the reader keeps it in mind while evaluating claims for restricting openness on the grounds that it harms specific interests.

23 Their use is found to be the less justified the higher the wage differences between the trade partners (Cordella and Grilo, 2001).

24 This policy mix is indeed the one chosen (more or less explicitly) by many national governments. See in this respect among others Hirschhausen and von Bitzer (2000).

25 In concluding this we do not think to take an ideological position, because more government involvement in creating good regimes is conducive to growth and private sector development. It is even consistent with more privatization and a reinforced role of markets.

4 The provision of global public goods

1 The analysis we make in this and the subsequent chapter is largely based on the so-called neoclassical writers of the school of New Institutionalism. See for a description of the relative position of these writers in the total tradition of institutionalism: Rutherford (1994). Particulary important in this group is North; a number of sentences of this section have been cited from his work (North, 1990a).

2 See for the change of property rights while going from a centrally planned economy to a capitalist economy, Weimer (1997).

3 There are other organizational forms to which we will not refer here (such as the association). What we would like to underline is that the various forms presented can be explained in terms of the differences in the cost of planning, adapting and monitoring task completion.

4 The aspects about transaction cost in economics that we have dealt with in the previous sections (see for instance, Williamson, 1989) take on a different character once applied to the public sector and notably to politics. Applied to the latter field they could be termed transaction cost policy. A start has been made by North (1990b), a much more elaborate exercise is given in Dixit (1998a), a more concise description of the most relevant aspects of the latter study is presented in Dixit (1998b). The text of the present sections is much indebted to the studies by Dixit.

5 Other examples abound of such cost of screening. One may but cite here chambers of commerce that give basic information about firms in their resort (legal structure, number of shareholders, size of the capital and bankruptcy records). Rating agencies give information about, for instance, the capital position of banks.

6 There are also cases where the private sector provides the institution that helps to bring down transaction cost. We may cite here (in the same vein as the exchange of students) the efficient international exchange of traineeships for students in economics and business organized by AIESEC. The organization provides for a market where traineeships are exchanged on standardized conditions for both participating firms and trainees.

7 In the literature, the term global public good (GPG) tends to get extended on two dimensions:

Means to realize the GPG. This is, for instance, the case with stability of conditions for doing international business. We may cite here the stability of exchange rates or the conditions under which goods will be traded internationally once a foreign investment project has come to fruition. Such GPGs are provided by a regime. The provision of such a regime can then be considered as an intermediate public good. In this book we will go along with this extended notion.

Anything that is politically desirable. In quite a few discussions about global problems the claim is made that solving the problem would be a global public good, usually followed by a claim for financial support of the international community. A list of subjects can be mentioned ranging from poverty reduction, health improvement, gender equality, etc. We will not go along with this extended view as it would imply a loss of analytical specificity leading to a loss of clarity of policy conclusions (Bezanson, 2002).

8 See in this respect the discussion about global commons in Hollick and Cooper (1997).

9 Based on Bezanson (2002).

10 Although it is already some time since Olson wrote his classic book on this subject and although much refinement has been made since, his main conclusions are still valid.
11 See Eden and Hampson (1997).
12 See, for example, for the environment Folmer *et al.* (1993) and Hanley and Folmer (1998).
13 Olson (1965: 48).
14 See, for instance, Dixit and Skeath (1999) in particular Chapter 11, Collective action games.
15 This section draws heavily on Dixit (1998a and b).
16 Given their importance for the development of institutions, we will specify the relevant principles for each regime in Chapters 7 to 11 and give an overview in Chapter 12.
17 A good example of such a solution was the European Monetary System. It created long-term stability of the exchange rates by specifying that the pivot rates of the participating countries could only be changed by mutual agreement. It provided for short-term flexibility by letting the market rates fluctuate within certain brackets; the limits of which were defended by the cooperating monetary authorities.

5 Types of institutions and their dynamics

1 Paramount among the authors we will cite is North (1990a and b) who won a Noble Prize for his work on the role of institutions. For other concepts used later in the chapter we will refer to textbooks, notably those of Kasper and Streit (1998) and of Furubotn and Richter (2000).
2 Examples abound of the use of the word *governance* in this sense: see the list of references. We refer here notably to CGG (1995) for the global level and to CEC (2001) for the regional (European) level. The word governance has a still somewhat different meaning in development economics: there good governance is defined as the provision of public institutions that are effective in enhancing economic and social development.
3 The term regulation is a source of much confusion. In the Anglo-Saxon literature it is often used (see, for example, Brathwaite and Drahos, 2000) in the sense we have defined institutions, including principles, norms, etc. In the French school around the 'Theorie de la Regulation' it applied essentially with 'capitalism and its transformations' (Boyer and Saillard, 2002).
4 The text of this section is partly based on IBRD (1992: 154)
5 The text of the rest of this section draws heavily on Williamson (1998: 26)
6 Here the objective is to gain insight into the way in which economic actors (players) come to coordination results on the basis of specified rules of the game on the basis of the information each player has (see also last section of the previous chapter).
7 This section is based on Alt *et al.* (1988: 446), Krasner (1983: 2) and Furubotn and Richter (2000: 429–30).
8 The term indicates the importance of internal consistency and provides for technical proficiency (Cooper, 1987: 2).
9 Compare in this respect the four levels of the scheme given in Table 5.1; the categories of norms would correspond to the first level; the principles would correspond to the second level and the rules and procedures to the levels 3 and 4.
10 Regimes apply also to national cases, where they can for instance apply to different sectors of activity see Campbell and Lindberg (1991). They can also apply to regional integration (see Molle, 2002).

11 See for complex interdependence of forces that contribute to the regime creation and development among others Cooper (1985) and Keohane (1993).
12 Among others Young and Osherenko (1993) and Efinger *et al.* (1993)
13 Political scientists view international regimes as an extension to national politics. In a game theoretic sense (see Alt *et al.*, 1988) as cooperative solutions to repeated collective action games.
14 Based on Keohane (1993), who uses the term institution in the same meaning as we use regime.
15 Of course the differences between the groups are rather a matter of intensity than a matter of principle.
16 Coordination is more difficult if it has to take place in an open negotiating setting, where the rules of the game, the agenda setting are often part of the negotiation. This will often imply cooperation to set up a new regime or a new organization.

6 Main organizations

1 Other specialized agencies, such as the ITU and ICAO (the International Civil Aviation Organization), have similar structures as IMO and will not be detailed in this chapter further. We briefly indicate their specific characteristics in the relevant sections of Chapter 10.
2 See for a general description, for instance, Winham (1998) and for an overview of the basic texts, other agreements and understandings and the procedure to apply for membership (www.wto.org/english/the wto_e/thewto_e.htm).
3 A detailed overview of the dispute settlement is given in Box 7.4.
4 The share of the US is some 17 per cent, the individual shares of the EU member states are much less but together they count for some 30 per cent. This must be compared with a share of the whole Asian region of some 18 per cent.
5 See Van Houtven (2002) for a critical assessment of the governance structure of the IMF.
6 See for more details the basic texts and other documents available from http://www.unep.org/about.asp and the annual document Global Environment Outlook.
7 See for more details the basic texts and other documents available from http://www.imo.org//about
8 See for more details the basic texts and other documents available from http://www.ilo.org/public/english/
9 See for a more detailed description of the role of the G8, Hodges *et al.* (1999) and for the G20, Kirton (2001).
10 Only in the course of the 1980s, long after the start of the EC. Compare for instance the European Union, where the European Council of heads of state and government was added to the institutional structure.
11 See for a review, Iwasaki and Prakash (2002).
12 See Box 11.1 for a concrete example of the way in which things that have been discussed without participation of NGOs can go wrong.

7 Trade in goods and services

1 Section based on Ethier (1998).
2 It implies that the free-rider problem is less important in trade matters than in other global regimes.

3 Economic theory also puts unilateral trade liberalization as more advantageous than protection. However, as governments tend to ignore this result, we will not introduce this aspect in the game.

4 Net benefits determine a country's position. These benefits do not need to be solely in monetary terms. A country can also gain in reputation from joining, which may work out positively on other policy fields (e.g. military protection by a major power). On the cost side, again there is not only the trade cost. For a small country the cost of setting up the administrative capacity to deal with world trade matters may be significant.

5 The market position of firms tend to determine their position in the trade issue.

   • Domestic firms that produce for the internal market tend to be in favour of protectionism;
   • Export-oriented firms tend to be in favour of free trade;
   • Importing firms (of intermediate goods) also have an interest in cheap imports, and thus in liberalization.

   As many MNFs are combinations of the latter two types they are in general in favour of free trade. However, some MNF that are exploiting their firm-specific advantages in the home markets of several countries can (like domestic firms), also have an interest in protection.

6 A complete overview of the objectives, rules and operational problems of WTO is given in Hoekman and Kostecki (2001). Students will also find here a number of interesting case studies of international trade disputes. Other general information can be found in Winham (1998), Krueger (1998) and Lloyd (2001). For a discussion on the future role we refer again to Hoeckman and Kostecki (2001) and Schott (2000).

7 See for services, for instance, Francois and Wooton (2001).

8 Although the WTO regime formally forbids quota, it has in practice accommodated many. The question is then: Why could they develop? The answer is because they are a substitute for tariffs. They are less efficient, but expedient. In institutional terms they could emerge and be maintained because they were often based on an agreement between protected home industries and rent-earning exporters. So there were no complaints.

9 LDCs differ in stage of development and are dependent on different goods for their export revenue.

10 In formal terms the General Council takes the decision. However, this body can only unanimously reject the findings.

11 A number of publications have expressed this concern. We cite here Bhagwati (2000), Oyejide (2000), Hertel *et al.* (2002) and the special issue of April 2000 of *The World Economy*.

12 Two of these subjects, viz., investment and competition will be discussed in Chapter 11. We do not discuss the other two subjects, as they seem obvious cases for WTO activity. Public procurement represents a considerable market. If access to that market is reserved for local companies or if local companies benefit from preferential treatment the principles of the WTO will be a dead letter. Trade procedures concern administrative obligations, certificates, cautions, etc. They are of considerable relevance in the daily practice of international traders and can add significantly to transaction cost.

13 It has been agreed that the competition issue would not be put on the negotiation agenda before 2004.

14 See for a presentation of the classical methods to analyse the welfare effects of introducing environmental concerns in trade matters, Anderson (1992).

15 We will discuss the issues of coordination in more detail in Chapters 11 and 12.

8 Finance

1 Morris (2000) presents an overview of the theoretical aspects of contagion. See also Sell (2001).

2 The more important the trade competition, the more likely self-fulfilling speculative crises and the larger the set of multiple equilibria. See Loisel and Martin (2001).

3 So there is a case for a soft procedure, whereby international bodies gradually step up their involvement in the support to countries encountering this type of difficulty.

4 It is a striking feature of the financial sector that the literature does not present us with clear principles, which differs much from the situation in other fields. All literature, for instance on trade mentions the basic principles there: liberalization, non-discrimination and MFN. The same applies to environment where the three principles of precaution, polluter pays and differentiated responsibilities are mentioned in all basic texts on the subject.

5 International standards have to be set and regularly adapted as innovations change the products and production technology. The international standard for bank capital arose out of discussions between the G10 regulators. It was adopted by the G10 as a result of the Basle Accord of 1998. It has subsequently been adopted by more than 100 countries.

6 It is indeed very difficult to get to an adequate interpretation of the data. The complex interplay of the international actors on one hand and the existence of multiple equilibria on the other mean that in the past many crises have not been foreseen, whereas many situations that might easily have led to crises have not done so. Moreover, there is actually a danger in the possibility of misinterpretation that if signals are wrongly understood that harmless information will trigger a crisis.

7 See, for instance, Mathieson and Schinasi (2000).

8 This view has given rise to the nickname 'It's Mainly Fiscal' for IMF. This position is in a sense the more astonishing as all developed countries have a strong institutional framework that copes with market failures and guides the economic actions of the private sector (Rappoport, 2002).

9 This has led to many critics naming the IMF as 'International Misery Fund'. Others prefer the name 'It's My Fault'; putting the accent on the fact that the IMF by prescribing in a number of cases the wrong therapy should be blamed for that and should actually waive the loans that it has given in these cases. As things now stand the poor LDC has eventually to pay for the errors of the arrogant staff of the Fund (Raffner, 2002).

10 See in this respect the special issue of the *Journal of Economic Perspectives* (here represented by the articles from Mishkin (1999) and Rogoff (1999)), the various contributions in Teunissen (2000) and the evaluation of a number of individual proposals as discussed in Kaiser *et al.* (2001). Moreover, many analyses of the problem also contain suggestions for improvement (see, for example, Chu and Hill (2001) and Sell (2001)).

11 Which means that particular attention should be paid to the effective regulation of the most volatile flows, such as portfolio investments.

12 There is an abundant literature on the subject. We base ourselves notably on Haq *et al.* (1996) and Artesis and Sawyer (1997).

9 Environment

1 The problems of depletion of renewable resources have been tackled in international environmental agreements concerning the seas (fisheries such as the

Convention on the Regulation of Whaling, and results of the United Nations Conference on the Law of the Seas. With respect to nonrenewable resources, such as the minerals of the ocean bed, an International Seabed Authority has been proposed to deal with this matter.

2 So it is of importance to come to a sustainable management of the use of the global commons (Hardin and Baden, 1977; Nordhaus, 1994).

3 For the relevance of these notions, see Chapter 5.

4 The precautionary principle, although applied in a number of international environmental agreements has not received universal acceptance. There is much discussion whether the principle is part of international law. LDCs are particularly concerned about the possibility that the principle is used as a disguise for protectionist measures by the highly developed countries.

5 Compare the set up of UNEP later in this chapter with the set up of WTO in Chapter 7.

6 This boils down to the putting of property rights on these goods; which indicates the relevance of the discussion of this item in Chapter 4.

7 See for a more detailed description of the international aspects of the design of emission trading the various contributions to Carraro (2000).

8 See for a much more detailed description of the causes and dynamics of these changes chapter 12 in Braithwaite and Drahos (2000).

9 For further details on the development and changed role of the NGOs in environmental matters see, for instance, McCormick (1999).

10 The EU has also cooperated with other countries to come to a better situation in the whole subcontinent. The Convention on Long Range Transboundary Air Pollution has set reduction targets for a range of pollutants. It monitors all nations' compliance with the protocols. The convention has been catalytic in promoting the understanding of causes and effects and by that has shown the road towards further reductions.

11 Their contribution to the production of greenhouse gases, both in absolute and in per capita terms is much less (by a very wide margin) than that of the developed world.

12 Their conclusion was, 'All in all, the Kyoto Protocol is an impractical policy focussed on achieving an unrealistic and inappropriate goal' (McKibbin and Wilcoxen, 2002: 127).

10 Transport and telecommunications

1 In a sense, this would have justified a very strong accent on transport in the economics of trade relations. This has not been the case; most of the accent has been on nonspatial aspects, such as tariffs, etc. Recently, more attention has been given to the relation trade and transport; see, for instance, Steiniger (2001).

2 See for a political economy approach to the fist three of these sectors, Zacher and Sutton (1996).

3 Countries, such as Britain, started very early in this respect by obliging wool traders to use British vessels.

4 Compare this role with the one of ICAO in air transport and of IPU in telecommunications.

5 The data abstract from ICAO is of a technical nature, on which we do not pronounce ourselves in this economic analysis.

6 No need is as yet indicated for public production.

7 Indeed, the Internet is in a state of considerable flux. It undergoes massive technical change. It entails large changes in industrial structure and ownership. Types of service change very rapidly.

8 In 1998, the EU has adopted a data protection directive laying down very stringent rules about the collection and transmission of personal data.

11 Complementing the system

1 See, for instance, the general view of Drahos and Braithwaite (2001) or the OECD (1992). The latter organization suggests the seting up of a wide-ranging framework for harmonization of national regimes and policies. An example is industrial policy, covering aspects such as technology, R&D, patents and subsidies.
2 This section is largely based on Dymond (2000), Johnston (2000) and OECD (1997c).
3 See for an early proposal Goldberg and Kindleberger (1970) and for a more recent view, Brewer and Young (1995).
4 See for a more detailed description of the structure and a comment on the position of various actors (such as developed countries UNCTAD (1999: 126–37).
5 This point has been one of the most controversial elements of the MAI.
6 See for the first view among others Carens (1987).
7 See for a review of these studies the section on migration in Chapter 3.
8 This section is largely based on and inspired by Straubhaar (2000), Ghosh (2000) and Nayyar (2002).
9 See the special issue of the *International Migration Review* (1991: 25–737).
10 See for a good overview of the discussion Bhagwati and Wilson (1989).
11 In this sense this proposal is comparable to the so-called Tobin Tax on international movements of capital (see Chapter 8).
12 This would have some resemblance with the idea of tradeable emission rights (see Chapter 9).
13 For this we refer to other parts of the literature, in particular Ghosh (2000).
14 Antidumping is obsolete as soon as competition policy is executed adequately. So the introduction of a multinational competition policy should limit the use of retaliation by trade policy measures (compare the situation in the EU; Box 12.4).
15 The OECD joint group on trade and competition found that the evidence for discrimination against foreign competitors in competition policy was very weak. Most countries tend to apply the same procedures to foreign and domestic companies alike.
16 This section has benefited much from the contribution of Feis to the ILO publication on International Labour standards (Sengenberger and Campbell, 1994).
17 The present section is largely based on OECD (1996).
18 For example, Cordella and Grilo (2001) prudently conclude 'that a social policy clause cannot be dismissed on domestic (or world) welfare grounds its case is weaker the higher is the domestic wage and the lower is the foreign wage'.
19 Some bilateral or regional arrangements go even further and impose actual fines in case a country does not observe labour standards (see Elliot, 2001).
20 See in this respect, e.g. Kolk *et al.* (1999).

12 Evaluation and outlook

1 Our point of departure is the observation that the present development of the global economy has created a number of good results but also some negative externalities. The problems need to be solved. This raises the usual 'why', 'which', ' who' and 'how' questions. Why have such problems emerged in the

first place, which problems need be addressed with priority, who should take action and in what way? Answering these questions is a task of heroic size and of bewildering complexity; anyway too large for this book. So we will limit ourselves to some essentials.

The citation of Stiglitz suggests that the answer to the 'why' question lies in the absence of sufficient guidance or 'government' to steer the operations of private actors in a socially acceptable way. The 'which' question has an answer in the sense that the most important problems have to do with sustainability, equity and volatility. With respect to the 'who' question, he suggests giving more voice to the LDCs and civil society. With respect to the 'how' question, he suggests taking a fresh look abstracting from the usual ideology, such as the Washington 'consensus' and reviewing the adequacy of the available battery of governance. Central in his citation is the plea for better government. All these elements have been touched upon in the previous chapters.

2　These notions refer in general terms to the discussions in Chapter 4.

3　This section refers to the elements presented in Chapter 6 and elaborated in the regime chapters.

4　Here we refer to the notions about the second layer of institutions distinguished in Section 5.3.2.

5　Referring to the third layer of institutions 'governance' of Section 5.3.2.

6　One might group the regimes for transport and telecommunication under this function, as they create the technical conditions for communication, a public good that is to a large extent creating the conditions for the operationality of others functions.

7　Special feature: European Court of Human Rights.

8　The OEEC as an organization did not amalgamate with the EU. It enlarged its membership to become OECD. However, its tasks for the western European countries have been taken over by the EU. The work of the Council of Europe has only very partly been taken over by the EU but cultural matters have mostly stayed with the national member states under the application of the subsidiarity principle.

9　There is a problem with this situation in the sense that the dominance of the free market model is often equated with the form it has taken in the US. Those making this mistake tend to overlook that other variants exist, that also perform well, and that are adapted to the specific cultural and institutional conditions of the country where it is applied.

10　Interesting in this respect is that Soros (2000), the chieftain of market speculators has become a convert and strongly criticizes the lack of capacity to check the negative side of free financial markets. His search for a new ideology respecting values of different parts of the world has resulted in the concept of 'Open Society'.

11　A case in point may be the Indian economy where the new economic policy recognized the need for participating in globalization and subsequently led to a change towards internal and external liberalization. However, other policies had to deal with regional equilibrium and labour and social issues (see, for example, Jauhari, 1996).

12　Notably problems in their access to markets for agricultural and labour-intensive goods.

13　'Institutions, especially those created to tackle the problems of globalism, come at particular moments of crisis under strains that are so great as to preclude effective operation. They become the main channels through which the resentments against globalization work their destruction' (James, 2001: 5).

14　There are many ways to organize such proposals. See an alternative set up also taking the UN into account Nayyar (2002b).

15 Our analysis will be problem-based not organization-based.
16 An example of such a plea is Moshirian (2002).
17 That is, not all countries need to participate in the same way, in all policy fields, at the same moment.
18 Similar proposals are made by Raffer and Singer (2001), Chapter 14.

References

Aghion, P. (1998) 'Inequality and economic growth', in P. Aghion and J.G. Williamson (eds). *Growth, Inequality and Globalization; Theory, History and Policy*, Cambridge: Cambridge University Press, 6–102.

Agiomirgianakis, G. and Zervoyianni, A. (2001) Globalization of labor markets and macro-economic equilibrium, *International Review of Economics and Finance*, 10(2): 109–33.

Aglietta, M. (1995) 'The international monetary system', in R. Boyer and Y. Saillard (eds). *Regulation Theory; The State of the Art*, London: Routledge, 64–71.

Alt, J.R., Calvert, R. and Humes, B. (1988) Reputation and hegemonic stability; a game theoretic analysis, *American Political Science Review* 82: 445–66.

Anderson, K. (1992) 'The standard welfare economics of policies affecting trade and the environment', in K. Anderson and R. Blackhurst (eds). *The Greening of World Trade Issues*, New York: Harvestor/Wheatsheaf, 25–48.

Anderson, K. and Norheim, H. (1993) 'History, geography and regional economic integration', in K. Anderson and R. Blackhurst (eds). *Regional Integration and the Global Trading System*, Hemel Hampstead: Harvestor/Wheatsheaf, 19–51.

Antweiler, W., Copeland, B.R. and Taylor, M.S. (2001) Is free trade good for the environment? *American Economic Review* 91(4): 877–908.

Artesis, P. and Sawyer, M. (1997) How many cheers for the Tobin tax? *Cambridge Journal of Economics* 21: 753–68.

Arthuis, J. (1993) Rapport d'ínformation sur l'íncidence economique et fiscale des delocalisations hors du territoire national des activites industrielles et de service, *Rapport d'information, No. 337 Senat*, Paris.

Atkinson, G. (1999) Developing global institutions; lessons to be learned from regional integration experiences, *Journal of Economic Issues* 33(2): 335–41.

Baer, W., Cavalcanti, T. and Silva, P. (2002) Economic integration without policy coordination; the case of Mercosur, *Emerging Markets Review* 3: 269–91.

Bairoch, P. (1993) *Economics and World History*, Brighton: Wheatsheaf.

Baldwin, R.E. and Martin, P. (1999) Two waves of globalization, superficial similarity and fundamental differences, *NBER Working Paper*, No. 8459.

Bakker, A. (1996) *International Financial Institutions*, London: Prentice Hall/Longman.

Barett, S. (1990) The problem of global environmental protection, *Oxford Review of Economic Policy* 6(1): 68–79.

Barett, S. (1999) 'Montreal versus Kyoto, international cooperation and the global environment', in I. Kaul, I. Grunberg, and M. Stern (eds). *Global Public Goods*, Geneva: UNDP, 192–219.

Batabyal, A.A. and Beladi, H. (eds) (2001) *The Economics of International Trade and the Environment,* Boca Raton: Lewis Publishers.

Bezanson, K. (2002) Global public goods; opportunities and threats, *EU LDC Network, Newsletter,* July 2–5.

Bertram, G. (1992) Tradable emission permits and the control of greenhouse gases, *The Journal of Development Studies,* 28 (3): 423–66.

Bhagwati, J. (ed.). (1976) *The Brain Drain and Taxation, Theory and Empirical Analysis,* Amsterdam: North Holland.

Bhagwati, J. and Wilson, J.D. (1989) *Income Taxation and International Mobility,* Cambridge, MA:, MIT Press.

Bhagwati, J.N. (1998a) The capital myth; the evidence between widgets and dollars, *Foreign Affairs* 3: 7–12.

Bhagwati, J.N. (1998b) 'Trade and wages; a malign relationship?' in O. Memedovic, A. Kuyvenhoven and W. Molle (eds). *Globalization and Labour Markets; Challenges, Adjustments and Policy Response in the European Union and Less Developed Countries,* Dordrecht: Kluwer, 31–66.

Bhagwati, J. (2000) After Seattle, free trade and the WTO, *International Affairs* 77: 15–30.

Bhalla, S.S. (2002) *Imagine There's No Country; Poverty, Inequality and Growth in the Era of Globalization,* Washington: IIE.

BIS (1997) Financial stability in emerging market economies, *Draghi Report of the Working Party on Financial Stability in Emerging Market Economies,* Basle.

Black, J., Levi, M.D. and de Meza, D. (1993) Creating a good atmosphere: mimimum participation for tackling the 'greenhouse effect', *Economica,* 60: 281–93.

Blackhurst, R. and Henderson, D. (1993) 'Regional integration agreements, world integration and the GATT', in K. Anderson and R. Blackhurst (eds). *Regional Integration and the Global Trading System,* New York/London: Harvestor/Wheatsheaf, 408–35.

Bordo, M.D. (ed). (1999) *The Gold Standard and Related Regimes; Collective Essays,* Cambridge: Cambridge University Press.

Bordo, M., Eichengreen, B., Klingebiel, D. and Soledad, M. (2001) Financial crises; lessons from the last 120 years, *Economic Policy; A European Forum,* 32: 53–82.

Bosello, F. and Roson, R. (1999) 'Carbon emission trading and equity in international agreements', in C. Carraro (ed.) *Efficiency and Equity in Climate Change Policy,* Dordrecht: Kluwer, 291–304.

Boyd, R. and Ibarraran, M.E. (2002) Cost of compliance with the Kyoto Protocol; a developing country perspective, *Energy Economics,* 24: 21–39.

Boyer, R. and Saillard, Y. (2002), *Regulation Theory; The State of the Art,* London: Routledge.

Braithwaite, J. and Drahos, P. (2000) *Global Business Regulation,* Cambridge: Cambridge University Press.

Brealey, R., Clark, A., Goodhart, C. Healey, J., Hoggarth, G., Llewellyn, D.T., Shu, C., Sinclair P., Soussa, F. (2001) *Financial Stability and Central Banks,* London: Routledge.

Brewer, T. and Young, S. (1995) Towards a new multilateral framework for FDI; issues and scenarios, *Transnational Corporations* 4(1): 69–83.

Brewer, T. and Young, S. (1996) Investment policies in multilateral and regional agreements; a comparative analysis, *Transnational Corporations* 5(1): 9–35.

Broadway, R. and Cuff, K. (2001), A minimum wage can be welfare improving and employment enhancing, *European Economic Review* 45(3): 553–76.

Brousseau, E. and Glachant, J.-M. (2002) *The Economics of Contracts*, Cambridge: Cambridge University Press.

Brown, D.K., Deardorff, A.V. and Stern, R. (2001) CGE modelling and analysis of multilateral and regional negotiating options, *Discussion Paper no 468*, Ann Arbor University.

Buchanan, J.M. (1991) *Constitutional Economics*, Cambridge, MA: Basil Blackwell.

Buonanno, P., Castelnuovo, E., Carraro, C. and Galeotti, M. (2000) 'Efficiency and equity of emission trading with endogeneous environmental technical change', in C. Carraro (ed.) *Efficiency and Equity in Climate Change Policy*, Dordrecht: Kluwer, 121–62.

Burkart, O. and Coudert, V. (2002) Leading indicators of currency crisis for emerging countries, *Emerging Markets Review* 3: 107–33.

Burtless, G., Lawrence, R.Z., Litan, R.E. and Shapiro, R.J. (1998), *Globaphobia; Confronting Fears about Open Trade*, Washington, Brookings Institute.

Button, K.J. (1999) 'Shipping Alliances; Are They the Core of Solving Instability Problems in Shipping?' in IAME. *Liner Shipping, What's Next?* Halifax: CIBS, 58–88.

Button, K. and Stough, R. (2000) *Air Transport Networks, Theory and Policy Implications*, Cheltenham: Edward Elgar.

Cahuc, P., Saint Martin, A. and Zylberberg, A. (2001) The consequences of the minimum wage when other wages are bargained over, *European Economic Review* 45(2), 337–52.

Calmfors, L. and Drifill, J. (1988), Bargaining structure, corporatism and macro-economic performance, *Economic Policy*, 13(6): 14–61.

Campbell, N.J. and Lindberg, L.N. (1991) 'The evolution of governance regimes', in N.J. Campbell, J.R. Hollingworth and L.N. Lindberg (eds). *Governance of the American Economy*, Cambridge, MA: Cambridge University Press.

Carens, J. (1987) Aliens and citizens, the case for open borders, *The Review of Politics* 47: 251.

Carlson, L.J. (2000) 'Game theory, international trade conflict and cooperation', in R. Palan (ed.) *Global Political Economy; Contemporary Theories*, London: Routledge, 117–29.

Carraro, C. and Siniscalco, D. (1993) Strategies for the international protection of the environment, *Journal of Public Economics* 52: 309–28.

Carraro, C. and Siniscalco, D. (1998) International environmental agreements; incentives and political economy, *European Economic Review* 42: 561–72.

Carraro, C. (2000) (ed.) *Efficiency and Equity of Climate Change Policy*, Dordrecht: Kluwer.

Cave, M. and Mason, R. (2001) The economics of the Internet; infrastructure and regulation, *Oxford Review of Economic Policy* 17(2): 188–201.

CEC (2001) *European Governance; A White Paper*, Brussels: Commission of the European Communities.

Chang, H-J. (2002) *Kicking Away the Ladder; Development Strategy in Historical Perspective*, London, Anthem Press.

Chirathivat, S., Pachusanoud, C.H. and Wongboonsin, P. (1999) ASEAN prospects for regional integration and the implications for the ASEAN legislative and institutional framework, *ASEAN Economic Bulletin* 16(1): 28–50.

Chu, Y.-P. and Hill, H. (eds) (2001) *The Social Impact of the Asian Financial Crisis*, Cheltenham: Edward Elgar.

CGG (1995) *Our Global Neighborhood, The Report of the Commission on Global Governance*, Oxford: Oxford University Press.

Cluitmans, M., van Nes, P.J. and Molle, W. (1999) *Survey on Impact of EMU on Labour Markets* (report for EC DGV), Rotterdam.

Coase, R.H. (1937 [1988]) The nature of the firm, *Economica*, 4: 386–405; reprinted as chapter 2 in: R.H. Coase (1988) *The Firm, The Market and The Law*, Chicago: University of Chicago Press.

Cooper R.N. (1985) *Economic Policy in an Interdependent World*, Cambridge, MA: MIT Press.

Cooper, R.N. (1987) *The International Monetary System; Essays in World Economics*, Cambridge, MA: MIT Press.

Cooper, R.N. (2000) International approaches to global climate change, *The World Bank Research Observer* 15(2): 145–72.

Cordella, T. and Grilo, I (2001) Social dumping and relocation, is there a case for imposing a social clause? *Regional Science and Urban Economics* 31: 643–68.

Crockett, A. (1996) The theory and practice of financial stability, *De Economist* 144(4): 531–68.

Crotty, J. and Lee, K.-K. (2002) Is financial liberalization good for developing nations? The case of South Korea in the 1990s, *Review of Radical Political Economics* 34: 327–34.

Dasgupta, I. and Osang, T.E. (2002) Globalization and relative wages: further evidence from US manufacturing industries, *International Review of Economics and Finance* 11: 1–16.

Daveri, F. and Tabellini, G. (2000) Unemployment, growth and taxation in industrial economies, *Economic Policy; A European Forum*, 30: 47–104.

Davidson, P.J. (2002) *ASEAN; The Evolving Legal Framework for Economic Cooperation*, Singapore: Times Academic Press.

De Freitas, G. (1998) 'Immigration inequality and policy alternatives', in D. Baker, G. Epstein and R. Pollin (eds). *Globalization and Progressive Economic Policy*, Cambridge: Cambridge University Press, 337–56.

De Gregorio, J. and Valdes, R.O. (2001) Crisis transmission; evidence from the debt, tequila and Asian flu crises, *World Bank Economic Review* 15(2): 289–314.

de la Fuente, A.(1997) The empirics of growth and convergence; a selective review, *Journal of Economic Dynamics and Control* 21: 23–73.

Dixit, A. (1998a) *The Making of Economic Policy; A Transaction Costs Politics Perspective*, Cambridge, MA/London: CES/MIT Press.

Dixit, A. (1998b) 'Transaction cost politics and economic policy: a framework and a case study', in M. Baldassarri, L. Paganetto and E.S. Phelps (eds) *Institutions and Economic Organization in Advanced Economies; The Governance Perspective*, Basingstoke: MacMillan, 139–75.

Dixit, A. and Skeath, S. (1999) *Games of Strategy*, New York/London: Norton.

Dobson, W, Hufbauer, G.C. ass. by Koo Cho, H. (2001) *World Capital Markets; Challenge to the G10*, Washington: Institute for International Economics.

Dolado, J., Kramarz, F., Machin, S., Manning, A. Margolis, D. and Teulings, C. (1996), The economic impact of minimum wages in Europe, *Economic Policy; A European Forum*, 23, 317–72.

Dollar, D. and Kraay, A. (2001) *Trade, Growth and Poverty*, Development Research Group, Washington: World Bank.

Dornbusch, R., Park, Y.C. and Claessens, S. (2000) Contagion, understanding how it spreads, *The World Bank Research Observer* 15(2): 177–97.

Drahos, P. and Braithwaite, J. (2001) The globalisation of regulation, *The Journal of Political Philosophy* 9: 103–28.

Dunning, J.D. (1993a) *Multinational Enterprise and the Global Economy*, Addison Wesley: Harrow.

Dunning, J.D. (1993b) *The Globalization of Business*, London: Routledge.

Dunning, J.D. (ed.) (1997) *Governments, Globalization and International Business*, Oxford: Oxford University Press.

Dymond, W. (2000) 'The MAI; back to the future', in MINEZ (eds) *From Havanna to Seattle and Beyond*, Den Haag: SDU, 175–85.

Eden, L. and Hampson, F.O. (1997) 'Clubs are trump; the formation of international regimes in the absence of a hegemon', in J.R. Holingworth and R. Boyer (eds). *Contemporary Capitalism; The Embeddedness of Institutions*, Cambridge: Cambridge University Press, 361– 94.

Efinger, M., Mayer, P. and Schwarzer, G. (1993) 'Inegrating and contextualizing hypotheses; alternative paths to better explanations of regime formation?' in V. Rittberger (ed.) *Regime Theory and International Relations*, Oxford: Clarendon Press, 252–81.

Eggertson, T. (1990) *Economic Behaviour and Institutions*, Cambridge: Cambridge University Press.

Eggertson, T. (1996) 'A note on the economics of institutions', in L.J. Alston, T. Eggertson and D.C. North (eds). *Empirical Studies in Institutional Change*, Cambridge: Cambridge University Press.

Eichengreen, B. (1995) *Golden Fetters, the Gold Standard and the Great Depression, 1919–1939*, Oxford: Oxford University Press.

Eichengreen, B. (2002) *Financial Crises, and What to Do about Them*, Oxford: Oxford University Press.

Elliott, K.A. (2001) Fin(d)ing our way on trade and labor standards? *International Economics Policy Briefs*, No. 01.5, Washington: IEE.

Ethier, W.J. (1998), Regionalism in a multilateral world, *Journal of Political Economy* 106(6): 1214–45.

Ethier, W.J. (1998) The international commercial system, *Essays in International Finance*, No. 210, Princeton.

Evrensel, A.Y. (2002) Effectiveness of IMF supported stabilization programs in developing countries, *Journal of Money and Finance*, 21: 565–87.

Faure, M. and Lefevere, J. (1999) 'Compliance with international environmental agreements', in N.J. Vig and R.S. Axelrod (eds). *The Global Environment; Institutions, Law and Policy*, Washington: CQ Press, 138–56.

Feenstra, R.C. (1998), Integration of trade and disintegration of production in the global economy, *Journal of Economic Perspectives* 12(4): 31–50.

Fischer, R.D. (2001) The evolution of inequality after trade liberalisation, *Journal of Development Economics* 66(2): 555–79.

Fitoussi, J.-P., Jestaz, D.P., Phelps, E.P. and Zoega, J. (2000) Roots of the recent recoveries; labour reforms or private sector forces? *Documents de Travail de L'OFCE*, No. 2000.4, Paris.

Florini, A. (2000) 'Who does what; collective action and the changing nature of authority', in R.A. Higgott, G.R.D. Underhill and A. Bieler (eds). Non State Actors and Authority in the Global System, *Warwick Studies in Globalization*, 1, London: Routledge, 15–30.

Folmer, H., van Mouche, P. and Ragland, S. (1993) Interconnected games and international environmental problems, *Environmental and Resource Economics* 3: 313–35.

Foreman-Peck, J. (1995) *A History of the World Economy; International Economic Relations Since 1850*, 2nd edn. New York/London: Harvestor/Wheatsheaf.

Foreman Peck, J. (ed.) (1998) *Historical Foundations of Globalization*, Cheltenham: Edward Elgar.

Francois, J. (2001) *The Next WTO Round; North South Stakes in New Market Access Negotiations*, Adelaide: CES/TI.

Francois, J. and Nelson, D. (1998), Trade technology and wages; general equilibrium mechanics, *The Economic Journal* 108: 1483–99.

Francois, J. and Wooton, I. (2001), Market liberalisation and the GATS, *European Journal of Political Economy* 17: 389–402.

Frankel, J.A. and Romer, D. (1999) Does trade cause growth? *American Economic Review*, 89(3): 379–99.

Franzini, M. and Pizzuti, F.R. (eds). (2001) *Gobalization, Institutions and Social Cohesion*, Berlin/Heidelberg: Springer.

Fratianni, M. and Pattison, J. (1982) The economics of international organization, *Kyklos* 35: 244–66.

Frey, B.S. (1984) The public choice view of international political economy, *International Organization* 38(1): 199–223.

Furubotn, E.G. and Richter, R. (2000) *Institutions and Economic Theory; The Contribution of the New Institutional Economics*, Ann Arbor: Michigan University Press.

Gartzke, E., Li, Q. and Boehmer, Ch. (2001) Investing in peace; economic interdependence and international conflict, *International Organization* 55(2): 391–438.

Ghai, D. (ed.) (1991) *The IMF and the South; The Social Impact of Crisis and Adjustment*, London: Zed Books.

Ghose, A.K. (2000), Trade liberalisation, employment and global inequality, *International Labour Review*, 139(3): 281–305; the full study is 'Trade liberalisation and manufacturing employment' (Employment paper 2000/3, ILO) (http://www.ilo.org/public/english/employment/strat/publ/ep00–3.htm)

Ghosh, B. (ed.) (2000) *Managing Migration; Time for a New International Regime?* Oxford: Oxford University Press.

Ghosh, B. (2000) 'New international regime for the orderly movements of people; what would it look like?' In B. Ghosh (ed.) *Managing Migration; Time for a New International Regime*, Oxford: Oxford University Press, 220–48.

Goldberg, P.M. and Kindleberger, C.P. (1970) Towards a GATT for investment; a proposal for supervision of the International Corporation, *Law and Policy in International Business*, 2(2): 295–325.

Goldstein, M. (2000) *IMF Structural Conditionality; How Much is Too Much?* Washington: IEE.

Graham, E.M. and Richardson, J.D. (1997) *Global Competition Policy*, Washington: Institute for International Economics.

Graham, E.M. and Wada, E. (2001) 'Foreign direct investment in China', in P. Drysdale (ed.) *Achieving High Growth; Experience of Transitional Economies in East Asia*, Oxford: Oxford University Press.

Graham, A. (2001) The assessment; economics of the internet, *Oxford Review of Economic Policy* 17(2): 145–58.

Griffith-Jones, S., Montes, M.F. and Nasution, A. (eds). (2001a) 'Managing capital surges in emerging economies'; in S. Griffith-Jones, M.F. Montes and A. Nasution. *Short-term Capital Flows and Economic Crises*, Oxford: Oxford University Press, 263–90.

Griffith-Jones, S., Montes, M.F. and Nasution, A. (eds). (2001b) *Short-term Capital Flows and Economic Crises*, Oxford: Oxford University Press.

Grimwade, N. (2000) *International Trade, New Patterns of Trade, Production and Investment*, London: Routledge.

Hanley, N. and Folmer, H. (eds) (1998) *Game Theory and the Environment*, Cheltenham: Edward Elgar.

Hanlon, P. (1999) *Global Airlines*, 2nd ed, Oxford: Butterworth/Heinemannn.

Hardin, G. and Baden, J. (eds). (1977) *Managing the Commons*, San Fransisco: Freeman.

Haq, M.U., Kaul, I. and Grunberg, I. (eds). (1996) *The Tobin Tax; Coping with Financial Volatility*, Oxford: Oxford University Press.

Haufler, V. (1993) 'Crossing the boundary between public and private; international regimes and non-state actors', in: V. Rittberger (ed.) *Regime Theory and International Relations*, Oxford: Clarendon Press, 94–111.

Heal, G. (1999) 'New strategies for the provision of global public goods, learning from international environmental challenges', in I. Kaul, I. Grunberg and M. Stern (eds). *Global Public Goods*, Geneva: UNDP, 220–39.

Hernandez, L.F. and Valdes, R.O. (2001) What drives contagion? Trade, neighbourhood or financial links, *International Review of Financial Analysis* 10: 203–18.

Hertel, T., Hoekman, B. and Martin, W. (2002) Developing countries and a new round of WTO negotiations, *World Bank Research Observer.*

Hertz, N. (2001a) *The Silent Take-over*, London: William Heinemann.

Hertz, N. (2001b) Speech given at the conference of the Belgian presidency of the EU, 30th October 2001.

Hirsch, S. (1981) Peace making and economic interdependence, *The World Economy* 4: 407–17.

Hirschhausen, Ch. and von, Bitzer, J. (eds). (2000), *The Globalization of Industry and Innovation in Eastern Europe; From Post-socialist Restructuring to International Competitiveness*, Cheltenham, Edward Elgar.

Hodges, M.R., Kirton, J.J. and Daniels, J.P. (eds). (1999) *The G8's Role in the New Millennium*, Aldershot: Ashgate.

Hoekman, B.M. and Kostecki, M.M. (2001) *The Political Economy of the World Trading System; the WTO and Beyond*, 2nd ed., Oxford: Oxford University Press.

Hoel, M. (1992) Carbon taxes, an international tax or harmonised domestic taxes, *European Economic Review* 36(2/3): 400–6.

Hollick, A.L. and Cooper, R.N. (1997) 'Global commons, can they be managed?' in P. Gasgupta, K.G. Maler and A. Vercelli (eds). *The Economics of the Transnational Commons*, Oxford: Clarendon Press, 141–71.

Hope, E. and Maeleng, P. (eds) (1998) *Competition and Trade Policies Coherence or Conflict*, London: Routledge.

Horn, H. and Mavroidis, P. (2001) Economic and legal aspects of the most favored nation clause, *European Journal of Political Economy* 17: 233–79.

Hufbauer, G. (1991) World economic integration; the long view, *Economic Insights* 30: 26–7.

Huysmans, J. (2000), The European Union and the securitization of migration, *Journal of Common Market Studies* 38(5): 751–78.

Huntingdon, S.P. (1997) *The Clash of Civilization and the Remaking of the World Order*, London: Touchstone.

IATCWG (1993) (International Antitrust Code Working Group) Draft International Antitrust Code, a GATT-MTO plurilateral trade agreement, *World Trade Materials*, 5 (September), 126–96; also published as: *BNA Antitrust and Regulation Report*, 64, No. 1628, Washington DC.

IBRD (1992) *World Development Report*, Washington.

IBRD (1997) 'The state in a changing world', in *World Development Report*, Washington.

IBRD (2000) *World Development Report*, Washington.

IBRD (2002) Building institutions for markets, *World Development Report*, Washington.

IMF (2000) *World Economic Outlook* (May), Washington: IMF, 149–63 and supporting studies, 1–19.

IMF (2001a) *IMF Surveillance; A Factsheet*; http://www.imf.org/exteranl/np/exr/facts/surv.htm.

IMF (2001b) *World Economic Outlook* (October), Washington: IMF, 152–73.

Irwin, D.A. and Tervio, M. (2002) Does trade raise income? Evidence from the twentieth century, *Journal of International Economics* 58: 1–18.

Irwin, G. and Vines, D. (eds) (2001) *Financial Market Integration and International Capital Flows*, Cheltenham: Edward Elgar.

Iwasaki, Y. and Prakash, B. (2002) ASEAN economic cooperation; a review, *Journal of Asian Economics* 13(3): 319–35.

James, H. (2001) *The End of Globalisation, Lessons from the Great Depression*, Cambridge, MA: Harvard University Press.

Jauhari, B.M (ed.). (1996) *Economic Liberalisation and Globalisation; an Indian Experience*, New Dehli: Commonwealth Publishers.

Jeanne, O. and Zettelmeyer, J. (2001) International bailouts; the IMF role, *Economic Policy; a European Forum*, 33: 407–32.

Johnston, D. (2000) 'Fostering international investment and corporate responsibility', in MINEZ (eds). *From Havanna to Seattle and Beyond*, Den Haag: SDU, 159–66.

Jungnickel, R. (1996) Globalization, exodus of German industry? *Intereconomics* 61: 181–88.

Kaiser, K., Kirton, J.J. and Daniels, J.P. (2001) *Shaping a New International Financial System; Challenges of Governance in a Globalizing World*, Aldershot: Ashgate.

Kantzenbach, E., Scharrer, H-E. and Wavermann, L. (1993) (eds). *Competition Policy in an Interdependent World Economy*, Hamburg: HWWA, Baden Baden: Nomos.

Kapur, D. (2002) 'Processes of change in international organizations', in D. Nayyar (ed.) *Governing Globalization; Issues and Institutions*, Oxford: UNU/WIDER, Oxford University Press, 334–55.

Kasper, W. and Streit, M. (1998) *Institutional Economics; Social Order and Public Policy*, Cheltenham: Edward Elgar.

Kaufmann, D., Kraay, A. and Zoido-Lobaton, P. (1999a) Aggregate governance indicators, *Policy Research Department Working Paper*, No. 2195, Washington: IBRD.

Kaufmann, D., Kraay, A. and Zoido-Lobaton, P. (1999b) Governance matters, *Policy Research Department Working Paper*, No. 2196, Washington: IBRD.

Kaufmann, D., Kraay, A. and Zoido-Lobaton, P. (2002) Governance matters II; updated indicators for 2000–2001, *Policy Research Department Working Paper*, No. 2772, Washington: IBRD.

Kaul, I., Grunberg, I. and Stern, M.A. (eds) (1999) *Global Public Goods*, Geneva: UNDP.

Kenwood, A.G. and Lougheed, A.L. (1999) *The Growth of the International Economy, 1820–2000*, 4th ed., London: Routledge.

Keohane, R.O. (1993) 'The analysis of international regimes; towards a European–American research programme', in V. Rittberger (ed.) *Regime Theory and International Relations*, Oxford: Clarendon Press, 23–45.

Killick,T. (1995) *IMF Programmes in Developing Countries; Design and Impact*, London: Routledge.

Kirton, J.J. and von Fuerstenberg, G.M. (2001) *New Directions in Global Economic Governance; Managing Globalization in the Twenty-first Century*, Aldershot: Ashgate.

Kirton, J. (2001) 'The G20, representativeness, effectiveness and leadership in global governance', in J.J. Kirton, J. Daniels and A. Freytag (eds). *Guiding Global Order, G8 Governance in the 21st Century*, Aldershot: Ashgate, 143–72.

Kolk, A., van Tulder, R. and Welters, C. (1999) International codes of conduct and corporate social responsibility; Can transnational corporations regulate themselves? *Transnational Corporations* 8.1: 143–80.

Kose, M.A. (2002) Explaining business cycles in small open economies; how much do world prices matter? *Journal of International Economics* 56: 299–327.

Krasner, S.D. (ed.) (1983) *International Regimes*, Ithaca, NY: Cornell University Press.

Krueger, A.O. (ed) (1998) *The WTO as an International Organization*, Chicago: University of Chicago Press.

Kuebler, F. (2002) The organization of global financial markets, *Journal of Institutional and Theoretical Economics* 158(1): 5–23.

Langhammer, R. (1992) The developing countries and regionalism, *Journal of Common Market Studies* 30(2): 211–31.

Lawrence, R.Z. (1996), *Single World, Divided Nations? International Trade and OECD Labour Markets*, Washington/Paris: Brookings/OECD.

Lee, E. (1996), Globalization and employment; is anxiety justified? *International Labour Review*, 135(5): 485–97.

Levinson, A. (1996) 'Environmental regulations and industrial location; international and domestic evidence', in J.N. Bhagwati and R.E. Hudec (eds). *Fair Trade and Harmonization; Prerequisites for Free Trade?* vol. 1, Cambridge, MA: MIT Press, 429–57.

Lipsey, R.E. and Muchielli, J.-L. (eds.) (2001) *Multinational Firms and Impact on Employment Trade and Technology; New Perspectives for a New Century*, London: Routledge.

Lloyd, P.J. (1998) Globalisation and competition policies, *Weltwirtschaftliches* Archiv, 134(2): 161–85.

Lloyd, P.J. (2001) The architecture of the WTO, *European Journal of Political Economy* 17: 327–53.

Loisel, O. and Martin, Ph. (2001) Coordination, cooperation, contagion and currency crises, *Journal of International Economics* 53: 399–419.

Lundborg, P. and Segerstrom, P. (2002) The growth and welfare effects of international mass migration, *Journal of International Economics* 56: 177–204.

Maddison, A. (2001) The world economy; a millennial perspective, *Development Centre Studies*, Paris: OECD.

Majone, G. (1997) From the positive to the regulatory state, *Journal of Public Policy* 17(2): 139–67.

Manne, A. and Richels, R. (2000) 'The Kyoto protocol; a cost effective strategy for meeting environmental objectives?' in C. Carraro (ed.) *Efficiency and Equity in Climate Change Policy*, Dordrecht: Kluwer, 43–62.

Mathieson, D.J. and Schinasi, G.J. (2000) *International Capital Markets; Developments, Prospects and Key Policy Issues*, Washington: IMF.

Mattoo, A. and Subramanian, A. (1997) Multilateral rules on competition policy; a proposal for early action? *Journal of World Trade*, 31(5): 95–115.

McCalman, P. (2002) Multi-lateral trade negotiations and the most favoured nation clause, *Journal of International Economics* 57: 151–76.

McCormick, J. (1999) 'The role of environmental NGOs in international regimes', in N.J.Vig and R.S. Axelrod (eds). *The Global Environment; Institutions, Law and Policy*, Washington: CQ Press, 52–71.

McKibbin, W.J. and Wilcoxen, P.J. (2002) The role of economics in climate change policy, *Journal of Economic Perspectives* 16(2): 107–29.

Meiklejohn, R. (1999) An international competition policy: Do we need it? Is it feasible? *The World Economy* 22(9): 1233–49.

Memedovic, O., Kuyvenhoven, A. and Molle, W. (eds). (1998) *Globalization and Labour Markets; Challenges, Adjustments and Policy Response in the European Union and Less Developed Countries*, Dordtrecht: Kluwer.

Memedovic, O., Kuyvenhoven, A. and Molle, W. (eds). (1999) *Multilateralism and Regionalism in the Post Uruguay Round Era; What Role for the EU?* Dordtrecht: Kluwer.

Menon, J. (2000) The evolving ASEAN free trade area; widening and deepening. *Asian Development Review* 18(1): 49–72.

Messerlin, P. (1999) External aspects of state aids, *European Economy* 3: 161–95.

Mishkin, F.S. (1992) Anatomy of a financial crisis, *Journal of Evolutionary Economics* 2(2): 115–130.

Mishkin, F.S. (1999) Global financial instability; framework, events, issues, *Journal of Economic Perspectives* 13(4): 3–20.

Molle, W. (2001) *The Economics of European Integration; Theory, Practice, Policy*, 4th edn, Aldershot: Ashgate.

Molle, W. (2002) Globalization, regionalism and labour markets; should we recast the foundations of the EU regime in matters of regional (rural and urban) development? *Regional Studies* 36(2): 163–74.

Moran, T.H. (1998), *Foreign Direct Investment and Development: The New Policy Agenda for Developing Countries and Economies in Transition*, Washington: IEE.

Morris, S. (2000) Contagion, *Review of Economic Studies* 67: 53–78.

Moshirian, F. (2002) New international financial architecture, *Journal of Multinational Financial Management* 12, 273–84.

Nayyar, D. (2002a) 'The existing system and the missing links', in D. Nayyar (ed.) *Governing Globalization; Issues and Institutions*, Oxford: UNU/WIDER, Oxford University Press, 356–84.

Nayyar, D. (2002b) 'Cross border movements of people', in D. Nayyar (ed.) *Governing Globalization; Issues and Institutions*, Oxford: UNU/WIDER, Oxford University Press, 144–76.

Neumann, M. (2001) *Competition Policy; History, Theory and Practice*, Cheltenham: Edward Elgar.

Nordhaus, W.D. (1994) *Managing the Global Commons*, Cambridge, MA: MIT Press.

North, D.C. (1990a) *Institutions, Institutional Change and Economic Performance*, Cambridge: Cambridge University Press.

North, D.C. (1990b) A transaction cost theory of politics, *Journal of Theoretical Politics* 2(4): 355–67.

OECD (1979) *The Impact of the Newly Industrialising Countries on the Production and Trade in Manufactures; A Report by the Secretary General*, Paris.

OECD (1987) *Competition Policy and International Trade*, Paris.

OECD (1992) *Globalisation of Industrial Activities*, Paris.

OECD (1994) *Jobs study; Evidence and Explanations*, two vols, Paris.

OECD (1995) *New Dimensions of Market Access in a Globalising World Economy*, Paris.

OECD (1996) *Trade, Employment and Labour Standards (A Study of Core Workers' Rights and International Trade)*, Paris.

OECD (1997a) www.oecd.org/publications/pol brief/1997/9702 pol.htm and also http://www.westgov.org/wga/publicat/maiweb.htm

OECD (1997b) *Employment Outlook*, Paris.

OECD (1997c) *The Multilateral Agreement on Investment* (state of play as of February 1997), *OECD Working Papers*, Paris.

OECD (1999a) *Action Against Climate Change; the Kyoto Protocol and Beyond*, Paris.

OECD (1999b) *International Emissions Trading under the Kyoto Protocol*, Paris.

OECD (2000) *A Multi Gas Assessment of the Kyoto Protocol*, Paris.

OECD (2001) The OECD guidelines for multinational enterprises, *OECD Observer*, June, 1–8 and www.oecd.org/def/investment/guidelines/index.htm.

Ohmae, K. (1995) *The End of the Nation State, The Rise of Regional Economies*, New York: The Free Press.

Olson, M. Jr. (1965) *The Logic of Collective Action; Public Goods and the Theory of Groups*, Cambridge, MA: Harvard University Press.

O'Rourke, K.H. and Williamson, J.G. (1999) *Globalization and History, The Evolution of a Nineteen Century Atlantic Economy*, Cambridge, MA: MIT Press.

Osakwe, P.N. and Schembri, L.L. (2002) Real effects of collapsing exchange rate regimes; an application to Mexico, *Journal of International Economics* 57: 299–325.

Oum, T.H., Park, J.H. and Zhang, A. (2000) *Globalisation and Strategic Alliances; The Case of the Airline Industry*, Amsterdam: Pergamon.

Oyejide, T (2000) Interests and options of developing countries and LDCs in a new round of multilateral trade negotiations, *G24 Discussion Paper*, No. 2, New York, UN.

Panagariya, A. and Krishna, P. (2002) On necessarily welfare-enhancing free trade areas, *Journal of International Economics* 57: 353–67.

Park, D. (2001) Recent trends in the global distribution of income, *Journal of Policy Modelling* 23: 497–501.

Park, Y.C. (2002) 'Beyond the Chang Mai initiative; rationale and need for a regional monetary arrangement in East Asia', in J.J. Teunissen (ed.) *A Regional Approach to Financial Crisis Prevention; Lessons from Europe and Initiatives in Asia, Latin America and Africa*, The Hague: Fondad, 121–47.

Park, Y.C. and Wang, Y. (2000) 'Reforming the international financial system, prospects for regional financial cooperation in East Asia', in J. Teunissen (ed.) *Reforming the International Financial System, Crisis Prevention and Response*, The Hague: Fondad, 70–84.

Pearce, D. and Turner, K. (1990), *Economics of Natural Resources and the Environment*, London: Harvestor/Wheatsheaf.

Pennings, E. and Sleuwaegen, L. (2000) International relocation; firm and industry determinants, *Economic Letters* 67: 179–86.

Perman, R.Y.M., McGilvray, J. and Common, M. (1999) *Natural Resources and Environmental Economics*, Essex: Pearson.

Petrakis, E. and Xepapadeas, A. (1996) Environmental consciousness and moral hazard in international agreements to protect the environment, *Journal of Public Economics* 60: 95–110.

Pizer, W.A. (2002) Combining price and quantity controls to mitigate global climate change, *Journal of Public Economics*, 85: 409–34.

Polacheck, S.W. (1980) Conflict and trade, *Journal of Conflict Resolution* 24: 55–78.

Pollard, S. (1997) *The International Economy Since 1945*, London: Routledge.

Putman, R.D. (1988) Diplomacy and domestic politics; the logic of two level games, *International Organization* 42(3): 427–60.

Raffer, K. (2002) Globalization and developing countries: global governance and the functioning of global financial markets. *Paper for EU/LDC Network Conference on Global Governance*, Chang Mai.

Raffer, K. and Singer, H.W. (1996) *The Foreign aid Business; Economic Assistance and Development Co-operation*, Cheltenham: Edward Elgar.

Raffer, K. and Singer, H.W. (2001) *The Economic North South Divide; Six Decades of Unequal Development*, Cheltenham: Edward Elgar.

Rao, P.K. (2002) *International Environmental Law and Economics*, Malden, MA, Oxford, UK: Blackwell.

Rappoport, L. (2002) Global governance and poverty reduction; the lessons of the Argentina case, *Paper for the EU LDC Network Conference on Global Governance*, Chiang Mai.

Reinhart, C.M. and Smith, R.T. (2002) Temporary controls on capital inflows, *Journal of International Economics* 57, 327–51.

Richards, J.E. (2001) Institutions for flying, how states built a market for international aviation services, *International Organization* 55(4): 993–1018.

Rodriguez, F. and Rodrik, D. (1999), Trade policy and economic growth, a skeptics' guide to cross national evidence, *NBER Working Paper*, No. W7081.

Rodrik, D. (1997) 'International trade and big government', in B.J. Cohen (ed.) *International Trade and Finance, New Frontiers for Research*, Cambridge: Cambridge University Press, 89–121.

Rogoff, K. (1999) International institutions for reducing global financial instability, *Journal of Economic Perspectives* 13(4): 21–42.

Rose, A.K. (2002) Do we really know that the WTO increases trade? *NBER Working Paper Series*, 9273, Cambridge, MA: NBER.

Rudra, N. (2002) Globalization and the decline of the welfare state in less developed countries, *International Organization* 56(2): 411–45.

Rutherford, M. (1994) *Institutions in Economics, The Old and the New Institutionalism*, Cambridge: Cambridge University Press.

Sapir, A. (1999) 'The impact of globalization on employment in Europe', in M. Dewatripont, A. Sapir and K. Sekkat (eds). *Trade and Jobs in Europe; Much Ado About Nothing*? Oxford, Oxford University Press, 172–89.

Scherer, F.M. (1994) *Competition Policies for an Integrated World Economy*, Washington: Brookings Institution.

Schiattarella, R. (2001) 'International relocalization and employment; an analysis for the traditional Italian industries', in: M. Franzini and F.R. Pizzuti (eds). *Globalization, Institutions and Social Cohesion*, Berlin/Heidelberg: Springer, 99–114.

Schneider, B. (2002) The road to international financial stability; are key financial standards the answer? *Paper Presented at the EU LDC Network Conference on Global Governance*, (also obtainable from Benu.Schneider@unctad.org).

Schott, J.J. (ed.) (2000) *The WTO after Seattle*, Washington: IEE.

Sell, F.L. (2001) *Contagion in Financial Markets*, Cheltenham, Edward Elgar.

Sengenberger, W. and Campbell, D. (eds) (1994) *International Labour Standards and Economic Interdependence*, Geneva: ILO.

Siddique, M.A.B. (2001) (ed.) *International Migration into the 21st Century*, Cheltenham, Edward Elgar.

Siebert, H. (1998) *Economics of the Environment; Theory and Policy* (5th edn), Berlin: Springer.

Simatupang, B. (1998) 'Association of South East Asian Nations' (ASEAN) Free Trade Area (AFTA); the changing environment and incentives', in A.E. Fernandez Jilberto and A. Mommen (eds). *Regionalization and Globalization in the World Economy, Perspectives on the Third World and Transitional Economies*, London: Routledge, 307–27.

Sjoestedt, G. (2000) 'How does economic theory interrelate with negotiation analysis for the understanding of international economic negotiation?' in V. Kremenyuk and G. Sjoestedt (eds). *International Economic Negotiation; Models versus Reality*, Cheltenham: IIASA/Edward Elgar, 329–42.

Sleuwaegen, L., Pennings, E., Mommaerts, G. and Van den Cruyce, B. (2000) *Delocalisatie, Innovatie en Werkgelegenheid*, Brussels: DWTC/FP.

Smith, S. (1992) Taxation and the environment; a survey, *Fiscal Studies* 13(4): 21–57.

Soros, G. (2000) *Open Society; Reforming Global Capitalism*, London: Little, Brown and Company.

Spar, D.L. (1999) 'The public face of cyberspace', in I. Kaul, I. Grunberg and M. Stern (eds). *Global Public Goods*, Geneva: UNDP, 344–362.

Srinavasan, T.N. and Bhagwati, J. (1999) *Outward Orientation and Development; Are Revisionists Right?* www.columbia.edu/'jb38/papers.htm.

Stanford, J. (1998) 'Openness and equity, regulating labor market outcomes in a globalized economy', in D. Baker, G. Epstein and R. Pollin (eds). *Globalization and Progressive Economic Policy*, Cambridge: Cambridge University Press, 245–70.

Steiniger, K.W. (2001) *International Trade and Transport: Spatial Structure and Environmental Quality in a Global Economy*, Cheltenham: Edward Elgar.

Stewart, F. (1995) 'Biases in global markets, can the forces of inequity and marginalization be modified?' in M.U. Haq *et al.* (eds). *The UN and Bretton Woods Institutions; New Challenges for the Twenty-first Century;* New York/London: St Martins Press, 164–84.

Stiglitz, J.E. (2002) *Globalization and its Discontents*, New York/London: Norton and Co.

Stiles, K.W. (2000) 'Grassroots empowerment; states, non-state actors and global policy formulation', in R.A. Higgott, G.R.D. Underhill and A. Bieler (eds). *Non State Actors and Authority in the Global System, Warwick Studies in Globalization*, 1, London: Routledge, 32–47.

Straubhaar, Th. (2000) 'Why do we need a general agreement on movements of people (GAMP)', in B. Ghosh (ed.) *Managing Migration; Time for a New International Regime*, Oxford: Oxford University Press, 110–36.

Swanston, T. and Johnston, S. (1999) *Global Environmental Problems and International Environmental Agreements; The Economics of International Institution Building*, Cheltenham: Edward Elgar.

Tapinos, G. and de Rugy, A. (1993) 'The macro economic impact of immigration; review of the literature since the mid 1970s', in SOPEMI, *Trends in European Migration*, 1993 report, Paris: OECD, 157–77.

Teubal, M. (1998) 'Regional integration processes in Latin America, Argentina and MERCOSUR', in A.E. Fernandez Jilberto and A. Mommen (eds). *Regionalization and Globalization in the World Economy, Perspectives on the Third World and Transitional Economies*, London, Routledge, 230–50.

Teulings, C. and Hartog, J. (1998) *Corporatism or Competition, Labour Contracts, Institutions and Wage Structures in International Comparison*, Cambridge: Cambridge University Press.

Teunissen, J.J (ed.) (2000) *Reforming the International Financial System, Crisis Prevention and Response*, The Hague: Fondad.

Teunissen, J.J. (ed.) (2002) *A Regional Approach to Financial Crisis Prevention; Lessons from Europe and Initiatives in Asia, Latin America and Africa*, The Hague: Fondad.

Tietenberg, T. (2003) 'Editors' introduction', in: T. Tietenberg (ed.) *The Evolution of Emissions Trading; Theoretical Foundations and Design Considerations*, Aldershot: Ashgate (awaiting this publication the article is available from the authors' website: www.colby.edu/personal/thieten).

Tietzel, M. (2001) In praise of the commons; another case study, *European Journal of Law and Economics* 12: 159–71.

Tinbergen, J. (1959) 'The theory of the optimum regime', in L.H. Klaasen, L.M. Koyck and H.J. Witteveen (eds). *Jan Tinbergen; Selected Papers*, Amsterdam: North Holland, 264–304.

Tussie, D. and Whalley, J. (2002) The functioning of a commitment based WEO: lessons from experience with the WTO, *The World Economy* 25(5): 685–95.

UNCTAD (1993, 2000, 2001) *World Investment Report*, Geneva: UN.

UNCTAD (1996/97) *Handbook of International Trade and Development*, p. 34.

UNCTAD (1999) *World Investment Report*; Foreign direct investment and the challenge of development, Geneva, UN.

UNCTAD (2001) *Handbook of Statistics*, p. 35.

UNCTAD (2002) *World Investment Report 2002, Transnational Corporations and Export Competitiveness*, Geneva: UN.

UNDP (1998) *Overcoming Human Poverty*, New York: UNDP.

van Bergeijk , P.A.G. and Mensink, N.W. (1997) Measuring globalization, *Journal of World Trade*, 31(3): 159–68.

Van Houtven, L. (2002) Governance of the IMF, decision making, institutional oversight, transparency and accountability, *IMF Pamphlet Series*, No. 53, Washington.

van Schendelen, R. (2002) *Machiavelli in Brussels; The Art of Lobbying in the EU*, Amsterdam: Amsterdam University Press.

Vaubel, R. (1986) A public choice approach to international organization, *Public Choice* 51: 39–57.

Walton, M. and Balls, E. (1995) Workers in an integrating world, *World Development Report*, Washington, IBRD.

Wavermann, L., Comanor, W.S., Goto, A. (eds). (1997) *Competition Policy in the Global Economy; Modalities for Cooperation*, London, Routledge.

Weimer, D.L. (ed.) (1997) *The Political Economy of Property Rights*, Cambridge/New York: Cambridge University Press.

Whalley, J. and Zissimos, B. (2002) An internationalisation-based World Environmental Organisation, *The World Economy* 25(5): 619–42.

Williamson, J.G. (1996) Globalization, convergence and history, *Journal of Economic History* 56(2): 277–306.

Williamson, J.G. (1998) 'Globalization and the labor market: using history to inform policy', in P. Aghion and J.G. Wiliamson (eds). *Growth, Inequality and Globalization, Theory, History and Policy;* Cambridge: Cambridge University Press, 103–201.

Williamson, O.E. (1989) 'Transaction cost economics', in R. Schmalensee and R.D. Willig (eds)/ *Handbook of Industrial Organization*, vol. 1, Amsterdam: North Holland, 135–82.

Williamson, O.E. (1998) Transaction cost economics: how it works, where it is headed, *De Economist* 146(1): 23–58.

Winham, G.R. (1998) The world trade organization, institution building in the multilateral trade system, *The World Economy* 21(3): 349–68.

Winters, L.A. (1997) What can European experience teach developing countries about integration, *The World Economy*, 20(7): 889–912.

Winters, L.A. (2001) Trade, trade policy and poverty: what are the links? *Paper Prepared for the EU LDC 2001 Conference*, Rotterdam: NEI.

Witherell, W.H. (1995) The OECD multilateral agreement on investment, *Transnational Corporations*, 4(2): 1–14.

Wood, A. (1995) How trade hurt unskilled workers, *Journal of Economic Perspectives* 9(3): 57–80.

Wood, A. (2002) Globalization and wage inequalities, a synthesis of three theories, *Weltwitschaftliches Archiv* 138(1): 54–82.

Wrigley, C. (ed.) (2000) *The First World War and the International Economy*, Cheltenham: Edward Elgar.

WTO (1998) Globalization and Trade, *WTO Annual Report*, Geneva.

WTO (1999), *WTO, the World Trade Organization*, 2nd edn. Available from: http://www/wto.org/english/the wto.

Wyplosz, Ch. (1999) 'International financial instability', in I. Kaul, I. Grunberg and M. Stern (eds), *Global Public Goods*, Geneva: UNDP, 152–89.

Young, O.R. and Osherenko, G. (1993) 'Testing theories of regime formation', in V. Rittberger (ed) *Regime Theory and International Relations*, Oxford: Clarendon Press, 223–51.

Zacher, M.W. and Sutton, B.A. (1996) *Governing Global Networks; International Regimes for Transportation and Communications*, Cambridge: Cambridge University Press.

Zimmermann, K.F. (1995) Tackling the European migration problem, *Journal of Economic Perspectives* 9(2): 45–62.

Index